Walking the Winds

^^^

Also by Rebecca Woods

Jackson Hole Hikes
A Guide to Grand Teton National Park
and Bridger Teton National Forest

Targhee Trails
A Guide to Targhee National Forest

Walking the Winds

A Hiking and Fishing Guide to
Wyoming's Wind River Range

by
Rebecca Woods

White Willow Publishing
1255 N. Iron Rock Road #6 • Jackson, Wyoming 83001

Warning

By their nature, outdoor activities can be dangerous. It is your responsibility to be aware of potential risks, have the proper equipment, and take safety precautions. Changing terrain and weather conditions present a wide range of hazards, including but not limited to: snow and ice fields, avalanches, landslides, caves, falling trees or limbs, high or rushing water, contaminated water, wild animals, severe weather, becoming lost or overexerted, dehydration and hypothermia.

Field conditions can and do change, and, while every effort has been taken to insure this book's accuracy, it may contain errors. This guide should not replace your own judgement or decision-making skills.

Table of Contents

Acknowledgments and Thanks

Author photo by Elizabeth McCabe. Photos on page 30 and 159 by Wade McCoy. Photo on page 35 by Wyoming Game & Fish. Photos on pages 45-46, 51, 61, 77, 82,111, 143, 162, 168-169 and 183 by Dick Dumais. All other photos by author.

Research for this guide was drawn from a large number of sources listed in the bibliography. Special thanks to Joe Kelsey, Finis Mitchell, and Orrin and Lorraine Bonney, whose initial efforts helped introduce the Winds to many people.

Personal thanks and gratitude to Rich Bloom
and Donna and Charlie Spurlock,
for everything.

First Printing July, 1994
Second Printing June, 1995
Second Edition, May 1998

Introduction

The most spectacular backpacking region in Wyoming is arguably the most spectacular in the entire Rockies: the Wind River Range. The range extends over 100 miles from Togwotee Pass to sage-covered foothills near South Pass, hugging the spine of the Continental Divide along its northwest to southeast course. Forty summits top 13,000 feet, led by 13,804 foot Gannett, the highest point in the state. Their upper slopes are draped with remnants of the last ice age: seven of the 10 largest glaciers in the lower 48 states are found in the Winds. Evidence of a much larger presence eons ago is seen in the jagged cirques, U-shaped valleys, and knife-edge ridges.

Over 1,600 lakes—and almost that many ponds and tarns— dot the alpine meadows, canyon floors, and valleys. Hundreds have been stocked with cutthroat, golden, brown, mackinaw and brook trout, making the range a mecca for anglers. The abundance of water also helps support a healthy wildlife population. On the Bridger Wilderness alone, there are an estimated 5,000 elk; 20,000 deer; 1,000 bighorn sheep; and 5,000 moose. Alpine meadows painted with wildflowers are standard.

ADMINISTRATION

Three agencies manage the 2.5 million acres that compose the range. The west slope is administered by Bridger Teton National Forest. Primary access into this forest is provided by Big Sandy, Boulder, Elkhart Park, New Fork Lake and Green River Lakes entrances. Sweetwater, Scab Creek, Half Moon, Spring Park and Willow Creek also provide entry points. A network of over 600 miles of trail connect the various west slope entrances, making extended trips along the length of the range an easy proposition. The Highline Trail is one of the popular choices.

Shoshone National Forest manages the north and south ends of the east slope. The east side offers some of the prettiest country in the range but draws fewer visitors, perhaps because there are fewer entry points. Major trailheads are located at Trail Lake, Dickinson Park and the Sinks Canyon/Loop Road entrances. The Glacier Trail in the Fitzpatrick Wilderness Area of Shoshone National Forest is a memorable 8-10 day trip that attracts backpackers from throughout the country. Over 200 miles of trail travel the east side. Trails up Hailey, Texas, and Washakie Passes, among others, allow backpackers to drop to the west side of the range.

Wind River Indian Reservation bisects Shoshone National Forest. The 2.2 million acre reservation borders the mid-portion of the range, spilling east into the Wind River Valley. Most of the reservation's mountainous 180,587 acre Wind River Roadless Area has been closed to backcountry use by the general public since 1974. Some areas may be visited if you hire a fishing guide or licensed outfitter. For addition information, consult the fishing section of this book, or contact the Joint Business Council, Shoshone and Arapaho Tribes, Box 217, Fort Washakie, Wyoming 82514.

REGULATIONS

Most of the range is protected by three designated wilderness areas: Bridger Wilderness on Bridger-Teton National Forest, and Fitzpatrick and Popo Agie wildernesses on Shoshone National Forest. To protect wilderness resources and values, both forests prohibit the use of vehicles, motorized equipment, mountain bikes, wheeled conveyances (with the exception of wheelchairs) and hang gliders in wilderness areas. Pets are allowed but must be kept under control. Aircraft may not pick people up or drop supplies off with out prior, written permission from the Forest Service.

Updated wilderness regulations and special restrictions are available at Forest Service district offices and at trailheads. At the time of this writing, the following regulations were in effect for the respective wilderness areas. Please become acquainted with the regulations to the area you will be visiting before your trip.

Bridger Wilderness Regulations

1. Group size is limited to 15 people and 25 pack and saddle stock.
2. Maximum length of stay is 16 days. After 16 days, campsites must be moved at least one mile away from the original site. Visitors may not return to the original campsite for at least five days. Campsites may not be left unattended for more than a 24-hour period.
3. Campsites must be located at least 200 feet from lakeshores or trails, and a minimum of 100 feet away from streams. This includes tethering and/or picketing of stock.
4. Organized groups (Scouts, church groups, clubs, school groups, etc.) must obtain a free visitor permit from the Pinedale Ranger District office at 29 East Fremont Lake Road in Pinedale. Groups are advised to plan well in advance to avoid scheduling conflicts with other groups.
5. Groups with pack or riding stock—including mules, llamas and goats—must

obtain a free visitor permit for overnight trips for the Pinedale office.

6. Pack and saddle stock must be tied in a manner that does not injure or damage trees, vegetation or soil.
7. Bulk hay or straw is not permitted in the wilderness. Processed hay is permitted at trailheads outside wilderness, but must be certified "weed-free." Use of hay promotes the spread of noxious weeds, and leftover hay is unattractive to other campsite visitors and not in keeping with "leave no trace" camping guidelines.
8. Camp structures such as hitching racks, tent frames, pegs and fire rings will be dismantled after the use period.
9. Non-burnable garbage will be packed out and no garbage will be buried.
10. Building, maintaining, attending or using an open fire above timberline is prohibited. Camp stoves, firepans or fireblankets are recommended below timberline to minimize fire scars on the land. If you must build a campfire, use only *dead, down* woody material. Standing live and dead trees provide homes and food for many wildlife species.

Fitzpatrick Wilderness Regulations

1. Group size is limited to 20 people and 30 pack and saddle stock.
2. Obey grazing closure and camping closure signs.
4. Camping within 100 feet of streams, lakes or trails is prohibited.
5. Campsite stay is limited to 16 consecutive days. At the end of that time, the group or individual must leave the site and not re-occupy it or another site within a five-mile radius of the original site for a minimum of seven days.
6. Fire Rings, hitching rails, and other camp structures must be dismantled.
7. Unburned refuse must be packed out.
8. Cutting switchbacks is prohibited.
9. Campfires and overnight camping with stock is not allowed off the Glacier Trail between the confluence of Dinwoody and Knoll Lake Creeks to the base of Dinwoody Glacier.

Popo Agie Wilderness Regulations

1. Group size is limited to 20 people and 30 pack and saddle stock. A free permit for recreational use of stock—including mules, goats and llamas—must be obtained from the Washakie Ranger District office in Lander.
2. Camping within 200 feet of streams, lakes or trails is prohibited.
3. Camping at signed closed areas is prohibited.
4. Campsite stay is limited to 14 consecutive days between Memorial and Labor days.
5. Shortcutting trails and switchbacks is prohibited.
6. Overnight camping and fires are prohibited within a quarter-mile of Lone some Lake in the Cirque of the Towers.

Registration and Permits

At the time of this writing, both forests are studying the possibility of instituting a fee permit system that would limit the number of people allowed into the wilderness any given day, and potentially charge a daily or overnight fee to visit the area. Check with the appropriate Forest Service District Office for updated information. Bridger-Teton and Shoshone National Forest currently ask that individuals register at the boxes located at major trailheads, and provide relevant comments at the conclusion of your trip. Comments alert fellow travelers to current trail conditions; registering helps managers gauge trail usage and gather information on visitor demand.

Individuals or organizations who provide paid service in the wilderness are required to have an outfitters/guide permit granted by the Forest Service. District offices maintain updated lists of licensed outfitters who provide catered trips, horseback or llama support, hiking and backpacking guides, photography trips, fishing trips, and climbing services. Contact the district to ensure your guide/ outfitter is authorized to operate in the Winds before paying your fee, or you could be fined for utilizing an illegal operator.

Trail Etiquette

When encountering horse parties on the trail, please give them the right-of-way. It is far easier—and causes less vegetation damage—for hikers and backpackers to move off the trail. If possible, move 15 feet off trail on the downhill side. Because horses can spook, talk softly and avoid sudden movements until the string has passed, unless the riders give other advice. If you are traveling with a pet, keep it close and quiet.

Grazing

Under the provisions of the 1964 Wilderness Act, grazing allotments are legally granted for both cattle and cattle on parts of the Bridger and Popo Agie wildernesses as a pre-existing use. Grazing typically occurs on the southern portion of Bridger Wilderness from mid-July to mid-September, dependent upon range readiness. Presently, allotments are granted for over 12,000 sheep and close to 5,000 head of cattle. This is considerably reduced from the almost 30,000 head of sheep that grazed in the range prior to Bridger Wilderness being officially recognized.

If you would rather not see cattle and sheep in the wilderness, contact the Pinedale Ranger District. Helpful staff will share the approximate location of sheep bands in the backcountry for your time frame. Please be aware, however, that herd movement is often contingent upon range conditions within the allotted area. Herds are typically encountered in meadowed areas from Cook Lakes south to Sweetwater River.

MINIMUM IMPACT

Above and beyond Forest Service regulations, backcountry users who adhere to minimum impact practices help keep our precious wild lands healthy. The "Leave No Trace" recommendations outlined below merit special emphasis.

Campsite Selection

If you are camping in a heavily-trafficked area, select a site that is obviously used rather than impact a new area. If you are camping in a rarely visited area, select a site that has no evidence of prior use. Sites that have been lightly impacted—obviously used but with vegetation surviving on the site—should be avoided. If you don't re-use them they will probably recover.

If choosing a pristine site, stay away from trails and waterways. Look for durable rock outcroppings, gravel areas, or snow. Avoid moist areas or vegetated forest floors and alpine zones that will register the impact of your feet. If you do camp on vegetation, look for grassy areas rather than terrain covered by bushes and woody-stemmed plants, and make your stay short. Alternate paths to water and your kitchen area to avoid formation of a use trail; similarly, wear "soft" shoes around camp. You'll know you've done a good job if no one will be able to tell you've been there when you leave.

Campfires

While campfires are permitted in most of the Winds below timberline, their use is not encouraged. Fires destroy organic matter in topsoil, and blackened rocks, half-burned wood and ash accumulation impacts the natural appearance of a site. Carry and use a backpacking stove. If you must build a fire, use only dead, down material. Use an existing fire ring or a firepan or fireblanket so you don't create another fire scar on the land. Don't construct a ring: Rings *do not* keep fires from escaping. Keep your fire small to reduce visual impact, wood consumption and forest fire danger. Never leave your fire unattended. Scatter unused firewood when you leave and make sure your fire is completely out. If you used an existing fire at a well-used campsite, leave it in place so another fire scar is not created.

Sanitation and Trash

Bury human waste at least 200 feet away from trails, campsites, waterways and other frequently used places. This prevents rain and snow run-off from carrying waste into lakes and streams, contaminating your source of drinking and cooking water. Dig a shallow hole 6-8 inches deep, make your deposit, and recover the hole. Carefully burn soiled toilet paper, or pack it out in a sealed plastic bag.

To protect lakes and streams, minimize the use of biodegradable soap for bathing and dishes. Lather and rinse at least 200 feet away from the water source with water carried to your washing site in a pot. This allows the soap to break down as it filters through the soil before re-entering the water system. Some campers prefer using sand and gravel to clean their dishes. This must also be done away from the water source so food particles don't pollute lakes and streams.

Aluminum does not burn, no matter how hot the fire. Don't attempt it unless you enjoy picking flakes out of ashes. Pack it out. Pack out all your trash, including cans, plastic and food scraps. Burying them doesn't cut it — animals dig them up. You're potentially affecting both their health and behavior patterns.

On the way out, when your pack is light and you're in great shape, pick up the gum wrappers, cans, foil and other items left by less conscientious backcountry users. It will help keep the wilderness pristine.

Backcountry Travel

Travel in the backcountry in a way that minimizes disturbance to others. Unless you are in bear country, walk quietly and avoid using brightly colored clothes and equipment to cut down on the likelihood others will see you and your camp (the exception to this, of course, is during hunting season). When you take a break, move away from the trail to a durable area such as rock outcroppings so others can pass by without contact. If possible, camp in a screened area so your site is not visible from the trail.

Walk in the middle of a path as much as possible, even if it is muddy. Walking on the edge of a trail to avoid a bog only makes the bog bigger by breaking down the trail edges and widening the mess. Similarly, snow patches on trails should be crossed rather than skirted to avoid creating small side trails. Trails switchback because the steepness of the slope and instability of the soils cannot hold a path that leads straight up. By shortcutting switchbacks, you're creating the very problem that they were intended to avoid: Erosion. Remember that it is illegal to cut switchbacks or portions of trail in the wilderness.

Respect the needs of wildlife. If you decide to approach an animal for a photograph or closer look, avoid sudden movement and stay downwind. If your behavior causes a reaction, you are too close. Keep in mind that you may cause an animal to abandon a nest, birthing site, water supply or feeding area—all of which have negative consequences. Give animals plenty of space.

Off-Trail Considerations

This book contains a number of unofficial routes and trails. Cross-country and off-trail travel demand a higher level of skill to protect both yourself and the environment. Should you travel off-trail? If you do not know how to use a map and compass, safely cross steep talus and snow, render emergency first-aid, or effect a rescue from a remote area, the answer is probably no—your skill level is not sufficient to keep you safe. Either go with other people who possess these skills or stay on well-traveled trails until you have acquired them.

If you do travel off-trail, minimize your impact on the environment. Use an existing path if available. If not, spread out instead of walking single file to avoid creating a new one. Even infrequent trampling can create an incipient trail, which will attract additional use. Choose a route that crosses durable surfaces such as rock or hard ground. Trails are more likely to develop on fragile vegetation, particularly above timberline. Avoid traveling in early season, when ground saturated from snowmelt deteriorates easily. Give the ground a chance to dry out. Don't mark your route by constructing cairns. Marking invites further use of that route, ultimately creating a new user trail. Finally, follow gradual ridges instead of cutting down steep slopes. If you must hike a steep slope, switchback to minimize erosion.

Stock considerations

Pack stock groups must be more conscientious than backpackers since animals tend to produce greater impact. The fewer animals taken, the less impact on the land. Keeping groups small and carrying lightweight equipment will help reduce the number of stock animals.

When selecting a campsite pay attention to available feed. If the area is overgrazed stock may remove feed needed by deer and elk during winter months. Also be aware of stock watering requirements. Loose herding for watering causes substantial streambank damage. Hitchlines, hobbles and staking are ways to confine pack animals. Only picket enough stock to keep others from straying, being sure to move pins every few hours to prevent overgrazing. Let stock graze freely during the day—hobbling if they need to be constrained—but attach to a hitchline at night. Protect bark by using straps or "tree saver" devices. Temporary corrals built of rope or portable electric fence can also be used, but must be moved twice daily.

Remember that it takes longer to naturalize an area impacted by pack animals. Scatter manure piles to aid decomposition and to be courteous to the next occupant. Fill areas dug up by animal hooves and remove excess feed.

SAFETY

It is beyond the scope of this book, nor is it my intention, to detail comprehensive safety aspects of backcountry travel: Entire volumes have been written on the subject. Visitors to the Wind River Range should be aware that, due to its remote location, rescue operations within the wilderness can be slow. Helicopter rescues are only authorized by forest supervisors for medical emergencies, and typically take at least an hour to reach the injured party once the rescue is initiated.

Because most Winds visitors prepare for their backcountry trips, on average there are only a half-dozen rescue operations any given year. These typically involve climbing accidents, heart attacks and strokes. There are, however, several safety considerations pertinent to travel in the Winds that deserve mention.

Weather

Be aware that it can snow in the Winds almost any day of the year and over the course of time probably has. Not only that it can snow on a day that began with 80° on the thermometer and bright blue skies. Be prepared to withstand sudden, severe weather changes in the mountains. On all but the simplest of hikes, carry a minimum of a wool hat and gloves, rain jacket, pile jacket or sweater, an emergency "space" blanket, sunscreen, sunglasses, a map and compass, and adequate food and water.

Afternoon thunderstorms are common in the Winds and with them, lightning. Every year approximately 200 people in the United States are killed by lightning strikes, more than the combined total of victims from floods, tornadoes and hurricanes. Lightning accounts for more than 6,000 forest fires each year. A single bolt carries 10 to 30 million amperes of current. To put this in perspective, the rail that powers Washington D.C.'s subway carries a charge of 750 volts.

This underscores the importance of taking refuge in a storm. Avoid meadows, ridges, lone trees, lakeshores, rock overhangs—where an electric charge can bounce to you at its base—and mountain tops. If available, seek refuge in groves of trees of uniform size or low-lying areas. Keep away from metal objects such as tent poles, pack frames and walking sticks that can act as lightning rods in an electrical storm.

While 20 percent of the people struck by lightning do not survive, if CPR is administered *immediately* to a victim of a lightning strike—even if they appear dead—chances are the victim may be revived.

Hypothermia & Dehydration

Hypothermia is the plunging of your body's core temperature; if the condition is not arrested it can lead to death. It often develops in wet, windy weather at or above 50 degrees, when most people aren't concerned about their bodies losing heat faster than it can be produced. When clothes become wet from rain or sweat they lose as much as 90% of their insulating value. Wind-driven cool air refrigerates the wet clothing by evaporating moisture from its surface. The body reacts by shivering to try to generate heat, and later, shunting blood away from the extremities and brain to keep the core more. This results in loss of coordination, memory lapses, poor judgment, unconsciousness and even death.

Treat initial symptoms seriously by getting out of the elements and into warm, dry clothes. After a long day of sweaty hiking, keep in mind that temperatures can plummet quickly when the sun sets. Change into dry, warm clothes before setting up camp or cooking dinner.

Dehydration is common at higher elevations. Every time you breathe, moisture is pulled from your lungs into the dry air. Sweat quickly evaporates in direct sunlight, making most people unaware of how much moisture they are losing. Make a conscious effort to regularly drink lots of fluids.

Altitude

High altitude is the leading cause of sickness for Bridger Wilderness visitors. Common symptoms of mild altitude illness, typically noticed around 10,000 feet, include headache, loss of appetite, a general "blah" feeling similar to the flu, poor sleep and nausea. Should these occur, drink plenty of water and don't go higher. If you are on a day hike the symptoms typically disappear shortly after you descend. If you are on a multi-day trip and your symptoms do not cease overnight, the safest course is to descend at least 2,000 feet or until your symptoms abate.

Underestimating Time and Energy

Many people underestimate the time and energy needed for hikes that gain significant elevation. As a rule of thumb add an "effort mile" to the overall mileage for every 500 feet gained. This will give you a more realistic approximation of how much energy the hike really takes. Give yourself enough time for your intended destination. If the hike is taking longer than you anticipated, don't push yourself to exhaustion; turn around. Many accidents in the mountains are the result of people becoming overly tired and losing their physical and mental acuity.

Contaminated Water

Giardia and other bacterial agents have become an increasing problem in the region's backcountry water supply. It is recommend that you treat all surface water before drinking it. A variety of methods can be used, including boiling water, treating water with iodine tablets, or using a filter/purifier. For the latter to be effective against giardia, they must filter to a minimum of .02 microns. While purifiers typically eliminate all microorganisms—including cysts, viruses and bacteria—filters may not remove all bacteria or viruses.

BEAR PRECAUTIONS

It would be rare, but within the realm of possibility, for Wind River visitors to see a grizzly bear. More probable is spying a black bear. While it can be a thrill to see a bear in the backcountry from a distance, you do not want to confront one. Contact the appropriate Forest Service district office for recent reports of bear activity prior to planning your trip, and adhere to the guidelines below.

1.   Don't surprise a bear. Near streams or bushy areas where visibility/hearing is limited, make your presence known by singing, talking, wearing bells or making other noises. Travel in groups and don't hike after dark.

2. Leave your dog at home when traveling in bear country. A dog can easily disturb a bear and lead it back to you.
3. If you see a bear but it doesn't see you, quietly leave the area.
4.. Food and odors attract bears. Minimize both.
   a. Keep a clean camp by storing food and garbage properly. "Food" includes canned items, pop and beer, cooking grease, and processed livestock and pet food. Store food/garbage out-of-sight , preferably in a bear-proof container. These are available on loan at the Pinedale Ranger District office. Otherwise place food/garbage in bags, back packs or panniers and hang them from a tree branch at least 10 feet above ground and four feet out from the tree trunk. Do not store food in tents.
   b. Avoid cooking smelly or greasy foods. Sleep uphill away from your cooking area and food storage site. Don't sleep in the same clothes you wore while cooking. Keep sleeping bags and personal gear clean and free of food odor.
   c. Store odorous items as though they were food. This includes sunscreen, toothpaste, lip balm, and soiled toilet paper or sanitary products stashed in a plastic bag. Don't use perfumes or deodorants.
   d Where hunting is permitted, keep game out of reach of bears. Dispose of fish entrails by puncturing the air bladder and dropping them in deep water where they will decompose naturally.
5. Horse pellets should be stored the same as food.
6. Before retiring for the night, note climbable trees in the area. Sleep in tents large enough to stack gear between you and the tent wall.

Encounter Guidelines

Even if you have taken all precautions you may still encounter a bear. The Interagency Grizzly Bear Committee, Wyoming Game & Fish Department and the U.S. Fish and Wildlife Service cooperatively developed guidelines for bear encounters in both the field and camp.

If you encounter the bear in the field, try to back out of the situation. Keep calm, avoid direct eye contact, back up slowly and speak in a soft monotone. Never turn your back on the bear and never kneel. Most encounters end with the bear leaving at this point. Do not climb a tree unless you have time to climb at least 10 feet before the bear reaches you. If you do have time to climb a tree, drop a non-food item such as a camera or jacket to distract the bear while you climb. Never run; this may excite the animal. It is unlikely you could outrun a black or grizzly bear.

If the bear charges stand your ground; it may be a mock charge. Bears often mock charge several times before leaving. Shooting a bear when it is charging is not recommended. The bear almost always lives long enough to severely maul the shooter.

As a last resort play dead. Lie on your stomach or side with your legs drawn up to your chest. Lace your hands over the back of your neck and tuck your head. If you have a backpack leave it on as it will help protect your back. If the bear swats you, roll with it. Stay in a tucked position and do not try to look at the bear until you are sure it is gone. Many people have survived bear attacks using this tactic.

Bear encounters in camp are different than those in the field. The encounters are potentially more dangerous because the bear is no longer avoiding confrontation with humans. If a bear enters your camp, stay calm and avoid eye contact. Get to safety as quickly as possible by slowly backing away while looking for suitable trees to climb. Climb as high as you can since some grizzlies can scale trees. Stay in the tree until you are sure the bear is gone. If you have kept a clean camp it will likely not stay long.

If the bear enters your tent or charges assume it is not a mock charge. Playing dead will not work in this situation, as the bear has made a conscious choice to attack you. Fight back by punching, slapping or using any object available as a weapon. Your best protection may be spraying it with one of numerous commercial repellants. Many of these are loaded with pepper. Make sure you know how to safely use these products before you are in a frightening situation. Spraying yourself in the eyes with concentrated pepper will make the scenario infinitely worse.

If there is enough daylight to strike camp following a bear visit, the best course is to leave. If the visit was at night, move to a different area in the morning. It is not recommended that you remain at a site visited by a bear.

Report all bear sightings and encounters, no matter how insignificant, to the appropriate district office. Your information may prevent someone else from having an encounter that endangers them or the species.

Λ

A FINAL WORD

This book is intended to serve as a general reference to hiking trails in the Winds, and not as a substitute for experience or one's own route finding abilities and skills. While reference points and intersections have been carefully selected to aid hikers, field conditions often change. This book should be used only as a reference and not as the final word in situations that require judgment calls.

I welcome comments, suggestions and recommendations. Please feel free to write me at 1255 N. Iron Rock Road #6, Jackson, Wyoming, 83001. I hope your time in the mountains brings you as much pleasure as mine has brought me.

The Range

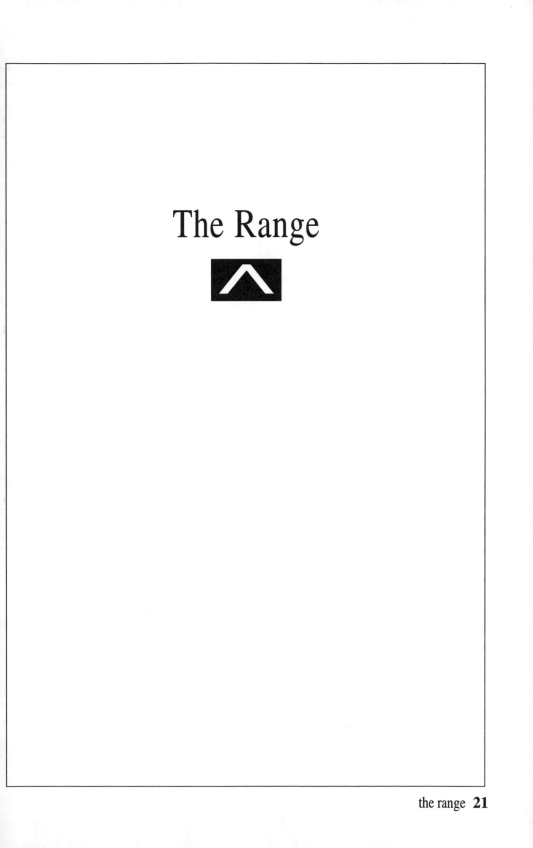

History

In 1803 President Jefferson negotiated one of the largest land deals in
history: the French agreed to sell
their continental holdings west of the
Mississippi. The $16 million transac-
tion, dubbed the "Louisiana Purchase,"
doubled the size of America. What was
there? There were few reports on the
little-explored, great western interior.

Jefferson intended to find out. An-
ticipating the purchase he had already
arranged for his personal secretary,
Meriwether Lewis, and Capt. William
Clark to try and find a route to the Pacific by heading up the Missouri to the
Columbia River, and hopefully, the
coast.

Lewis and Clark left St. Louis the
spring of 1804. They made it to the
Mandan Indian Villages in present
North Dakota before winter forced them
to stop. While wintering over they met
a disagreeable French-Canadian trapper
named Toussaint Charbonneau. In
Charbonneau's company was a
Shoshone woman he had purchased
from the Minnetaree Indian Tribe.
Sacajawea, born in the late 1700s, had
been captured from her tribe by the
Minnetarees and taken to their village,
a spoils of war who was later sold.

Lewis and Clark recognized her
value to their expedition. She could
serve as interpreter, knew how to live
off the land, and—perhaps most impor-
tantly—would help provide the expedition with safe passage through Indian
territory. As H. D. Del Monte noted in
*Early History of Lander, Wyoming and
the Wind River Valley,* it was "traditional
among the Indians that no women
should accompany a war party...her
presence alone guaranteed a friendly re-
ception by most of the Indians they
met."

The expedition agreed to hire
Charbonneau on the stipulation that
Sacajawea, who later became one of his
many wives, would accompany the
group. Only two months before they
were to leave she gave birth to a son,
Baptiste, whom she carried on her back
throughout the arduous 17-month journey. (Clark became so attached to the
infant that he later wrote Charbonneau
to request his permission to raise and
educate the boy, which was granted.)
The expedition made it to the Pacific
the fall of 1805 and wintered near the
mouth of the Columbia before return-

ing to Missouri the following spring. On their way back to St. Louis, Lewis and Clark's men encountered two trappers who intended to spend the winter hunting the Upper Yellowstone. John Colter, a member of the expedition, was granted permission to join them. The venture floundered and the trio dissolved the spring of 1807. Colter was returning to St. Louis when he met a party led by fur trader Manuel Lisa near the mouth of the Platte. The 40-man outfit was headed upstream to build a trading fort at the confluence of the Bighorn and Yellowstone Rivers (Ft. Raymond was completed late the fall of 1807). Once again Colter turned around, this time hired by Lisa to travel throughout the region to invite Indians to trade furs at the fort.

Colter made his legendary journey in late 1807 and 1808. He left few records, but from Lewis and Clark's 1814 published account, it is believed he traveled up the Big Horn, crossed Union Pass at the north end of the Wind River Range, and wandered through parts of what is now Yellowstone and Jackson Hole, making him the first known white man to visit the area.

Fur Trade

It was Lewis and Clark's report and tales brought back by a handful of trappers that prompted American entrepreneurs to try their hand at the western fur business, dominated by the Hudson Bay and North West fur companies of Canada. New York businessman John Jacob Astor formed a subsidiary of his American Fur Company, Pacific Fur, and sent Wilson Price Hunt overland to scout possible sites for a series of trading posts. He was instructed to retrace Lewis and Clark's route to the mouth of Columbia, where he would remain to manage a post being built by Astor's sea-going expedition. Hunt's group started late and did not cross Union Pass until late September. They endured a horrendous winter trip to the coast, finally reaching Fort Astoria in February of 1812. Hunt sent his first dispatches back to Astor via Robert Stuart. The 27-year-old Scotsman, who had arrived at Astoria by ship, was selected to lead a party of seven overland to St. Louis. They left in June.

In an attempt to avoid skirmishes with the Crows and other hostile tribes, Stuart left Lewis and Clark's route and promptly got lost. In subsequent wandering the party inadvertently "discovered" South Pass, a 20-mile, wide divide that marks the southern end of the Winds.

The pass would be the site of the largest overland migration in history less than 30 years later. At the time Stuart did not appreciate its significance, but a hint of things to come was reported in the *Missouri Gazette* on

April 30, 1813, shortly after he reached St. Louis: "By information received from these gentlemen, it appears that a journey across the continent of N. America, might be performed with a wagon, there being no obstruction in the whole route that any person would dare to call a mountain..."

While Stuart was making his way back, American fur trade west of the Mississippi had come to a virtual standstill. Escalating conflict over territory between the British and Americans exploded into war. Both sides attempted to garner support from the Indians, creating what historian Tom Bell called "confusion and animosity ... Trappers met Indians on the warpath everywhere."

It was not until the early 1820s that the fracas had cooled enough for businessmen to look westward once more. Missouri Lieutenant Governor William Ashley and Andrew Henry, owner of the Missouri Fur Company, decided to try their luck in 1822. They placed an ad in the *Missouri Gazette & Public Advertiser,* seeking "100 Enterprising Young Men" to "ascend the river Missouri to its source, there to be employed for one, two or three years." Jim Bridger, Jedediah Smith, William Sublette, Jim Clyman, and Tom Fitzpatrick were among the stellar group that responded.

Their legendary mountain man status was earned not on the Missouri, but in Wyoming. Exploits on the Missouri almost sank the Ashley-Henry partnership from the onset. An overturned boat cost $10,000; marauding Indians killed 16 men, and wounded another 50. The party decided to split up, leave the ill-fated river, and trap what is now Wyoming. Bell notes that between the two groups, the men "probably explored and trapped most of the Wind River Basin."

Reports sent back to Ashley were encouraging. He ventured to the Green and arranged to reprovision and meet with his trappers in the Uintas on July 10, 1825. Through misfortune on the Missouri, Ashley realized he could resupply his trappers at a gathering place and avoid the expense of maintaining a post. The Rendezvous was born. For trappers it was a chance to socialize, get paid for pelts, buy supplies, and raise cane. The Rendezvous would often go on for two weeks, a wild affair punctuated by gambling, fights, foot races, drunken escapades and what Wyoming historian T. A. Larson called "grappling of squaws in lust and love." It was, perhaps, a needed release from dangerous work: one-third of Ashley's trappers died pursuing their trade.

The Rendezvous, and the fur trade that gave it birth, were not to be long-lived. In the early 1830s fashion turned her fickle head from beaver to silk hats, and the demand for pelts dropped. The animals themselves were virtually trapped out. By 1840 —the year of the last Rendezvous—less than 120 trappers and traders were in attendance. In reality, it had never been a big business. H.M. Chittenden estimated in *American Fur Trade of the Far West* that under 3,000 men were involved in fur trade activities west of the Missouri, and most of them earned under $400 a year.

But oh, the romance of it! Capt. B.L.E. Bonneville was a johnny-come-lately on the scene. He secured leave from the army, ostensibly to establish an outpost but more likely to enter the fur trade. On May 1, 1832, he led 110 men and 20 wagons loaded with ammunition and goods over South Pass, and proceeded to build a fortified camp near the site of that year's Rendezvous. The outpost was dubbed "Fort Nonsense" by the trappers and Indians, who knew its location would not survive a winter. They were right; it closed within a month. Bonneville was discharged from the army for overstaying his leave. He did explore the surrounding mountains, and may have made the first ascent in the range. That said, his place in history was earned by confirming what a St. Louis reporter had suspected 20 years earlier: Wagons could be taken over South Pass.

Emigration Flood

In 1831 four Indian chiefs traveled to St. Louis in search of the "Book of Heaven." Believing the Indians wanted to be converted, the Methodist church began sending missionaries west. Dr. Marcus Whitman, his wife and another missionary couple crossed South Pass July 4, 1836, on their way to Oregon. Four more missionary couples crossed the divide in 1838. "The safe passage of these six women did not go unnoticed in the eastern United States," a historian wrote in the Oct./Nov. 1991 issue of *Wind River Mountaineer.* "Where these women went, others could go."

Emigrants began to join the missionaries. Some sought to escape the financial depression of 1837. Others were drawn by the promise of free land, and the concept of "Manifest Destiny" espoused in Washington, D.C.: America was *meant* to extend from sea-to-sea. Towards that end, the government began funding expeditions to survey routes for wagons and military posts.

The emigration turning point came in 1843 when missionary Whitman returned to Missouri to lead the Applegate church group to Oregon. Over 1,000 people, 120 wagons and 5,000 head of cattle bid good-bye to Independence and headed west that spring. Guided by William Sublette, they reached their goal in September. It had been shown beyond doubt that wagon trains could not only negotiate South Pass, they could travel the route all the way to the coast. The emigration floodgates had been opened.

The discovery of gold in California in 1848, as well as Mormons seeking a homeland to avoid religious persecution, added to the stream of those seeking different lives. It is estimated that over 300,000 people traveled through South Pass between 1841 and 1868 on their way to California, Oregon, and Utah. Drovers trailed a million cattle and sheep over the same routes.

During the peak gold rush years the route suffered the modern equivalent of bumper-to-bumper traffic. In his comprehensive study of the Oregon Trail, *Plains Across,* John Unruh wrote that the swath "(was) often so dusty that overlanders donned goggles to see, and so crowded that traveling partners and relatives became separated in the vast multitudes passing east and west."

Yet for all the traffic, few emigrants remained in what is now Wyoming. It was viewed as inhospitable country to get through as quickly as possible. The route was arid. It lacked the scenic beauty of the Tetons and did not have the lure of gold or fertile farmland. On the other side of the pass, the Winds lay undisturbed—but not unaffected.

In the mid-1800s close to 90% of the region's residents were Indians. Most of the Oregon Trail cut through their land, and as settlers passed through or stopped to homestead in Nebraska and Kansas, they depleted supplies of buffalo, grass and timber. Other trails were forged as gold was discovered in Montana, further impacting the once undisturbed plains. As traditionally nomadic tribes were squeezed into smaller areas, intertribal battles and conflicts with emigrants threatened to explode. In anticipation of an uprising, the federal government appointed mountain man Tom Fitzpatrick High Plains Indian agent in 1847 to hear complaints and help keep the peace. Fort Laramie was purchased and garrisoned two years later. In 1851, Congress authorized a massive peace treaty council near Laramie. Ten thousand Indians attended the historic meeting at Horse Creek. Tribes were compensated for depletion of their resources, and offered $50,000 to permit the establishment of military roads and posts.

The peace did not last long. A series of inept military decisions escalated tensions, resulting in the 1854 Grattan Massacre. Feeling their entire way of life was threatened, tribes fought each other, attacked emigrants along the trail (roughly 400 were killed from 1840 to 1860), burned stage and freight stations,

and tore down the transcontinental telegraph line. The government's response was to built more forts.

Railroads and Reservations

It was in this climate that demands for a transcontinental railroad gained momentum. The massive influx of people to California, Oregon and Utah had created the need for better postal and transport services between the east and west coasts. A railroad was proposed in the 1850s, but it did not receive serious consideration until after the Civil War. The Union Pacific and Central Pacific Railway Corporations woed senators by offering to transport government supplies, troops and mail at reduced rates. They also proposed promoting settlement of the area by granting investors land for each completed mile of track.

Congress took the bait and passed the Pacific Railway Acts in 1862 and 1864. To get the project started, the railroads were offered 30 year loans of $16,000 for every mile of track completed across the plains, $32,000 for track laid in the foothills, and $48,000 for each mountain mile. It was a significant investment, one the government did not want compromised by the "Indian problem." Its solution was to place tribes on reservations away from the lines and new settlements. The Sioux were granted land in western Dakota. The Shoshones, whose leader Chief Washakie had maintained friendly relations with the emigrants, were granted desirable land on the east side of the Wind River Range in 1868, both as a thank-you from the government and to help control the Sioux.

Given the perspective of the time, the Sioux needed controlling. In a July 29, 1867 report to F.H. Head, Superintendent of Indian Affairs, Indian agent Luther Mann argued that Shoshone occupancy of the Wind River Valley,

"with suitable protection from the government, would prevent the raiding war parties of Sioux from interfering with the development of mines just discovered and being opened in the vicinity of South Pass...

The entire range of country west from the South Pass to the Mormon settlements on Weber River is almost destitute of game, and while these friendly (Shoshone) Indians are obliged, during the summer months, to subsist on the small game of this vast area of sagebrush, the powerful and hostile Sioux are roaming unmolested over the beautiful valleys east and north of the Wind River chain of mountains, with grass and game at their disposal, which enables them to murder and rob with impunity the soldiers near their garrison, the almost defenseless emigrant crossing the plains in search of a new home, and the hardy miners who are tolling to develop the mineral resources which constitute the base of our national wealth."

When the government agreed to deed the Wind River Valley to the Shoshone Indians, the tribe accepted being placed on the reservation. Washakie realized there were few other options. Most tribes, however, did not willingly give up their homeland, or surrender prime hunting ground to settlers. It would be another dozen years before the Indian Wars abated. But the concept of reservations had been established, and with it, the future of a large segment of the east side of the Wind River Range.

Tie Hacks, Cowboys, and Herders

The impact of the transcontinental line on the Winds extended far beyond establishment of the reservation. Track had to be laid on wood beams, or ties. Because wood was scarce across the prairie, a booming logging business on the Green and Wind Rivers sprang up almost overnight. The ties were cut in winter, stored on the banks, then floated downstream to the nearest railhead. Charles Deloney contracted with Union Pacific in 1867 to flood ties down the Green to Green River City, an operation that ran for two years. The Wyoming Tie and Timber Company near Dubois produced over 10 million ties for Chicago and Northwestern Railroad during its 40 years of operation. The company floated logs 100 miles down the Wind River to Riverton. Eventually, portable sawmills and reduced demand made the tie business obsolete.

The business that was to endure was ranching. The railroad provided a means to get beef to eastern markets. Moreover, the government had created a demand for beef at its military posts and Indian reservations: Native Americans could no longer rely on diminishing buffalo herds to feed themselves. Ranching, like logging, became a viable entity with the completion of the line. Enormous herds were trailed north from Texas to fatten up in the newly-formed territory before being shipped to market. Cattlemen, railroad promoters, and politicians were shameless in their promotion of the "open range," and overgrazing soon occurred. In 1885 it was estimated that there were 1.5 million head of cattle in Wyoming. Disaster struck the winter of 1886-87, when ceaseless blizzards stranded the animals on the range. Unable to forage or protect themselves, the dead stacked up against each other like cords of wood.

The financial loss was staggering. It forced Swan Land & Cattle, the largest cattle company in Wyoming, into bankruptcy. Others soon followed. Ranchers still in the business struggled for survival—a struggle worsened by the coming of homesteaders who fenced the range, and an increasing influx of sheep. In 1870 the territory supported fewer than 7,000 woolly-backs. Forty years later, the count reached five million.

Five million! The "woolly monsters" were eating grass to the roots on land cattle had overgrazed for 20 years. Belatedly realizing there was a limit to Wyoming's grasslands, intense feuding broke out between the ranchers and sheepmen. Over 2,000 sheep were murdered in an ambush near Raid Lake, one of many incidents. Writes historian Charles Whittenburg:

"Herders were tied to trees and their wagons burned... occasionally wagon-wheel spokes were used to club the sheep to death. Some were poisoned or shot, or blown up by dynamite..."

In 1909, three herders were murdered near Tensleep. Ironically, it eased the intense feuding. Both sides realized the situation was out-of-hand, and agreed to compromise. The end of the open range was acknowledged. Cattle and sheep herds were reduced and grazing was eventually regulated under the Taylor Grazing Act of 1934. (The historic use of the Winds as "open range" explains why cattle and sheep are still permitted to graze in designated wilderness areas. They were an acknowledged pre-existing use.)

Dudes and Climbers

In the open range shakedown some ranchers discovered it was more profitable to host wealthy Easterners than run cattle. The visitors, nicknamed dudes, paid handsomely to participate in ranch activities, or have someone guide and cook for them. The first dudes had come years before on the heels of the fur trappers. Capt. William Drummond Stewart of Scotland paid William Sublette $500 in 1833 "for the right to tag along with the party," wrote bemused historian Charles Roundy in a 1973 *Annals of Wyoming* article. Jim Bridger was similarly employed in 1854 by Sir George Gore, an Irish nobleman who spent two years trophy hunting in Wyoming. It was, again, the arrival of the railroad that made staying on a ranch a possibility for a significant number of people. The rails gave access to far-off Wyoming.

Why the interest? America was, quite simply, in love with the West. Yellowstone National Park was created in 1872. By 1929 the fledgling park had already drawn 260,000 visitors. President Arthur sparked interest in the Winds on a well-publicized 1883 business trip through the region, an interest fed by Owen Wister's *Virginian.* His popular 1901 novel went through 14 printings in its first year. Roundy noted that the book was the precursor of "literally thousands of 20th century 'Westerns' in print and film."

Ranchers who had struggled to make ends meet discovered folks willing to pay for their daily experience. Dubois became a thriving dude ranch town in the 1920s, as did Pinedale. Business dropped off significantly with the advent of World War II, and many dude ranches ceased operation. By then, however, the range had been discovered not only by dudes but by mountaineers and hikers.

In 1929 Robert Underhill and Kenneth Henderson began climbing peaks around beautiful Titcomb Basin. Henderson wrote a series of articles for *Appalachia* in the 1930s entitled, "The Wind River Range of Wyoming." Portions of the existing Bridger Wilderness were designated a primitive area on February 9, 1931, one of the first such designations in the country. The intent of the designation, as defined in the *1995 Bridger Wilderness Action Plan*, was "to preserve the primitive conditions of environment, " "to make it possible for people to detach themselves, at least temporarily, from the strain and turmoil of modern existence," and "to afford unique opportunities for physical, mental and spiritual recreation or regeneration." The area was expanded in May of 1937 to include the southern portion of the Winds, a region thoroughly explored by Frank and Notsie Garnick of Rock Springs and Orrin Bonney in the 1940s. Bonney, too, wrote of their discovery in *Appalachia*, drawing the attention of numerous mountaineering clubs. The Chicago Mountaineering Club, Iowa Mountaineers and Wisconsin Hoofers explored the range extensively through the 1950s and 1960s, climbing many of the peaks.

Towards the end of the decade the U.S. Geological Survey began producing 15 minute maps of the peaks, lakes and Indian trails. The maps opened the doors for thousands of recreational backcountry users.

Geology

Geology tells the history of the earth through textbooks written in stone. Rock in the Winds is far more complex than the space available here to describe it: the text fills an encyclopedia, not a guidebook. The jumble of igneous, sedimentary and metamorphic slabs holds mysteries geologists have yet to decipher.

Much is known, however. We'll start near the end of the present chapter, about 600 million years ago. The plains of western Wyoming were slowly but steadily being submerged by an ancient sea, a process that continued for over 350 million years. As the sea advanced it dropped sand, mud and calcium carbonates. The weight of the deposits compacted the lower layers and formed sedimentary rock.

Laramide Revolution

The thick layer of sediment lay undisturbed during a long period of geologic calm before massive activity began brewing in the west. The earth's crust started buckling in what is now southern California 80 million years ago. Rock "shock waves" spread eastward like ocean waves, reaching the Winds 15 million years later. Here, horizontal compression pushed the land up in great bulges. The compression was so great it literally broke the rock, folding it over itself at the southwest end of the range. In what pre-eminent geologist Dave Love called "the greatest localized vertical displacement known anywhere in the world," the earth-moving forces also weakened ancient fault lines, uplifting blocks of granitic rock over 40,000 feet, exposing some of the oldest known rocks of earth. Carbon dating estimates they are almost three-and-a-half billion years old.

The Winds were never two miles higher than Everest. As massive blocks of rock were slowly being uplifted, steepened streambeds began to vigorously erode the new mountains. For 30

A hiker relaxes in front of massive Mammoth Glacier, seen from the west flank of Gannett Peak.

million years the mountains were carried away, bit by bit, and deposited in canyons and streambeds. The range was literally buried in its own debris, once again little more than an undulating plain with a few peaks poking above sediment thousands of feet thick.

Like a swinging pendulum, the process was reversed approximately 10 million years ago when a new series of uplifts occurred. As the mountains rose reactivated streams began carrying ancient deposits downstream. Protected by position or capped with flat rock not easily eroded, tongues of the ancient sediment held fast. Goat Flat, Ram Flat and Horse Ridge are all remnants of the ancient plain that had buried the high peaks.

Glaciers

The uplifted range was a hodgepodge of hulking blocks and broken mounds. The jagged peaks, pinnacles and cirques that characterize the rugged range we know today are a new addition, carved within the last 250,000 years. Five different times—for periods lasting thousands of years—temperatures cooled enough in the region to form glaciers and massive ice caps in the mountains. The largest cap in the Winds extended 50 miles down the Green River Valley, a river of ice over eight miles long and 1,000 feet thick. When temperatures warmed, the glaciers began to melt and move, polishing granite walls and carving deep canyons and cirques in their path. The weight of the ice created hollows filled by melting ice chunks, forming many of the range's myriad lakes. Others were created when meltwater was impounded by moraines, or, as is the case with piedmont lakes at the mouth of canyons, the glaciers deepened and widened existing river chasms, creating deep lakes on the canyon floor. Fremont, New Fork, Green River Lakes, Willow Lakes, and Boulder Lake are all examples of the latter phenomenon.

Evidence of past glaciation is seen virtually everywhere in the range. Researchers believe glaciers in the Winds all but disappeared 5,000-7,000 years ago, reforming during a mini ice-age around 1400.

These new icefields have been receding the last 150 years. Today most of the range's glaciers are located on less-exposed, north or northeast facing slopes or steep, shadowed cirques. Their retreat, easily seen by new moraines at their toe, is closely monitored: three-quarters of all fresh water in the world is stored in glaciers. It has been estimated that the July-August stream flow from Wyoming's glaciers is 35 billion gallons of water. The Winds contain 60 of the state's 80 glaciers. Collectively, the permanent snowfields comprise the largest glaciated area in the U.S. outside of Alaska. Seven of the 10 largest glaciers in the United States are in the range, most of them clustered around 13,804 foot Gannett Peak on the east side of the Continental Divide.

Extensive glaciation, both past and present, gives the range much of its beauty. Ultimately, the erosive power of the many glacier-fed streams in the range will also be its demise, reducing it once again—millions of years hence—to a pile of rubble.

Wildlife

Wyoming's wildlife outnumbers its human population. Elk, bison, moose, deer, bear, pronghorn antelope, bighorn sheep, dozens of smaller mammals, and over 200 species of birds and waterfowl inhabit the state. A large portion of the menagerie roams through it's northwest corner, an immense tract of relatively undeveloped land that includes the Teton, Absaroka, Gros Ventre, Wind River and Wyoming mountain ranges. This impressive chunk of real estate is administered by two national parks, five national forests, an Indian reservation, and two national wildlife refuges. Collectively it forms the largest wildlife preserve in the lower 48 states.

Wildlife species aren't evenly dispersed in the ecosystem. Wind River backcountry users will likely not see grizzly bears. Nor are bison high profile mammals. Other species of wildlife, however, commonly inhabit the range. Some of the more noticeable residents are listed below.

Bighorn Sheep

The Whiskey Basin Habitat Area at the northern end of the Wind River Range is home to the world's largest bighorn sheep population. Over 1,000 sheep migrate in late fall/early winter from the high country to critical winter range four miles outside of Dubois. Come spring, the sheep return to the rugged, high terrain west of the upper Green River. Deep canyons, snow fields, glaciers, and rocky cliffs characterize the region's 100 square miles.

The sheep management unit has been jointly run by Wyoming Game & Fish, the U.S. Forest Service, and the U.S. Bureau of Land Management since 1969. It was originally formed by Game & Fish in the 1940s when bighorns were in danger of being wiped out. Historically, as many as two million wild sheep ranged from Canada to Mexico. When trapper Osborn Russell traveled through the area in 1835 in search of beaver pelts, he wrote in his journal that, "thousands of mountain sheep were scattered up and down... feeding on the short grass which grew among cliffs and crevices."

The bountiful population plummeted in the late 1880s, decimated by unrestricted hunting and introduction of domestic livestock. Cattle and sheep competed for scarce forage and carried disease that wiped out entire herds. By 1940 the once thriving wildlife species had dwindled to less than 3,000 animals statewide. It was thought that only 500 bighorns were left in the Wind River mountains.

Alarmed, the Game & Fish Department began working with private land-owners and other government agencies to protect critical habitat near Whiskey Mountain. Two large land purchases, totaling over 3,200 acres, were made in 1954 and 1957. (Now, approximately 8,500 acres has been set aside.) The agency also tightened its hunting regulations and livestock management policies.

The sheep population rebounded successfully enough for wildlife agencies to transplant animals to other herds. Over 1,200 sheep have been relocated since 1949. The National Bighorn Sheep Interpretive Center in Dubois offers insights on both the management program and the magnificent animals. It is open daily in the summer from Memorial Day to Labor Day weekend.

It is a thrill to see bighorns in the backcountry. The brown to gray-brown rams have creamy white rear ends and massive horns that coil backwards, out, then forward to form an arc. The horns aren't shed. They grow from the base, forming annual "rings" that help age the sheep. A three-quarter curl indicates that a ram is about 10 years into its 15 year life expectancy. Mature rams stand 40 inches high at the shoulder and weigh around 250 pounds. Ewes are comparative lightweights, capping out around 150 pounds. Rut peaks in December; lambing, six months later in June.

Elk

The elk, or wapiti, is a magnificent looking animal. Standing 4-5 feet tall, the males weigh a hefty 700-1,000 pounds; the smaller females 500-600 pounds. They have a reddish-brown summer coat, buff colored rump patch, and a distinctive dark brown neck cape. Mature males sport spreading antlers that reach maximum size in early autumn, typically about 5 1/2 feet across. The antlers may weigh as much as 25 pounds. They are shed each spring and quickly "recycled" by mice and other rodents who consume the calcium rich bone.

Elk have keen senses and are easily spooked by the sight or scent of humans. The cows and calves give out a high-pitched squeal, or bark, when threatened, and the whole herd will flee en masse if frightened. Generally however, elk are slow-moving walkers.

Since grasses account for over three-fourths of their diet, elk are usually seen in open meadows where they feed at dawn and dusk. Typical feeding areas are fringed by forest, providing quick escape for the herd and cover at night. Elk use the same nocturnal migration routes, forming well-worn paths to and from their feeding areas.

Backcountry users traveling in September and early October may hear bull elks bugling. The high-pitched mating call punctuates crisp autumn days and nights as the rutting season nears its peak. Rubbing their antlers against trees to remove the last vestiges of summer velvet and sparring with rival bulls are all part of the mating behavior. The results of the rut are evident in June when females drop their single, 30 pound calves. The calves are mobile within hours of birth and by six months of age may weigh as much as 250 pounds.

Backcountry users should be aware

that elk are hunted in the range. Wearing "hunter orange" is a recommended safety precaution if traveling in popular hunting units during hunting season. Check with the district administering the area you are considering.

Mule Deer

Mule deer can be found throughout the range, though their population has declined in recent years. Their coat is reddish brown in the summer, a duller gray during the winter months. Black-tipped, large ears and dichotomous antlers that "V" into equal parts distinguish them from other species of deer. Males are typically 3-4 feet tall and weigh roughly 250 pounds. The smaller females range from 100-150 pounds. Mulies are most active at dawn and dusk and, like elk, follow definite trails to and from their feeding areas. Unlike elk, however, the primary component of their diet is not grass but shrubbery and browse herbage. For this reason deer are often spotted in brushy terrain that contains both open meadows, scattered aspen groves and rocky ridges.

The mating season begins in late fall. It is usually completed by the end of December, when bucks may band loosely together. Does and young form their own winter herds. One or two fawns are dropped, typically in July. The weak, spotted young are "hidden," with the mother returning to them only to nurse. They gain enough strength to follow their mother in a couple of weeks and are weaned from her by autumn.

Coyotes

Coyotes resemble medium-sized German shepherds. Their nose is slightly more pointed and their tail fuller, the latter held between their back legs while running. The animal is gray to reddish-gray in color with a whitish throat and underbelly.

This prodigious member of the dog family has a short gestation period of two months and drops a litter of 5-7 pups. The hairless babes grow quickly in their burrows, partly because coyotes will eat anything. Porcupines, skunks, mice, birds, snakes, woodrats, weasels and crickets all satisfy a coyote's voracious palate. The animal establishes a typical 10 mile hunting route but will range up to 100 miles if food is scarce. They tend to hunt in pairs, using clever teamwork to kill their prey.

Despite ranchers' persistent efforts to eradicate it, the coyote has thrived. Key to its survival is its adaptability. The animal will travel through all kinds of terrain in search of food and water. Typically, however, it is seen in open meadows and broken forest country rather than in dense woodlands. Chiefly nocturnal, backcountry users often hear rather than see coyotes. Their nighttime serenade begins with sets of short yips followed by a long, mournful howl.

Black Bear

Opportunistic bruins habitually fatten up in the summer months near heavily-used campgrounds and trailheads at Green River Lakes and Big Sandy. The past several years black bears have set up housekeeping in the vicinity of Smith, Middle, Cathedral and Cook lakes. Different sites have been targets for "problem" bears over

The estimated deer population in the Greater Yellowstone Ecosystem approaches 88,000. Some biologists believe populations have been declining in the Winds.

the years. The real problem, of course, is humans not maintaining clean camps. With their keen sense of smell, bears are drawn to food and garbage. The easy pickin's at unsecured sites disrupts the bears' normal diet of insects, nuts, berries, small mammals and carrion. It also changes their pattern of ranging up to 15 miles per day for food. They become far more stationary, increasing the chance of a possible human/bear confrontation. While black bears seldom attack they will react aggressively if startled or with cubs. You don't want to tangle with these bruins. At maturity they stand 5-6 feet high, are 2-3 feet wide at the shoulder, and weigh 200-475 pounds. They can charge at speeds up to 30 mph in short spurts. Assume the bears are where you are, and follow recommended procedures to avoid trouble.

Pronghorn Antelope

Over half of the world's population of pronghorn antelope reside in Wyoming. Thousands of animals browse on the vast, rolling sagebrush hills and plains that characterize much of the state. Visitors to the Winds are likely to spy small herds of 12 or more on approach drives to the trailheads, notably near Pinedale, Boulder and Lander.

The tan and white animals stand roughly three feet high and weigh between 75-130 pounds. Their underside and rump are white, as are a pair of bands across their throat. Both sexes grow short, gently curved horns with a single prong that projects forward. Noticeably large eyes help them spot potential predators. They give birth to one to three kids in late spring/early summer.

Graceful pronghorns are the race car drivers of the plains. Their ample lungs allow them to easily maintain a pace of 30 mph, almost double that for short bursts. Quick escape helps them compensate for a sense of curiosity that permits hunters to approach too close for safety. For their own protection, pronghorn hunting is now strictly regulated.

Moose

Moose are most likely to be spied in wet, bushy terrain. It is hard to mistake this large mammal with any other. Large and dark brown with grayish legs, it has a prominent snout and a pendant of fur hanging from its throat. Its massive body—moose stand five to six-and-a-half feet high and can weight 850-1,100 pounds—perches on spindly legs, giving it an ungainly appearance.

They are anything but. In water moose can keep pace with two men paddling a canoe; on land they attain speeds of up to 35 miles per hour. They are mainly active at night, but also browse during the day. Moose feed primarily on aquatic vegetation in the summer and are thus often seen in or near water. In winter they eat bark, sapling, twigs and woody herbage.

Pronghorn are frequently sighted on the sagebrush flats.

Living up to 20 years in the wild, female moose begin breeding between the ages of two and three. The fall rutting season is in September and October; a single calf is born in the spring following an eight month gestation. Occasionally a cow will give birth to two calves. Newborns are a light reddish brown. Though wobbly at birth, by three days they are strong enough to follow their mother.

The male species sport massive antlers that can spread over 70 inches from tip to tip. They drop their antlers every year, typically from December to February, and rapidly grow a new set covered in soft hair called velvet. The velvet is shed and/or rubbed off by late summer in preparation for rut, an activity called "horning."

Smaller Mammals

Some of the smaller residents of the Wind Rivers are just as interesting as the big game. One of the most endearing is a little fellow called the pika. This tiny member of the rabbit family is a 6-8" ball of brownish-gray fur with a tail so short it looks like it doesn't own one. Its hind legs are only marginally bigger than its front ones and, unlike its larger relatives, its ears are small and round.

Pikas live in rock slides and talus slopes above treeline. Their size and coloring make them difficult to spot but they usually give themselves away with a shrill squeak or bark. A closer look reveals them hunched near small piles of "hay" they store for winter under overhanging rocks. Frenetic gathering of herbs and grasses begins in mid-July and continues until it snows. While not much is known about the pika, biologists theorize that the animals don't hibernate. Instead, they build tunnels under the snow to connect their storage rooms and live off their collected food supply until spring.

Marmots are a second small mammal that backcountry visitors are likely to see — like it or not. They are known for raiding the food supply of unattended camps. This large member of the squirrel family is the size of a porcupine without its quills. Marmots range in color from tan to reddish-brown to almost black, and sport dark faces and light underbellies. The shrill alarm emitted when danger approaches has earned them the nickname "whistle pig."

Marmots live in small colonies typically consisting of a male, his harem, and their offspring. They often inhabit sub-alpine meadows studded with large boulders, denning in burrows at the boulder's base.

When the sun comes up marmots breakfast on green vegetation. Mid-morning they are often seen soaking up sunshine on top of boulders or logs. They retire to their burrows mid-day, reappearing in the afternoon to bask and eat again. In his book *Rocky Mountain Mammals*, David Armstrong compared their behavior to that of "tourists on well earned vacations...they eat or they sunbathe, then they sleep."

Marmots hibernate in late September/early October. They surface from their burrows in early spring to begin breeding; average litters of 4-5 are born roughly five weeks later. The young stay in the burrow for a month before emerging.

Unlike marmots and pikas, nocturnal beavers are rarely seen during the day. Stick and mud dams, chewed trees and burrows announce their presence. In the Winds beavers' handiwork is found near low-lying trailheads, particularly at Boulder and New Fork Lakes.

The industrious animals supplement their diet of grass and herbage by eating the inner bark and small twigs of the trees they down. The larger branches and logs are used to construct their underwater lodges and dams. A beaver often fells more than 200 trees a year to meet its food and shelter requirements.

Beaver live in small colonies of parents, yearlings and new kits. Two-year-olds are booted out or leave to establish their own lodge, usually within a few miles of the parental home. Average litters of two to four kits are born once a year in the spring/early summer. Occasionally, a female will drop nine or more.

The beaver population in the western United States was virtually exterminated by trapping in the late 1800s. The population has slowly but steadily recouped and is no longer in danger of becoming extinct. This is good news for wildlife who use the still water of the animal's ponds for their homes: ducks, muskrats, mink, and shorebirds among others.

The above is only a sampling of the wildlife that live in the range. Weasels, mink, martens, otters, badgers, foxes, bobcats, rodents of all size and description, skunks, snakes, birds and waterfowl are all on the lengthy list.

Beaver dams are seen far more frequently than their nocturnal inhabitants.

The Hikes

How To Use This Book

The hikes in this book have been arranged by entrances into the range. Please refer to the map on the following page. A network of trails—old trails, new trails, use trails not shown on maps, and game trails—criss-cross the range. Some of the destinations can be accessed from a different entrance. I chose what made sense to me. Driving instructions are detailed on the entrance page at the front of the section, rather than repeated in each write-up. The entrance page also describes the nearest town for services, places to camp near the trailhead, the agency administering the area you are visiting, and, best of all, where you can get a shower when you return to civilization.

Hike descriptions start with an information capsule at the top of the page, followed by a written narrative to give you a general feeling of the route. The first component in the information capsule is distance. This is just what the name implies: the number of miles you will cover one-way on the hike. For off-trail routes the distance given is the best approximate available. The next three categories in the information capsule are elevation gain, elevation loss, and maximum elevation. The one-way gain and loss and maximum elevation figures should help you determine how strenuous the hike will be. They are important in assessing time and energy needed for the trip. Average walking pace on level ground is two miles per hour. On steep terrain it drops to 1.5 miles an hour. Altitude and uneven cross-country terrain further reduce speed.

Maps are the next item in the information capsule. Unless otherwise noted all topographic maps listed are USGS 7.5", 1:24.000 scale quadrangles. Topographic maps are the map of choice for their detail. The U.S. Forest Service publishes large maps of Bridger-Teton and Shoshone National Forests. Earthwalk Press also sells popular commercial maps of the range, divided into northern and southern portions. These maps are good for trip planning and providing an overview of the entire region, but their scale limits use for off-trail, cross-country travel. The appropriate Earthwalk map has been designated for each hike, as well. The line maps included in this book are for quick trail junction reference, and to pinpoint names of geographic features.

Backcountry users should be aware that trails shown on the topo maps, many surveyed over 30 years ago, may not be on the ground; that the maps don't show game or popular use trails; and that there are a number of errors on the Earthwalk maps. These are often pointed out in the hike's text.

Finally, the information capsule lists the type of fish found in various lakes enroute.

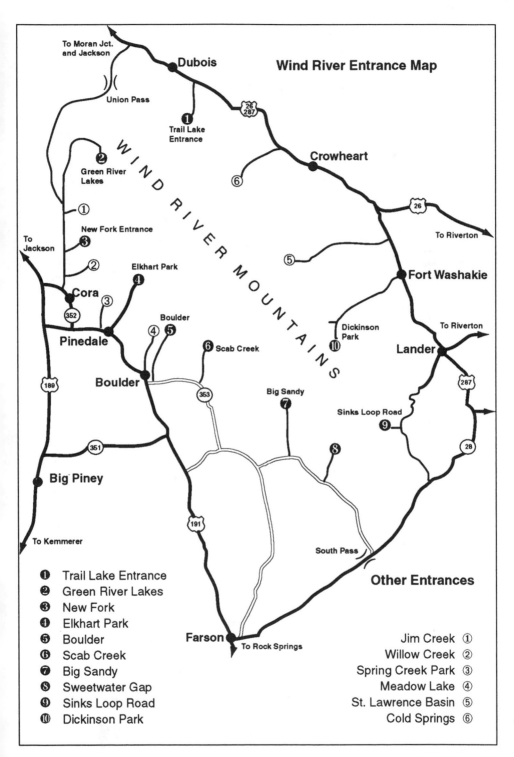

Wind River Entrance Map

To Moran Jct. and Jackson

Dubois

Union Pass

❶ Trail Lake Entrance

26 287

❷ Green River Lakes

Crowheart

①

New Fork Entrance

❸

②

Elkhart Park

❹

Cora

③

352

Boulder

④ ❺

Pinedale

❻ Scab Creek

Boulder

353

Big Sandy

❼

189

351

Big Piney

To Kemmerer

To Jackson

⑥

⑤

26

To Riverton

Fort Washakie

Dickinson Park

❿

Lander

To Riverton

287

Sinks Loop Road

❾

28

❽

191

South Pass

Other Entrances

Farson

To Rock Springs

❶ Trail Lake Entrance
❷ Green River Lakes
❸ New Fork
❹ Elkhart Park
❺ Boulder
❻ Scab Creek
❼ Big Sandy
❽ Sweetwater Gap
❾ Sinks Loop Road
❿ Dickinson Park

Jim Creek ①
Willow Creek ②
Spring Creek Park ③
Meadow Lake ④
St. Lawrence Basin ⑤
Cold Springs ⑥

Other Entrances

Most of the trails in the Wind River Range can be accessed by the entrances covered in this guide. Driving directions are given below for minor entrances not included in the hiking write-ups, and for entrances on the Wind River Indian Reservation. Winds visitors are reminded that they must have a permit/guide to travel on the reservation.

① Jim Creek Road

Drive 23.3 miles down Green River Lakes Entrance Road to the signed intersection with Jim Creek Road. The road dead-ends at poorly maintained Jim Creek Trail, which the Forest Service has abandoned.

② Willow Creek Entrance

Drive the Green River Lakes Entrance Road for eight miles to a signed turn-off to Willow Creek. Turn right onto the dirt road and drive nine miles to Willow Creek guard Station. A short distance beyond the guard station the trail to Section Corner and Trapper lakes begins near the creek.

③ Spring Creek Park Entrance

At the west end of the town of Pinedale is a signed turn-off to Soda and Willow Lakes. Turn north onto this road and drive 10 miles to a "T" intersection. Turn right here and drive three miles to Spring Creek Park on a rough road that worsens as you near the entrance.

④ Meadow Lake

Timico Lake Trail begins at this entrance. To reach it drive one mile north of Boulder of U.S. Hwy. 191 and turn north onto a dirt road. It is approximately 12 miles to Meadow Lake and a gate beyond it, typically locked. Park off-road near the gate, where you'll find the start of the trail.

Reservation Entrances

⑤ St. Lawrence Basin

Travel north of Fort Washakie 7.7 miles on U.S. Highway 287 to a signed intersection with a paved road to St. Lawrence Basin. Turn west onto the road. Continue straight at an intersection with another paved road. The pavement ends in 8.2 miles. It is another 11 miles via dirt road to a ranger station. The road continues a short distance beyond the station to the trailhead for Paradise Basin. A permit/guide is required.

⑥ Cold Springs

A mile north of Burris on U.S. 287 Gannet Peak Road turns west. Go straight past a ranch turn-off to reach Cold Springs Entrance, the start of the Ink Wells Trail. Ink Wells is the shortest route to Gannett Peak. A permit/guide is required.

Trail Lake Entrance

Trails
Glacier Trail
Lake Louise
Bomber Lake and Falls
Whiskey Mountain
Ross Lake

Administering Forest Service District
Wind River Ranger District
Shoshone National Forest
Box 186
Dubois, Wyoming 82513
307-455-2466

Nearest Town
Dubois (pop. 900+). Pronounced DO-boys. Full range of services, including gas, groceries, backcountry supplies, fishing licenses, maps. Forest Service office is located at 209 E. Ramshorn. Chamber of Commerce is at 616 W. Ramshorn (455-2556). Attractions include the Dubois Museum, adjacent National Bighorn Sheep Center, and Welty's General Store. Built in 1889, the store is on the National Register of Historic Sites. Due to a death in the owner's family, it has been open only sporadically in recent years. Two Ocean Books carries a nice selection of regional titles; Green River Traders has a good selection of beads and beading supplies. The Yellowstone Garage is a popular local eatery.

Driving Directions
Follow U.S. Highway 26/287 east out of Dubois. From the population sign it is three miles to Fish Hatchery Road (#411) on your right. Turn onto this dirt road, staying left at the immediate fork. At 2.3 miles you cross a cattle guard and sign to the Whiskey Basin Wildlife Habitat area. An information turnout is reached .2 miles further. Cross the cattle guard past the turnout and stay left where the road forks. Here it becomes rocky and rough as it travels through a portion of signed private land. Go slow, particularly if you have a low-clearance vehicle. Cross another cattle guard at three miles, then a private drive to Torrey Lake Ranch Road on your left. A public boat access road to the left is reached at 5.5 miles. Pass left-hand turnoffs to a private residence and Ring Ranch Road before reaching public parking areas/camping spots to the left of the road at 7.2 and 7.6 miles. The road forks near a state conservation camp at eight miles. Turn right and drive another 1.6 miles to the large parking lot, 9.6 miles from U.S. Highway 26/287. Two picnic tables, a handicap accessible restroom, information map and trail register are located at the end of the access road. No water is available; fill your water bottles in Dubois or bring water with you.

Area Camping

You can camp for free along the access road at pull-off sites near the lakes. The sites are basically a place to park and outhouses. There is no piped water. Circle-Up Camper Court in downtown Dubois was 15 tent sites and RV spots. The Forest Service maintains two public campgrounds: Horse Creek is located 12 miles north of Dubois, reached via Horse Creek Road in town. Falls Campground is 23 miles west of town off U.S. Hwy. 26/287.

Showers

Non-campers can buy a shower at Circle-Up or Red Rock Lodge 13 miles east of Dubois on U.S. Hwy. 26/287.

Bomber Peak rises above the shores of sparkling blue Bomber Lake. The lake is in a remote area reached by a strenuous route.

The Glacier Trail

Close-up views of the highest peak in Wyoming, the largest glacier in the U.S. outside of Alaska, picture-perfect meadows and a riot of wildflowers have earned the Glacier Trail its' reputation of being one of the best backpacking trips in Wyoming, and in many ways it meets and surpasses the superlatives used to describe it.

Unfortunately, its very attractiveness has led to overuse. Hikers flock to the trail, joining the large number of climbers who use it to access Gannett Peak. Local outfitters frequently horse pack people into the upper meadows. Hiking the Glacier Trail in July or August is almost guaranteed to not be a "wilderness experience." Those with time, however, can find both solitude and stunning scenery on the many side-trips off the main route. And if you don't mind company, it is unquestionably a fine choice.

The trail description has been divided into two portions. Phillips Lake Basin is a common first-night destination, not because people are fond of walking over 10 miles when their packs weigh the most, but because there is scarce potable water before the lake.

The second half of the trail takes you from Phillips to Wilson Meadows below Gannett Peak. The division is for description only. Ideally, you will have a week to 10 days or more to explore the surrounding terrain. Towards that end, four hiking options off the main trail are described in this section: Goat Flat, Downs Lake, Echo Lake/Horse Ridge, and Klondike Creek.

Frothy Torrey Creek tumbles down its steep gorge near the start of the Glacier Trail.

1 Phillips Lake

Distance:
  Dinwoody Trail: 10.1 miles
   Upper Phillips Lake: 10.5 miles
Elevation gain: 3,950 feet
Elevation loss: 540 feet
Max. elevation: 10,895 feet
Topo maps:
  Torrey Lake, Ink Wells
  Earthwalk Map: Northern
Fish: Brook, Cutthroat

∧∧∧

Phillips is one of nine lakes nestled in a pretty amphitheater formed by the eastern ramparts of Goat Flat. Meltwater from glaciers high above the lakes contributes to the lushness of the basin. Phillips, a rancher for whom two of the lakes are named, stocked the area with trout years ago and fishermen today still enjoy the result of his efforts. Good campsites are found around both Phillips and Upper Phillips lake, as well as the more secluded Golden Lake.

That's the good news. Less cheery is the hike's length, lack of dependable water for miles, and monotonous uphill grade. On a hot day the grandeur of the panoramic view fades as you slog to a saddle 3,000 feet above you. Be assured that it is worth the effort.

The Glacier Trail begins at the north end of the parking lot at the signed trailhead, sharing the same start with all other trails in this section. Its plotting on the 1968 Torrey Lake map is no longer accurate. A huge landslide the

fall of 1976 resulted in almost four miles of the trail being re-routed. The Earthwalk map, published in 1989, still shows a separate trailhead off a spur from the access road. Outfitters often use the old trail, although the Forest Service no longer maintains it. The description below is for the new trail originating at the trailhead parking lot.

The well-trod path travels southwest through a desert micro-environment of sage and prickly pear cactus as it switchbacks up the southern slope of Whiskey Mountain. At .5 miles a sometimes signed trail to the right leads to Ross Lake and Whiskey Mountain. The name "Whiskey Mtn." is an attractive one for sign-baggers. It's a 50-50 proposition the sign will be in place.

Stay left at the junction and continue ascending through impressive stands of Douglas fir, Engelmann spruce and wind-twisted limber pine. The steady, upward course takes you through a swampy area at .7 miles before regaining firm ground a short distance further.

Reach a signed junction at one mile. The trail to Lake Louise heads right. Take the left fork, descending to a sturdy bridge spanning Torrey Creek. There, the creek cascades in thundering froth down the narrow chasm. Beyond the bridge the path climbs at an easy but steady grade northeast for .3 miles to a ridge, offering good views of Whiskey Mountain and West Torrey Creek Valley to your right (NW). The trail hugs the ridge for a short distance then drops down to an intermittent tributary, skirting a pleasant meadow to reach the signed trail to Bomber Falls at three miles. Continue straight (S).

Monkshood thrives at Phillips.

The Glacier Trail gradually ascends a draw to the base of Arrow Mountain before beginning a seemingly endless, switchbacking climb up the same. A small grove of trees in the middle of the open expanse, halfway up the 1,200 plus foot climb, provides a welcome place to take a break at five miles.

Continuing its ascent at an easier grade, the path crests a small rise at seven miles, distinguished by rock outcroppings to the right and old horse corrals below you. After dropping slightly to an intermittent tributary it climbs to the day's high point: a 10,895 foot saddle between two rubble mounds, each just under 11,700 feet. Goat Flat rises above you to your right (SW), while Horse Ridge defines the horizon. It's a great place to enjoy the view before hoisting the pack one more time.

The trail drops off the saddle to Burro Flat and crosses a tributary at 9.8 miles before reaching a faint junction at 10.1 miles. Stay right. (The little-used Dinwoody Trail to your left heads due east and enters the Wind River Indian Reservation at 6.5 miles.)

The Glacier Trail crosses Burro Flat Creek at 10.3 miles, the first reliable water source since the parking lot. Be heartened: from here to the end of the trail water is plentiful. Walking downhill through pine trees, you'll soon cross a bridged tributary to reach Upper Phillips Lake. A use trail follows the inlet creek upstream to the lake. It continues around the north side, crosses its inlet, then climbs steeply up to hidden Golden Lake, roughly .7 miles beyond Phillips.

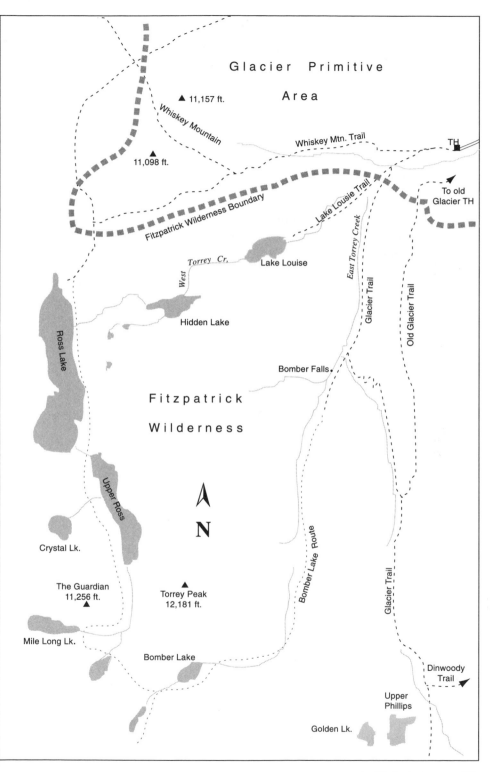

Glacier Primitive Area

▲ 11,157 ft.
Whiskey Mountain
▲ 11,098 ft.
Whiskey Mtn. Trail
TH

To old Glacier TH

Fitzpatrick Wilderness Boundary
Lake Lousie Trail

West Torrey Cr.
Lake Louise
Hidden Lake
East Torrey Creek
Glacier Trail
Old Glacier Trail

Ross Lake
Bomber Falls

Fitzpatrick
Wilderness

Upper Ross

N

Crystal Lk.

Bomber Lake Route

Glacier Trail

The Guardian
11,256 ft.
▲

Torrey Peak
12,181 ft. ▲

Mile Long Lk.

Dinwoody Trail

Bomber Lake

Upper Phillips

Golden Lk.

2 Wilson Meadows

Distance from Phillips Lake Outlet to:
  Double Lake: .6 miles
  Star Lake: 1.7 miles
  Honeymoon Lake: 2.9 miles
  Downs Fork Trail: 5.3 miles
  Big Meadows: 7.5 miles
  Ink Wells Trail: 8.8 miles
  Klondike Creek: 10.4 miles
  Wilson Meadows: 11.3 miles
Elevation gain: 860 feet
Elevation loss: 400 feet
Max. elevation: 10,330 feet
Topo maps:
  Ink Wells
  Earthwalk: Northern
Fish:
  Double: Splake, Brook, Cutthroat
Star: Cutthroat
  Honeymoon: Cutthroat

∧∧∧

The Glacier Trail crosses a bridge at Phillips Lake's outlet and climbs a short distance before dropping 200 feet to the outlet of Double Lake in .6 miles. It follows that lake's rocky eastern shore, crosses its far inlet at a wide, shallow ford, then switchbacks up 200 feet to a bridge spanning Double Lake Creek at 1.5 miles. Star Lake lies .2 miles further. The rocky walls to the west of the lakes dominate this section of the hike. The glacier-hung amphitheater provides a stunning backdrop to the mountain bluebell, monkshood and scores of other wildflowers that thrive on the basin floor. Wildflower enthusiasts will definitely find themselves lingering.

Beyond Star Lake the trail weaves through wooded, rocky terrain for three-quarters of a mile before crossing Honeymoon Creek. It follows that creek for .3 miles, recrossing it before dropping to Honeymoon Lake at 2.9 miles, a favorite destination for fishermen and fall huckleberry hunters. The trail stays left of Honeymoon's outlet creek for one

As hikers near the end of the Glacier Trail, they enter Floyd Wilson Meadows.

mile before dropping steadily via switchbacks to a third crossing of the creek at four miles. Shortly afterwards you come to a signed junction. The trail to the left leads to Dinwoody Falls. Leave your pack and walk .5 miles northeast to the waterfall. This beautiful drop of almost 100 feet is worth the side trip. The falls, lakes, glacier, and creek were named after a member of the U.S. Cavalry stationed at Ft. Washakie in the 1800s. Ironically, his name wasn't "Dinwoody," but Lt. William A. Dinwiddie.

Beyond the junction to Wilson Meadows the trail climbs a short distance before dropping into the northern end of Downs Fork Meadows at 4.5 miles. It skirts its right side to avoid an exceptionally mucky bog in the middle. At 5.3 miles you reach a signed junc-

tion to Downs Fork Valley and Downs Lake. Beyond is a bridged crossing of Down's Creek. Cross an unbridged tributary of Dinwoody Creek .6 miles further and continue walking south through wooded Dinwoody Creek Valley. The trail bends west (right) around an unnamed 10,204 foot peak at 6.8 miles. A half-mile further it enters Big Meadows.

There are many good places to camp between Big Meadows and Floyd Wilson Meadows three miles further. The trail continues south, reaching the junction with the Ink Wells Trail at 8.8 miles. Here, Gannett and the jagged peaks surrounding her finally come into view.

Klondike Creek flows into Dinwoody Creek 1.6 miles past the Ink Wells trail junction. Cross Klondike

Phillips Lake to Wilson Meadows

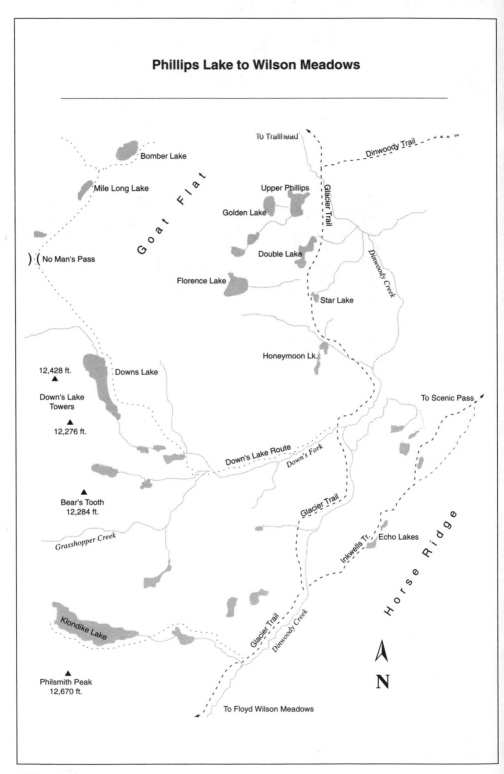

Bomber Lake

Mile Long Lake

Goat Flat

No Man's Pass

Upper Phillips

Golden Lake

Double Lake

Florence Lake

Star Lake

Glacier Trail

Dinwoody Trail

Dinwoody Creek

To Trailhead

Honeymoon Lk.

12,428 ft.

Downs Lake

Down's Lake Towers

12,276 ft.

Down's Lake Route

Down's Fork

Glacier Trail

To Scenic Pass

Bear's Tooth 12,284 ft.

Grasshopper Creek

Inkwells Tr.

Echo Lakes

Horse Ridge

Klondike Lake

Glacier Trail

Dinwoody Creek

Philsmith Peak 12,670 ft.

To Floyd Wilson Meadows

N

Creek, gradually gaining elevation as you skirt meadowed terrain before dropping down to Floyd Wilson Meadows at 11.3 miles, 21.8 miles beyond the trailhead. Wilson, for whom the area is named, horsepacked climbers and other interested parties into an elaborate base camp he provisioned in the meadows in the 1940s. The venture proven to be economically unfeasible.

From the meadows it is possible to continue walking south another mile, cross Gannett Creek (be careful here—this can be dangerous), and walk 2.5 miles to the toe of Dinwoody Glacier. Dinwoody is the most frequently vis-ited glacier in the range because of its accessibility, but it is not the biggest. Neighboring Gannett, Mammoth, Sacajawea and Knife Point Glaciers are all larger. Dinwoody measures approximately two miles wide and one-and-a-half long and encompasses 660 acres.

Hikers can also reach the toe of Gannett Glacier by following Gannett Creek from its confluence with Dinwoody Creek. A rough path can be found on the right (N) side of Gannett Creek for about half a mile. The trail crosses the creek just below its split into two streams and continues up the left side of the south stream.

∧

3 Goat Flat

Distance:
    From Saddle: 4.1 miles
    From Glacier Trailhead:
    12.8 miles
Elevation gain:
    From Saddle: 1,593 feet
Elevation loss: Negligible
Max. elevation: 12,488 feet
Topo maps:
    Ink Wells, Downs Mtn.

∧∧∧

Goat Flat draws few visitors. The off-trail trek to this high plateau gains 1,500 feet in 4.1 miles. Piece of cake , except you first have to gain 3,400 feet over 8.7 miles to get to the starting point. But for those camping near Phillips Lake, the route up Goat Flat is worth the small backtrack to the saddle. Hikers are treated to an incredible expanse of weathered stone slabs as flat and fitted as a tile floor. Glaciated Gannett Peak and Downs Mountain rise above its southwest terminus, offering an unrestricted view of some of the most impressive peaks in the range.

To access Goat Flat follow directions for Phillips Lake, hike no. 1. At 8.7 miles you reach an obvious saddle. Leave the trail here, walking right (SW) up the grass and rock covered slopes of Goat Flat. The grade steepens after about a mile until you reach vast rock slabs around 12,000 feet, approximately

2.3 miles from the saddle. It is an additional 1.8 miles to the end of southwestern end of the plateau. Here, rocky cliffs drop north to East Torrey Creek and south to Downs Lake.

Goat Flat is named not for mountain goats but bighorn sheep, which are occasionally (and incorrectly) called goats. The Torrey Rim Herd migrates from Whiskey Basin south to Ross and Daphne lakes and Goat Flat during the summer months.

∧

4 Downs Lake

Distance from Glacier Trail Jct.
    to lake: 4.2 miles
Elevation gain: 1,660
Elevation loss: Negligible
Max. elevation: 10,960 plus feet
Topo maps:
    Ink Wells, Downs
    Earthwalk: Northern

∧∧∧

Mile-long Downs Lake is sandwiched between peaks and plateaus that rise over a thousand feet above its shoreline. Nice camping spots near the east side of the lake, relative seclusion, the close-up views of half a dozen glaciers make this a worthwhile day hike or overnight side-trip off the Glacier Trail.

The start of the trail is easily missed if you are not looking for it. At the far end of Downs Fork Meadow the Glacier Trail crosses a bridge over Downs Fork Creek, 15.8 miles from the trailhead. Don't cross the bridge. The trail to the lake is a faint path that continues straight up the north side of the creek. It crosses an intermittent stream at .9 miles and again at 1.2 miles before entering a narrow canyon and crossing to the south side of Downs Fork at 1.5 miles. The wooded canyon gradually widens as the trail nears the junction of Downs Fork and Grasshopper Creek. The latter is the outflow of Grasshopper Glacier above you. The striking black cone to your left is 12,294 foot Bear's Tooth.

The topo map shows the path ending at this junction but on the ground a distinct path crosses Grasshopper Creek at the two mile mark and switchbacks 300 feet up to Lake 9900.

After crossing that lake's outlet it heads northwest, climbing over a thousand feet to a saddle north of Point 11,006 before dropping to Downs Lake's eastern shore at 4.1 miles.

Downs Fork, lake, glacier and mountain are believed to be named after John Downs of Lander, an early settler. The mountain is little more than a big pile of rubble first climbed by the USGS in 1906. Finis Mitchell erected a cairn on the summit in 1961.

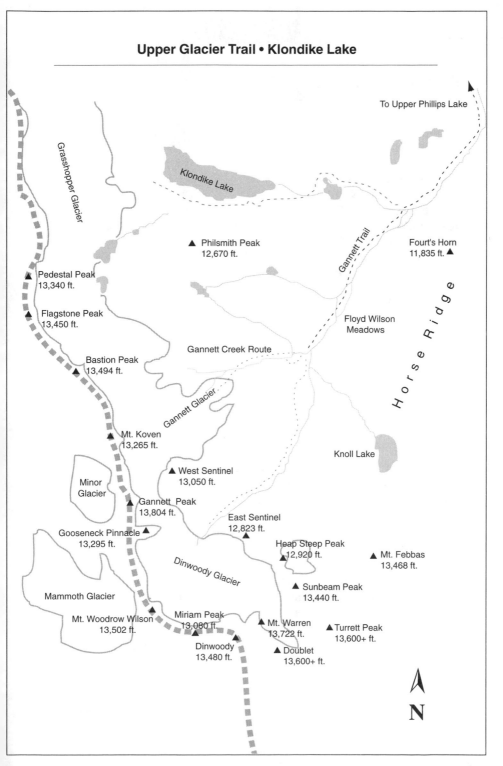

Upper Glacier Trail • Klondike Lake

To Upper Phillips Lake

Grasshopper Glacier

Klondike Lake

▲ Philsmith Peak
12,670 ft.

Gannett Trail

Fourt's Horn
11,835 ft. ▲

▲ Pedestal Peak
13,340 ft.

▲ Flagstone Peak
13,450 ft.

Floyd Wilson
Meadows

H o r s e   R i d g e

Gannett Creek Route

▲ Bastion Peak
13,494 ft.

Gannett Glacier

▲ Mt. Koven
13,265 ft.

Knoll Lake

Minor
Glacier

▲ West Sentinel
13,050 ft.

▲ Gannett Peak
13,804 ft.

Gooseneck Pinnacle ▲
13,295 ft.

East Sentinel
12,823 ft. ▲

Dinwoody Glacier

Heap Steep Peak
▲ 12,920 ft.

▲ Mt. Febbas
13,468 ft.

Mammoth Glacier

▲ Sunbeam Peak
13,440 ft.

Mt. Woodrow Wilson
13,502 ft.

Miriam Peak
13,080 ft. ▲

▲ Mt. Warren
13,722 ft.

▲ Turrett Peak
13,600+ ft.

Dinwoody
13,480 ft.

▲ Doublet
13,600+ ft.

N

5 Klondike Lake

Distance:
 From junction: 1.8 miles
Elevation gain: 1,535 feet
Elevation loss: Negligible
Max. elevation: 11,215 feet
Topo maps:
 Fremont Peak South
 Gannett Peak
 Earthwalk: Northern

ΛΛΛ

The route to Klondike Lake is short but challenging, gaining over 1,500 feet in under two miles. It involves steep grades and crossing a creek that at peak flow can be dangerous. When doable, however, the adventurous hiker enjoys spectacular views of Grasshopper Glacier and Klondike Peak, a 13,114 foot summit two miles west.

The easiest route to the lake begins where Klondike Creek crosses the Glacier Trail. Do not cross the creek; instead, walk up its right (N) side. At .4 miles you'll reach a waterfall. Stay to the right here and climb above the falls until you reach the outlet of Lake 10,860 at .7 miles. If it is safe to do so, cross the outlet and walk around the left (S) side of the lake. At 1.4 miles you cross an intermittent stream, then ascend the left side of the main stream to its outlet at the east end of Klondike Lake. There are several nice spots to camp along the south side of the 1.3 mile long lake.

How the creek, lake and peak got their names is debatable. Orrin and Lorraine Bonney claim the lake was named by a Burris man, who thought the country looked like the Klondike. Veteran mountaineer Joe Kelsey says the creek was named after an early attempt at mining gold, and the name was later applied to the lake and the mountain. Wyoming historian Mae Urbanek believes all were named for "Klondike" Jones, a Johnson County man who traveled to Alaska during the gold rush, made a modest fortune, and returned to live on a ranch with his in-laws.

6 Horse Ridge

Distance:
   From Glacier Trailhead Jct.:
   Echo Lake: 1.2 miles
   Knoll Lake: 12.1 miles
   Mt. Febbas: 13.7 miles
Elevation gain: 4,068 feet
Elevation loss: Negligible
Max. elevation: 13,468 feet
Topo maps:
   Ink Wells, Fremont Peak North
Fish:
   Echo: Brook
   Ink Wells: brook
   Knoll: none
   Earthwalk: Northern

∧∧∧

A walk up Horse Ridge gives non-climbers access to what some have called the best panoramic views in the entire Wind River Range. From 10,960 foot Scenic Pass, the ancient sedimentary ridge gradually rises in its nine mile course to 13,468 foot Mt. Febbas, then turns left and runs another 2. 5 miles to its eastern terminus overlooking Dry Creek Ridge and Indian Pass. The sharply-defined ridge drops off abruptly to both the east and west: a meander to either side unveils spectacular views of numerous lakes, glaciers and rugged peaks, including Klondike, Flagstone, Koven, and Gannett. Snowfields, springs, meadows and 12,165 foot Knoll Lake lie on the ridge itself. There are no trees or obvious camping spots, but as Winds veteran Finis Mitchell

noted years ago, you can drop a sleeping bag just about anywhere.

Shortest access to this marvelous ridge is from Scenic Pass via the Ink Wells Trail in the Wind River Indian Reservation. Although this access is only 3.5 miles, it involves securing a permit and hiring an Indian guide. The directions given below are for public access, which starts at the intersection of the Glacier Trail with the western end of the Ink Wells Trail in Shoshone National Forest, 19.8 miles from the Glacier trailhead.

Turn left (E) onto the Ink Wells Trail and soon cross a bridge over Dinwoody Creek. The steep trail quickly gains 800 feet as it climbs through wooded terrain to Echo Lake at 1.2 miles. After passing a second small lake on your right, it continues to ascend to a junction at 2.1 miles. The left branch drops 200 feet to the Ink Well Lakes, then climbs back towards Scenic Pass. The right fork bypasses the lakes and climbs more directly towards the pass. The forks merge at four miles. Those interested in fishing or a camping spot near water should take the left fork.

Where the forks rejoin hikers may continue straight for another three-quatrers of a mile to Scenic Pass or leave the trail and head right (SE) up the slopes of Horse Ridge. While the view from the pass is memorable, comparable views can be had further up Horse Ridge. From either starting point the route is straightforward and obvious. Most of it lies close to or above 12,000 feet. The terrain gradually ascends, the exception being a slight drop as you near Knoll Lake at 12.1 miles.

Steep snowfields hang above the south side of the lake. To continue to the ridge's high point, walk left (E) above the lake, cross the snowfield below Chimney Rock and head right (W) up Mt. Febbas' northeast slopes. Impressive views of the northern end of the range await you on the summit, including close-ups of Dinwoody Glacier and Gannett.

The peak was named after a local wrangler who guided English dudes from Wells Dude Ranch on the Green River near the turn of the century. Some historians believe Horse Ridge was first ascended by Captain Bonneville in September of 1833. Famed mountaineer Arthur Tate is credited with the first ascent of the ridge's high point in 1920.

Horse Ridge can also be accessed from Floyd Wilson Meadows by following the outflow of Knoll's Lake. This option is quite steep.

∧

7 Lake Louise

Distance: 2.3 miles
Elevation gain: 1,100 feet
Elevation loss: 260 feet
Max. elevation: 8,520 feet
Topo Maps:
  Torrey Lake
   Earthwalk: Northern
Fish:
  Lake Louise: Brook, Rainbow
  Hidden: Rainbow

∧ ∧ ∧

Perhaps nowhere else in the Winds does a short day hike provide such a clear example of why Indians called the range "The Shining Mountains." Polished smooth by glaciers, the granite walls of Middle Mountain and cliffs surrounding Lake Louise glow silver-white in the midday sun. That, plus rugged Torrey Creek, superb fishing, and a crystalline body of water reminiscent of its famous Canadian namesake make the destination one of the most popular in the northern end of the range.

The path begins at the signed trailhead north of the parking area. It travels southwest through a desert micro-environment of sage and prickly

Rock-bound Lake Louise's beauty mirrors that of its Canadian namesake.

pear cactus as it switchbacks up the southern slope of Whiskey Mountain. At .5 miles a trail to the right leads to the summit of that peak and Ross Lake.

Stay left and continue ascending through impressive stands of Douglas fir, Engelmann spruce and wind-twisted limber pine. The steady, upward course brings you to a second junction at one mile. The Glacier Trail to your left descends to a 50 foot bridge spanning East Torrey Creek. (Note: It is worth the short diversion to walk to the bridge to view the impressive cascade.)

Hike right at the junction to reach the lake. Over the next mile you ascend west through stands of trees and numerous rock-studded meadows that characterize Bomber Creek Basin. The now common appellation replaced Torrey Creek Valley after a WWII fighter pilot crashed on a training run in 1942 and

ignited a forest fire. The stark results of a more recent fire are evident shortly before reaching the lake. After crossing a tributary at 1.9 miles and passing a pretty stretch of cascades on West Torrey Creek, the trail climbs a series of rock benches marked by cairns. The view before you is marred by blackened stumps and snags, grim testament to an improperly extinguished campfire that escaped its fire ring the summer of 1976. Fueled by stiff winds and dry ground cover, the blaze consumed close to 1,700 acres during its four-day burn, decimating the area.

The outlet of Lake Louise is reached at 2.3 miles. It is possible to cross to good campsites on the southern side of the lake by carefully negotiating a log jam at the outlet, adding roughly .4 miles to the total mileage.

8 Bomber Falls/Lake

Distance:
    Bomber Falls: 3.8 miles
    Bomber Lake: 8 miles
Elevation gain:
    Bomber Falls: 1,430 feet
    Bomber Lake: 2,930 feet
Elevation loss: 180
Max. elevation:
    Bomber Falls: 8,680 feet
    Bomber Lake: 10,180 feet
Topo maps:
    Torrey Lake
    Ink Wells (Bomber Lake), Downs Mt. (Bomber Lake)
    Earthwalk: Northern
Fish: None

∧∧∧

A quiet walk through forest and pretty meadow country brings you to Bomber Falls, a difficult-to-see drop of over 150 feet. Bomber Lake is a sparkling blue body of water surrounded by glaciated 12,000 foot peaks. Secluded and rarely visited, it's a great place to set up base camp and foray to Mile Long Lake, Turquoise Lake, and the headwaters of East Torrey Creek.

Follow the trail directions to Lake Louise, hike no. 7, until you reach the signed junction at one mile. Here, take the left fork and continue on the Glacier Trail (Bomber Falls is not identified on the sign). The trail abruptly drops down to a sturdily-constructed bridge spanning a small gorge over East Torrey Creek. An impressive cascade above you plunges 100 feet down a narrow gorge before flowing under the bridge.

The trail climbs out of the gorge and travels through the rocky slabs, broken domes and glacial erratics that characterize this end of the range. After roughly 45 minutes of walking you'll enter a pleasant mixed forest of conifer and pine. East Torrey Creek can be seen through the trees to your right. At 2.2 miles the trail switchbacks a short distance above the stream then enters a pleasant meadow. Distant Bomber Falls can be seen ahead at the two o'clock position. The trail stays left of a meadow and crosses the base of a talus slope before entering a stretch of forest and reaching a signed trail junction at three miles. The Glacier Trail continues left; take the right fork to reach

Because it is not easily reached, Bomber Lake usually offers solitude for those seeking a quiet corner of the Wind River Range.

Bomber Falls. The "trail" is lush grass bent by pedestrian traffic. It turns into a dirt path as you near a fringe of trees. The trail is lightly used and tends to fade in-and-out of a carpet of pine needles. Pay attention to your route, which stays left of East Torrey Creek.

The falls is reached at 3.8 miles. Although it drops over 150 feet, it twists out of view and is more easily heard than seen. Experienced hikers can get a closer view by scrambling up rocks next to the falls.

To continue to the lake stay left of the rockfall and climb one of the numerous eroded use trails to the top of the wooded hillside. Head right (W) to East Torrey Creek. The route follows the left bank of the creek. It is easy but slow walking across talus slopes and around downed trees. The route crosses several intermittent run-off tributaries flowing down Arrow Mountain on your left. A mile before reaching Bomber Lake, the canyon and creek bend west. Consult your map: it's a good idea to cross East Torrey before the bend to avoid crossing a rocky moraine.

Spectacular peaks surround Bomber Lake, including 12,254 foot Spider Peak to the southwest, 12,058 foot Runelbick to the west, and the high plateau of Goat Flat to the south.

This lovely place hardly seems to merit a name as incongruous as "Bomber Lake." In 1942 a B-17 crew training to fly missions in W.W. II crashed near here, killing 11 people on board and starting a forest fire in the vicinity. Hence, the name.

9 Whiskey Mountain
10 Ross Lake

Distance:
    Whiskey Mtn.: 4.8 miles to summit
    Ross Lake: 6 miles
Elevation gain:
    Whiskey Mountain: 3,674 feet
    Ross Lake: 3,020 feet
Elevation loss:
    Whiskey Mountain: Negligible
    Ross Lake: 900 feet
Max. elevation:
    Whiskey Mountain: 11,157 feet
    Ross Lake: 10,320 feet
Topo maps:
    Torrey Lake, Simpson Lake
    Earthwalk: Northern
Fish:
    Ross: Rainbow, Cutthroat
    Upper Ross: Cutthroat

ΛΛΛ

The possibility of spotting bighorn sheep—and the certainty of great views of the northern Winds—lures hikers up high, windswept Whiskey Mountain. Its grassy south ridge is the westernmost extension of Torrey Rim, home of the largest herd of bighorn sheep in North America. The sheep graze in the nearby drainages of Jakey's Fork and Torrey Creek, protected by the deep canyons, glaciers and high plateaus that characterize the area. In late spring and early summer, a segment of the herd migrates from Whiskey Basin to the higher elevations of Goat Flat to the south. By fall they return to the more hospitable basin. Hikers often see majestic rams and small bands of ewes on the mountain. Bring a spotting scope or telephoto lens so you can observe the sheep without disturbing them.

The first three miles of trail to Whiskey Mountain are shared by hikers heading to Ross Lake. Tucked un-

Ram Flat, seen along the Whiskey Mountain Trail.

derneath Ram Flat 2,500 feet above, the two-mile long, rock-enclosed lake is home to sizable cutthroat and rainbow trout. Unfortunately, the steep rock walls make lakeside travel difficult. Those wishing to explore Ross' southern reaches and Upper Ross Lake are advised to pick a route on the east side of the lakes to avoid numerous avalanche sloughs along the precipitous slopes sweeping above their western shores. Even on the east side of the lakes it is not easy walking. From Upper Ross Lake, it is possible to follow Torrey Creek upstream for .5 miles, cross a 10,600 foot saddle to the southwest, and drop down to Bomber Lake, returning to your vehicle via Bomber Basin.

The path begins at the signed trailhead north of the parking area. It travels southwest through a desert micro-environment of sage and prickly pear cactus as it switchbacks up the southern slope of Whiskey Mountain. At .5 miles a trail to the left leads to Lake Louise. Stay right and continue a steady westward climb, shortly reaching a large wooden sign identifying the area as the Fitzpatrick Wilderness. This segment of Shoshone National Forest was designated wilderness in 1976. It is named after famed mountain man, guide, and fur trapper Thomas "Broken Hand" Fitzpatrick. Wed to a Northern Arapaho Indian, Fitzpatrick was appointed High Plains Indian Agent by the federal government in 1846 in an attempt to ease escalating tensions between Indians and whites on emigrant trails.

At one mile impressive views of Torrey Creek valley and the apricot-colored, limestone slopes of Arrow Mountain to your left are gained. Continuing its steep climb, the well-used path crosses the base of a talus slope before re-entering a shady conifer forest at two miles. Here the grade lessens somewhat as the trail traverses small meadows fringed with young aspens and crosses two intermittent run-off streams before reaching a boggy spring at 2.6 miles. The sweet scent of indigo forget-me-nots and white phlox greets hikers early to midsummer along this section of trail. Above the spring, the terrain opens up to expansive views and alpine meadows graced by prairie smoke, delicate slimpod shooting stars and lavender pasque flowers. The latter were used by Native Americans to relieve itching associated with skin rashes. These 2" wide blossoms, distinguished by a fine covering of silk-like hair on the backside of their petals, typically appear early season when the snow begins to recede.

Beyond the wildflower laced meadows the trail gains a wind-swept ridge that yields views of 12,242 foot Ram Flat and four large glaciers draping it's steep eastern side. At three miles an old wooden sign (probably doomed) and a large rock cairn mark the Whiskey Mountain Trail junction.

To reach Whiskey Mountain

At the junction take the faint path to the right and head uphill towards a wooden pole. It is likely to be windy, as the exposed ridge is blasted from glacier-cooled, northwest winds. Bring a hat, gloves and windbreaker, even on warm days, so you can comfortably linger on the ridge to look for sheep and enjoy the view.

From the pole the trail becomes a route through a spectacular sea of grass, hay and meadow forbs. A series of large rock cairns point the way. Generally speaking, the route stays left near the ridge line, climbing from 10, 240 feet at the junction to a wide saddle just below 11,000 feet. The saddle, 4.1 miles from the trailhead, lies between Whiskey Mountain's double summit. The smaller summit of 11,098 feet is to your left (W), while the higher summit of 11, 157 feet rises .7 miles to the east. A large surveyor's cairn marks that zenith.

Although it is fun to claim a summit, the openness of the terrain yields a comparable view from the saddle. On a clear day the Grand Teton and Mount Moran can be seen to the northwest. The jagged pinnacles of the Absaroka Range command attention to the north, while to the east Crowheart Butte juts above the plains.

The trail drops .9 miles off the saddle to a junction with a jeep trail that heads south towards Ross Lake. The Whiskey Mountain Trail continues straight, descending to Wasson Creek then climbing to Soapstone Lake, 4.4 miles beyond the Ross Lake junction. Simpson Lake lies another 2.7 miles further.

In *Wyoming Place Names,* historian Mae Urbanek notes that Whiskey Creek and mountain were named for a still and caches of whiskey found on the mountain before the turn of the century. The still was apparently used by early settlers who discovered making moonshine was far cheaper than buying it. Prohibitionist Charles Beck started a camp for Quaker children at the base of the mountain in the early 1900s. And that, one presumes, was the end of the still.

To reach Ross Lake

Bear left at the three mile junction, descending slightly southwest as the

As you crest a ridge on the trail, Ross Lake comes into view.

trail crosses another open expanse. The faint, rocky trail is testimony to its relatively scant use. It passes through a skeletal forest of trees—victim of a 1976 forest fires that started on the shores of Lake Louise—then levels and enters a flat, boggy area around four miles. A striking granite pinnacle borders the right side. It is easy to lose the scant trail here. Stay near timberline to your left. You'll pass a small pond to your far right at 4.7 miles, then pick up a more clearly defined trail inside treeline at the far southwest corner of the meadow. The trail then heads south across a wooded ridge, affording a fine view of Ross Lake at five miles. From here, it steeply drops via a series of small, tight switchbacks before leveling at a small saddle, then more gradu-

ally descending through forest to the northern end of the lake.

Ross and Upper Ross Lakes were both named in honor of Nellie Tayloe Ross, the first woman governor in the United States. She served from 1925-27, completing the term of her husband, Gov. William B. Ross. Ross had served half of the four-year term he had been elected to in 1922 when he died unexpectedly of complications following an appendectomy. Mrs. Ross was elected to finish the end of her husband's term. Her re-election bid was unsuccessful.

Wyoming became the first state to grant women the right to vote on July 10, 1890, when statehood was bestowed on the territory. The territory had previously granted women the right to vote in December, 1869.

Notes

Green River Lakes & New Fork Entrances

Clear Creek Natural Bridge

Trails

Roaring Fork to Faler Lake
Osborn Mountain
Clear Creek
Slide Lake
Twin, Shirley and Valaite
New Fork Trail

Administering Forest Service District

Pinedale Ranger District
Box 220
Pinedale, Wyoming 82941
307-367-4326

Nearest Town

Pinedale (pop. 1,200+). Full range of services available, including lodging, gas, groceries, backpacking supplies, fishing licenses and maps. There is also a small store at Cora, four miles in on the access road. Fishing licenses and beer can be purchased enroute at The Place, a popular bar. The district office for Bridger-Teton National Forest is located at 210 W. Pine St. in Pinedale. The Chamber of Commerce is at 35 S. Tyler (367-2242). Special attractions include the Museum of the Mountain Men and Faler's General Store, which has a huge collection of trophy heads scattered throughout the store.

Driving Directions

Drive six miles east of Pinedale on U.S. 187/191 to Wyoming Highway 352. Turn north onto the paved road and drive past Cora at four miles. The Willow Creek access road is eight miles in; New Fork Lakes turn-off is reached in 14.7 miles. If you are going to New Fork Lake, turn right here and follow the rough entrance road five miles to the end of a loop in Narrows Campground, where you'll see the trailhead sign. To continue to Green River Lakes, drive north past the New Fork Entrance. The Place is passed at 20.7 miles, Moose Gypsum Road at 25.5. Shortly after this the pavement ends near a turn-around and small restroom. Drive on gravel road past the turn-off to Whiskey Grove Campground at 27.9 miles. A signed junction with Union Pass is half a mile up the road. Stay right here, passing a turn-off to Moose Creek Road at 41.1 miles and Green River Lakes Campground before reaching the parking area, 45.7 miles from U.S. 187/191.

Area Campgrounds

Forest Service campgrounds are located at New Fork Lake, Whiskey Grove, and Green River Lakes. All have water. Green River Lakes usually receives a lot of traffic. Less-visited Whiskey Grove has nine pleasant sites right on the river and is a nicer alternative. There are two private campgrounds in Pinedale: Campground of Wyoming at 204 S. Jackson Street and Lakeside Lodge, located three miles NE of town on Fremont Lake, reached via Fremont Lake Road.

Showers
Campground of Wyoming sells showers to non-campers.

Forlorn Pinnacle

11 Roaring Fork to Faler Lake

Distance:
    Native Lake: 10.2 miles
    Faler Lake: 12.4 miles
Elevation gain: 3,080 feet
Elevation loss: 860 feet
Max. elevation: 11,000 feet
Topo maps:
    Green River Lakes, Big Sheep Mountain, Downs Mountain
    Earthwalk: Northern
Fish:
    Native Lake: Cutthroat
    Faler: Golden
    Crescent Lake: Cutthroat
    Upper Crescent: Cutthroat

∧∧∧

The Roaring Fork Trail traverses the long, scenic east-west corridor between Three Waters Mountain to the north and Osborn Mountain to the south. Numerous alpine lakes at its head make it a good choice for fishermen and backpackers. Relatively easy grades and access to water provides favorable backcountry access for hunters, outfitters, and other stock users. Its length, however, deters most one-day excursion parties, protecting it from overuse. It's a nice way to explore this pretty corner of the Winds.

From the Green River Lakes parking area walk left .4 of a mile around the northern end of Lower Green River Lake. Cross the bridge over its outlet and turn left at the signed junction onto the Highline Trail, soon passing the log remains of the Osborn cabin. Osborn homesteaded the property following his service in the Union Army during the Civil War.

The trail parallels the Green for about three miles before veering north and climbing 800 feet to a ridge. Here, it divides at the 4.1 mile mark. The left branch heads west and eventually intersects a four-wheel drive road that leads to the Green River Lakes entrance road. Bear right to reach Faler Lake.

Three-quarters of a mile beyond the junction the trail crosses the Roaring

Roaring Fork • Osborn Mountain
Clear Creek Natural Bridge • Slide Lake
Twin, Shirley and Valaite Lakes

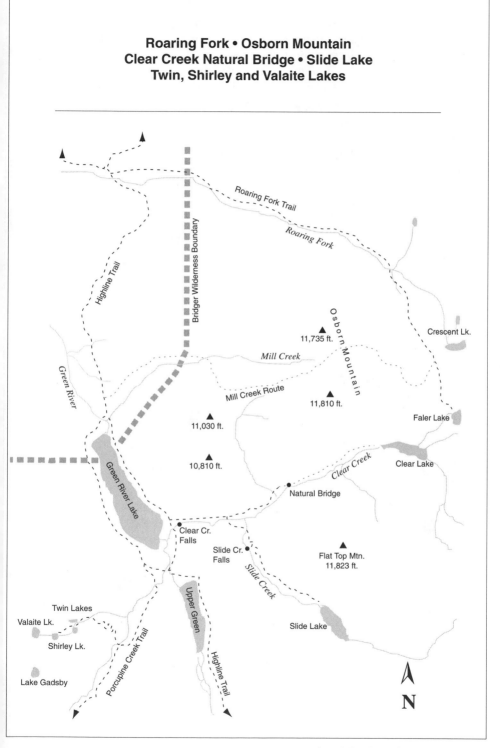

Roaring Fork Trail

Roaring Fork

Bridger Wilderness Boundary

Highline Trail

Green River

Osborn Mountain

11,735 ft.

Crescent Lk.

Mill Creek

Mill Creek Route

11,810 ft.

Faler Lake

11,030 ft.

10,810 ft.

Clear Creek

Clear Lake

Natural Bridge

Clear Cr. Falls

Slide Cr. Falls

Flat Top Mtn. 11,823 ft.

Slide Creek

Green River Lake

Upper Green

Twin Lakes

Valaite Lk.

Shirley Lk.

Slide Lake

Lake Gadsby

Porcupine Creek Trail

Highline Trail

N

Fork and shortly intersects the Roaring Fork Trail. You have now officially left the Highline. Turn right and begin walking east up the wooded corridor. The trail stays to the left of meandering Roaring Fork to avoid swampy areas near the creek and damp stretches of an unnamed meadow further along. After passing a series of ponds at 7.8 miles, it offers relatively flat walking as it continues east towards the head of the corridor. There it ascends to Alexander Park.

At the far end of the pleasant park it ascends again, climbing 500 feet to the eastern shore of 9,925 feet Native Lake, 10.2 miles from the trailhead. Parties often camp near the lake's eastern shore and day hike to Faler Lake, or walk up the steep slopes east of Native to 10, 739 foot Crescent Lake, source of the Roaring Fork.

From Native the trail heads southeast, gaining over 1,000 feet in its 1.1 mile course to an 11,000 foot saddle east of Osborn Mountain. This high vantage point offers great views to the south of Bear Creek Basin and a panorama of glaciated peaks. The final leg of trail descends 800 feet from the saddle to Faler Lake, 12.4 miles from the trailhead.

While the trail officially ends here, the possibilities for cross-country travel are just beginning. Consult the Downs Mountain topo. One option is to walk south beyond Faler's eastern shore until you reach an intermittent stream. Follow it up a steep draw. The route tops out in Bear Basin, prime summer range for bighorn sheep. Bring binoculars or a spotting scope.

The Roaring Fork Trail parallels its namesake. The vigorous creek and the lakes that feed it offer fine fishing opportunities.

12 Osborn Mountain

Distance:
  Osborn Summit: 4.4 miles
  Faler Lake: 7.8 miles
Elevation gain: Approx. 3,920 feet
Elevation loss: Negligible
Max. elevation: 11,880 feet
Topo map: Green River Lakes
  Earthwalk: Northern
Fish:
  Faler: Golden

∧∧∧

If high, alpine walking with unobstructed views appeals to you, Osborn Mountain is a good choice. The route is made doubly attractive by the chance of seeing elk or mountain sheep instead of other people. (For the same reason, think twice about hiking Osborn during hunting season).

Although not a maintained trail, the Mill Creek Route up Osborn is quite doable for experienced hikers. From Green River Lakes parking lot walk left .4 of a mile around the northern end of Green River Lake and cross the bridge over its outlet. Turn left (N) at the signed junction and walk downstream on the Highline Trail for roughly 1,800 feet. To the right of the trail a faint, unsigned path heads up the open hillside towards a large glacial erratic. Take this path, which soon parallels the left side of Mill Creek. If you can't find the path leave the trail and head towards the boulder and you'll soon pick it up.

The path follows the creek for about two miles then crosses it and heads south through timber for .4 miles to a small saddle between Point 11,030 to your right (W) and the main plateau of Osborn Mountain on your left (E). Here the dirt path disappears in the rocky slopes. Head left across the plateau. Roughly 1.6 miles beyond the saddle—4.3 miles from the start of this hike—you reach the plateau's high point. Glorious views of Green River Lakes, the White Rock Range, Flat Top Mountain, Squaretop, and a sea of lesser peaks stretch south.

There are a number of game trails in the vicinity that won't get you to the top of Osborn. Heed the above directions and consult your topo map to stay on route.

The Mill Creek Route is often used to access Faler Lake. To reach that popular destination walk to the far eastern point of the plateau (about 6.1 miles from the start), and descend a narrowing ridge .7 miles to a small saddle west of Crescent Lake. Here you'll intersect the Roaring Fork horse trail. Follow the trail to the lake, a total of 7.8 miles from the start.

13 Clear Creek Natural Bridge
14 Slide Lake

Distance:
   Natural Bridge: 4.3 miles
   Slide Lake: 5.7 miles
Elevation gain:
   Natural Bridge: 320 feet
   Slide Lake: 1,530 feet
Elevation loss: Negligible
Max. elevation:
   Natural Bridge: 8,280 feet
   Slide Lake: 9,490 feet
Topo map: Green River Lakes
   Earthwalk: Northern
Fish:
   Lower Green River Lake: Mackinaw, Grayling, Whitefish
   Upper Green: Mackinaw
   Clear Lake: Golden trout
   Slide Lake: Brook trout

∧∧∧

The hike to Clear Creek Natural Bridge or Slide lakes offers a nice day outing or the start of a multi-day trip for the avid fisherman/backcountry explorer. Tucked at the base of surrounding mountains, the hike to sapphire blue Slide Lake offers the additional bonus of a tumbling waterfall.

The trail to both begins at Green River Lakes parking area. Walk to the obvious trailhead sign and turn left. Follow the well-worn path around the northern end of Lower Green River Lake and cross a bridge over the outlet at .4 miles. On the other side of the bridge turn right at the signed junction and begin a pleasant, rolling walk along the lake's eastern shore. The trail cuts through open grasslands and sage hillsides that can be quite hot in July and August. Small, scattered aspen groves and sparse cottonwoods add to the scenery but provide little shade. An early morning start is rewarded not only with cooler temperatures, but often mirror reflections of Squaretop Mountain in the still waters of the lake. This granite monolith—one of the most photographed landmarks in Wyoming—dominates the skyline as you bear southeast around Lower Green.

At two miles the trail splits at a signed junction. The right branch is a continuation of the Highline Trail. Bear

Clear Creek meadows, enroute to Clear Creek Natural Bridge. Forlorn Pinnacle is visible to the left.

left onto the Clear Creek Trail and switchback up a small hill. Noisy Clear Creek Falls spills down the deep river canyon to your right, hidden from view. At the head of the small canyon the trail levels out and follows the left side of a lush meadow fed by Clear Creek. Impressive 11,823 foot Flat Top Mountain dominates the skyline. The trail divides again at 3.2 miles.

To reach Clear Creek Nat. Bridge

Hike left at the junction. The clear trail weaves through fringes of lodgepole forest as it skirts the large, open park to your right, paralleling meandering, placid Clear Creek. A rainbow palette of wildflowers colors the peaceful ley most of the summer, but is particularly appealing in July, when delicate blue harebells add their hue to a palette of fiery scarlet gilia, sunny yellow cinquefoil and omnipresent yarrow. The tiny, pearly white flowers of the latter low-growing plant are an important component in the diet of sage grouse. Keep a sharp eye out for these large birds as you cross the expanse.

At the far end of the meadow the trial bends right (E) through lodgepole pine forest burned in 1988 following a lightning strike. Young saplings pushing their way through the forest floor are visible reminders that lodgepole pines "replant" themselves after being burned. The tree's cones open when exposed to intense heat, scattering their seeds over charred terrain.

Cross a log bridge over a tributary stream at four miles. Here, jagged

Flat Top Mountain dominates the view as you hike towards the natural bridge and Slide Falls.

11,640 foot Forlorn Pinnacle rises prominently to the northeast. Clear Creek Natural Bridge is reached .3 miles further, a total of 4.3 miles from the trailhead. Walk up the trail to the east side of the bridge, which is far more impressive. Spirited Clear Creek has worn an arch a dozen yards wide through a block of soft limestone.

A trail of sorts exists past the bridge to Clear Lake, although the recent fire has made following it a hit-or-miss, difficult affair. Walk cross-country using the outlet stream as your reference point. It is somewhat easier to stay to the left (N) of the stream as the canyon narrows. Traverse the rocky hillsides above it and drop back down to the lake at its outlet.

The lake is 1.8 miles beyond, and 700 feet higher, than the natural bridge.

To continue to Slide Lake

Turn right at the signed junction at

Slide Lake is surrounded by peaks that soar almost 2,000 feet above it.

3.2 miles and cross a jouncing log bridge over Clear Creek. A bit dicey in all conditions, the logs are especially tricky when wet. The bridge itself is subject to being washed out. If this is the case, or you are not comfortable, stay on the Clear Creek Trail and scout a safe crossing upstream.

Beyond the crossing the trail follows a series of log posts bisecting a grassy meadow before fording frothy Slide Creek at 3.6 miles (again, exercise caution here) and ascending a dozen or so steep, wooded switchbacks that snake around the chasm cut by Slide Creek, largely hidden by fir, spruce, pine and thick understory foliage.

Midway up the climb, the path bears close to the creek for your first view of Slide Creek Falls, a sheath of water that pours off its tilted limestone bottom, cascading in stages over 200 feet.

At the top of the canyon the trail crosses a small, wet bench whose unfettered skyline reveals both Lost Eagle Peak and Flat Top mountain, then re-enters the trees and resumes climbing to Fish Bowl Springs at 5.3 miles. This delightful deep pool is home to fingerling trout. Slide Lake lies .4 miles further and 340 feet above the springs.

It is possible to climb 11,868 foot Flat Top Mountain by following the inlet to Slide Lake until you see a small stream coming down on the left (N). Follow it to a basin containing several small lakes then head left (N) to gain the summit plateau. The peak was first ascended by Finis Mitchell in 1962.

15 Twin, Shirley & Valaite Lakes

Distance:
  Twin Lakes: 6.3 miles
  Shirley Lake: 6.7 miles
  Valaite Lake: 6.9 miles
Elevation gain:
  Twin Lakes: 2,080 feet
  Shirley Lake: 2,240 feet
  Valaite Lake: 2,280 feet
Elev. loss: 200 feet (all)
Max. elevation: 10,040
Topo map: Green River Lakes
  Earthwalk: Northern
Fish:
  Twin, Shirley: Cutthroat
  Gadsby: Cutthroat
  Valaite: Cutthroat

∧∧∧

Twin, Shirley, and Valaite Lakes receive less traffic than the Highline Trail. The trio of small, glacier-formed lakes rest at the foot of Big Sheep Mountain, the northeast terminus of a massif that includes Gypsum and Battleship mountains. The scenic backdrop, good fishing, and option of a cross-country trek to seldom-visited Lake Gadsby make this trail a good choice for either a long day hike or a backpacking trip.

From the parking area walk right (W) along the northern end of Lower Green River Lake to a large wooden directional sign for Porcupine Creek, Twin Lakes, Summit Lake, etc.. Follow the arrows and head south on the Porcupine Creek Trail through a shady,

mixed spruce and fir forest. The trail climbs 200 feet up a small bench before dropping closer to the lake's western shore. Numerous run-off streams flowing down Big Sheep Mountain are crossed enroute. Distinctive Flat Top Mountain fills the eastern skyline to your left.

A small sandy beach near the end of the lake is an appealing place to rest, try your luck fishing, or have lunch. Beyond the lake's west shore the trail stays right of a large park between Lower and Upper Green lakes; elk often herd here in late summer/early fall before the start of the rut. At 2.4 miles an unmarked trail heads left (E) across the far end of this open expanse. It joins the Highline Trail on the other side of the park, completing a loop trail around the lake. To get to Twin, Shirley, and Valaite lakes continue straight, soon reaching the first of two crossings over broad, shallow Porcupine Creek at 2.8 miles. A huge log spans the creek about 15 yards upstream if you don't want to get your feet wet. Selective rock hopping at the second crossing will accomplish the same goal.

After the second crossing the trail begins a moderate but steady climb of 800 feet through shady pine and spruce forest to the junction with Twin Lakes Trail at 4.2 miles.

The sign marking the cut-off is up a rise on the other side of Porcupine Creek. Since the trail you are on continues to Porcupine Pass, the poorly-signed junction is easy to miss. As the Porcupine Trail bends closer to the creek look to your right and you'll see a wooden sign post up a small draw. Cross the creek here and climb the draw to the post, anchored in the middle of a beautiful meadow blazoned by showy green gentian, Indian paintbrush, silky phacelia, and silvery lupine early to midsummer. With alpine peaks as a backdrop and water nearby, this is a seductive place to camp for those who got a late start or dislike carrying a pack very far.

From the meadow the Twin Lakes Trail swings northwest and steadily climbs switchbacks through magnificent limber pine forest. These contorted trees—with irregular, drooping branches and smooth, light gray bark—are virtually indistinguishable from whitebark pine. The dark green, rather stiff needles of both are clustered in groups of five; their elevation range, bark appearance and typical height of 25-50 feet are almost identical. Which is which? Examine the trees' cones. Limber pinecones are tan or light brown. The non-prickly scales open at maturity, and the cone itself is only slightly gummy, or sticky. Whitebark cones are a darkish purple and gummy; their scales remain closed, though squirrels and rodents often chew the cones to get to the seeds, leaving remains that resemble a husked ear of corn.

As the trail gains elevation, views of the northern end of the range unfold, a panorama that includes impressive snow-capped Desolation Peak, Mt. Solitude, Flagstone, and Squaretop.

Cross Twin Lakes Creek at the six mile mark. The "Twins," two pretty, small lakes separated by a narrow strip of land, lie just .3 miles further up the trail. Squeaking through a narrow strip of land between the two, the trail heads due west for .4 miles to Shirley Lake. Although the topo map shows the trail ending here, a path goes around the north side of Shirley and continues west to Valaite Lake, 6.9 miles from the trailhead. All three of the lakes offer good camping options.

Lake Gadsby is a great side-trip for those who enjoy walking cross-country. Climb the slope due south of the Twins, then contour southwest to a draw that leads to Gadsby's east shore, a total distance of one mile. Gadsby is semi-enclosed by the flanks of Battleship and Big Sheep mountains to the south, west and north. The impressive view to the east is filled with snow-covered peaks. Cutthroat thrive in the stocked lake.

16 New Fork Trail

Distance: 16 miles
Elovation gain: 3,790 feet
Elevation loss: 2,240 feet
Max. elevation: 10,940 feet
Topo maps:
    New Fork Lakes, Kendall Mtn., Squaretop Mtn., Gannett Peak
    Earthwalk: Northern
Fish:
    New Fork Lakes: Brook
    Lozier Lakes: Brook
    Clark: Rainbow

∧∧∧

The New Fork Trail ascends a striking canyon, crosses a beautiful park, then climbs to a high saddle before dropping over a thousand feet to Trail Creek Park and intersecting the Highline Trail. Hiking New Fork Trail and taking either the Porcupine Pass Trail or the Highline back to Green River Lakes makes a memorable 3-4 day backpacking trip. You may also want to consider by-passing Green River Lakes and starting a traverse of the range from this comparatively lightly-visited, but worthwhile, trail— contained by perhaps the most dramatic canyon walls in the entire range.

From the signed trailhead at the Narrows Campground the trail gradually climbs through aspen groves then hot, open sage-covered slopes above Upper New Fork Lake before descending to a stretch of appealing beach at its northeast corner. Beyond the lake it stays left of a marshy area created by the New Fork River, reaching a signed intersection with the Lowline Trail at two miles. Continue straight (NE), hiking through scattered pine and aspen to a bridged tributary crossing at 2.6 miles. The trail jogs north then southeast in a peculiar semi-circle before crossing the forest boundary into wilderness area at 3.4 miles, ascending just enough to notice several times enroute. Ford a large tributary .7 miles after entering Bridger Wilderness. Beyond, the canyon begins to narrow, its sheer rock walls rising precipitously above you.

The trail transects stretches of lodgepole forest and crosses minor tributaries at 4.6 and 4.7 miles before climbing a rise that obscures views of the river below. It drops off the rise and descends to two unbridged crossings of the river, the first at 5.4 miles, the second at 6.1. While the crossings aren't problematic when the river level is low, during high water they can be quite tricky and potentially dangerous. If you don't feel comfortable negotiating the

New Fork Trail

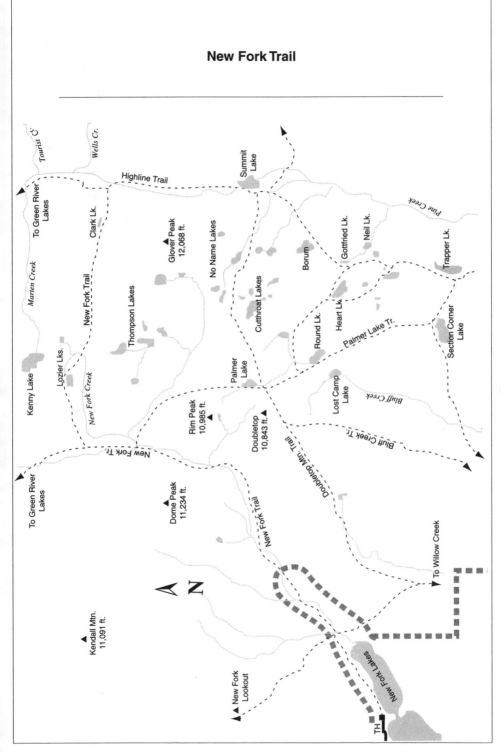

New Fork River Canyon rises steeply above the river that helped carve it.

river stay on the north side and pick a route through large boulders for about half a mile before reaching easier walking near the river.

Beyond the crossings the trail travels northeast, gradually ascending to open New Fork Park at 6.4 miles. The impressive mile-long pinnacled walls of Dome Peak Range rise above you to the left. To the right, the sheer walls of an unnamed 10,985 foot peak dominate. Numerous potential campsites are found throughout the park.

Cross wide but comparatively shallow Dodge Creek, a tributary of New Fork River, at 8.1 miles. The signed trail junction to Palmer Lake Trail lies 20 yards ahead. Stay left here and climb through conifer forest to an intersection with the Porcupine Pass Trail a mile further.

The New Fork Trail bears right (NE) and begins a steep, switchbacking climb to Lozier Lakes, 2.5 miles and 1,200 feet above the junction. Cross an outlet to the upper lake at 11.6 miles then descend to a crossing of a lower lake's outlet at 12.2 miles. Climb more gradually past that lake to a 10,940 foot pass at 13.8 miles, the high point of this hike. In season, Lozier Lake Basin is dressed in one of the most spectacular alpine wildflower displays in the Winds—and the all-encompassing sweep of glacier-clad peaks from the pass is second to none.

From the pass the trail drops steeply to Clark Lake at 14.6 miles. There are numerous nice places to camp on the south side of the lake. The trail descends past the lake through pine forest, crossing and recrossing Clark Creek, then Trail Creek, on its way to Trail Creek Park and a junction with the Highline Trail at 16 miles.

Boulder & Scab Creek Entrances

A hungry moose

Trails
Boulder Creek
Horseshoe Lake
Scab Creek

Administering Forest Service District
Pinedale Ranger District
210 W. Pine Street
P.O. Box 220
Pinedale, Wyoming 82941
307-367-4326

Nearest Town
Boulder (pop. 70). Limited service. Hotel, gas, small store. More complete facilities and services available in Pinedale, 12 miles north on U.S. 187/191.

Driving Directions:
From Pinedale, drive 12 miles SE on U.S. 187/191 to Boulder. Turn east onto Wyoming Highway 353 and drive 2.5 miles to a signed junction with Boulder Lake Road. To continue to:

Boulder Entrance: Turn left at the junction and drive five miles to an intersection with Stokes Crossing. Stay right here and continue to Boulder Lake parking area, 10.6 miles from the town of Boulder.

Scab Creek Entrance: Stay right past the Boulder Lake Turn-off and drive to the signed Scab Creek access road at 6.7 miles, just below a group of government buildings. Turn left onto the access, then left again in 1.5 miles. From here it is 7.3 miles to the parking area. Or, park at the Scab Creek campground .4 miles further. The signed trailhead is located near the campground.

Area Campgrounds
Forest Service Campgrounds at Boulder Lake and Scab Creek. No water. Ox-Yoke Campground near town of Boulder.

Showers
Showers are available for a fee at Ox-Yoke.

Boulder Creek • Horseshoe Lake

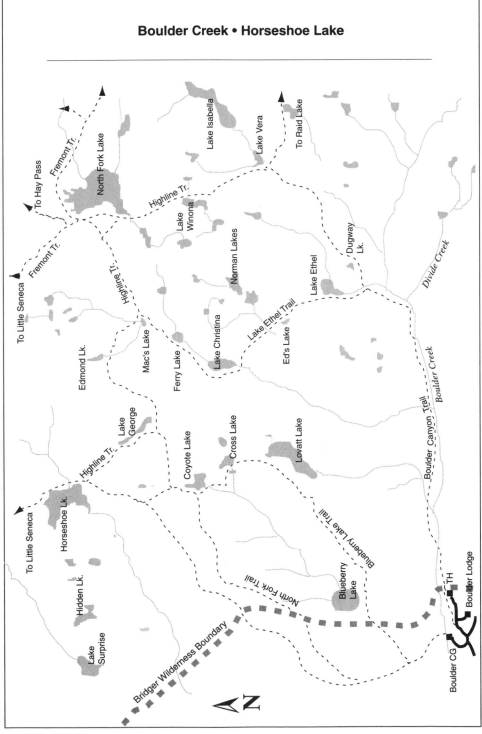

17 Boulder Canyon

Distance: 9.3 miles
Elevation gain: 2,360 feet
Elevation loss: Negligible
Max. elevation: 9,640 feet
Topo maps:
 Scab Creek, Halls Mountain, Horseshoe Lake
 Earthwalk: Southern
Fish: Cutthroat in Vera, Boulder

∧∧∧

Boulder Canyon is a popular trip with fishermen, horse packers and backpackers. Pretty Boulder Creek flows on the floor of the wooded chasm. Nice camping spots on the lower portion of trail and still, green pools teeming with trout still draw a fair number of recreationists, despite the fact the upper half of the trail was scoured by a large forest fire in 1988. Numerous extended trips can be made from Lake Vera, including spectacular jaunts to Halls Lake or Europe Canyon.

From the parking area walk on the road past Boulder Creek Ranch and a signed cut-off to the North Fork Trail to the start of the hike up Boulder Canyon, marked by a register at .7 miles. The trail heads east and crosses a bridge to the north side of Boulder Creek at one mile. It winds on a mostly level course through pleasant conifer and aspen forest to an open area and tributary crossings at 1.6 and 1.7 miles before skirting a large marshy area and crossing another tributary near two large beaver ponds at 2.6 miles. Here the canyon begins to narrow.

Hop numerous small tributaries before crossing larger Mac's Creek at 3.1 miles. The trail climbs at a moderate grade through conifer forest that opens to views of rock walls above you. At roughly 4.5 miles, you enter forest burned in the 1988 Fayette Fire, a huge conflagration that scorched much of the terrain between here and Lake Vera, the end of this hike.

Pass North Fork Falls (in reality, a cascade) at 4.8 miles and begin a sustained, switchbacking climb to a signed junction with the Ethel Lake Trail at 5.9 miles. Stay right at the junction, cross the bridge and ascend through burnt forest to Dugway Lake at 6.3 miles. Continue climbing through forest to a narrow section of woods strewn with large boulders. Pass a small pond on your left at 7.4 miles and climb east via switchbacks to Pipestone Creek Valley. Here the trail bears north and hops a tributary at 9.1 miles before dropping to appealing Lake Vera at 9.3 miles. The fire spared most of the lodgepole pine surrounding the lake.

18 Horseshoe Lake

Distance:
    Coyote Lake: 5.3 miles
    Horseshoe Lake: 7.2 miles
Elevation gain: 2,360 feet
Elevation loss: 140 feet
Max. elevation: 9,620 feet
Topo maps:
    Scab Creek, Horseshoe Lake
    Earthwalk: Southern
Fish:
    Coyote: Grayling
    Horseshoe Lake: Brook

∧∧∧

Three different trails south of Horseshoe Lake lead to this popular fishing destination: an unnamed trail to the west, the North Fork Trail, and the Blueberry Lake Trail (Blueberry Lake is called "Ruff" Lake on old Forest Service maps). The North Fork Trail described below cuts through mule deer country. Hikers often spot that graceful animal and occasionally moose on their way to Coyote and Horseshoe lakes.

From the parking area follow the directional signs to the North Fork Trail, reached by crossing a bridge over the river to a campground not shown on the topo map. The trail begins near the north end of the campground loop. It heads northwest through aspen to a tributary crossing at .2 miles then climbs at a moderate grade above Boulder Lake.

Reach a signed junction with the Blueberry Trail at .7 miles. Take the left fork and climb steeply to a nice overlook of the lake. The trail levels then climbs again to an intersection with the Lowline Trail at 1.7 miles. Bear right, following wood posts through an expanse of sage-covered terrain where the trail is difficult to follow. It becomes obvious as it leaves the flats and climbs a wooded draw to the signed Bridger Wilderness Boundary at 2.8 miles.

Shortly cross a tributary and climb then drop over a rise. Here, a use trail not shown on the map drops right to Blueberry Lake. Continue straight, climbing the ridge above the lake before contouring then dropping to cross its inflow creek at 3.7 miles. Recross the creek at 3.8 miles and climb steeply through pine to the west right of a boggy area. The trail skirts the bog only to bear right (E) at 4.2 miles and cut through the middle of one above it. It crosses two tributary streams then winds in-and-out of marshy areas fed by numerous small ponds and tributaries before reaching the west shore of Coyote Lake at 5.3 miles. Here the trail splits. The right fork is the Blueberry Trail, which will take you back to the parking area, a nice loop option for day hikers. Turn left to continue to Horseshoe Lake. This trail soon splits again. Both forks re-join in .4 miles near a junction with the Horseshoe Lake Trail. Turn left and hike north past two ponds as you gradually drop through forest to the southeast end of Horseshoe Lake and an intersection with the Highline Trail at 7.2 miles.

∧

19 Scab Creek

Distance
    Toboggan Lakes: 4 miles
    Little Divide Lake: 5 miles
    Highline Trail: 9.8 miles
Elevation gain: 2,080 feet
Elevation loss: 80 feet
Max. elevation: 10,120 feet
Topo maps:
    Scab Creek, Raid Lake
    Earthwalk: Southern
Fish:
    Toboggan Lakes: Brook
    Divide/Little Divide: Brook, Rainbow
    Lightning Lake: None
    Scab Creek: Brook

∧∧∧

The Lowline/Scab Creek Trail is not particularly appealing. While there is good fishing enroute, the trail is often muddy with few compensating scenic oohs and aahs. Views of the high peaks to the east don't open up until the last mile or so of trail as you approach its high point near Raid Lake. Herds of domestic sheep graze the area for sig-nificant portions of the summer. The trail is included in this book because it provides direct access to the middle section of the range, offering numerous extended trip options.

From the trailhead at Scab Creek Campground the trail climbs an open hillside to a junction with the Lowline Trail at .3 miles. Stay right (N) and con-

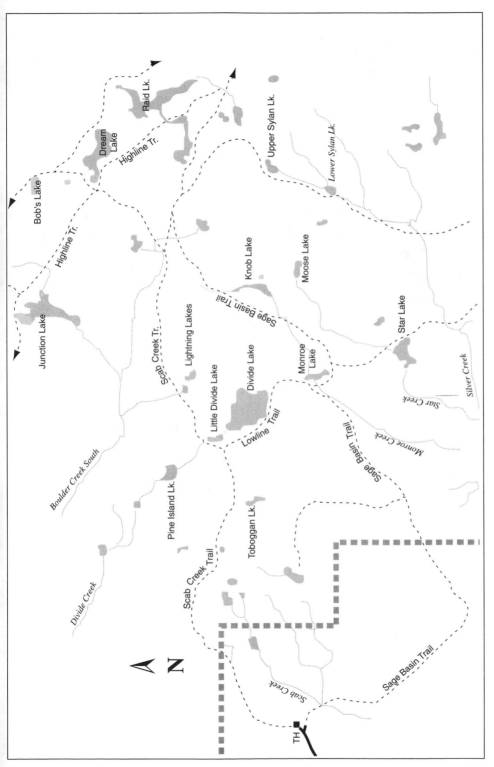

tinue to climb past the ruins of an old cabin at .8 miles to a stream crossing .2 miles further. Here the trail climbs at a steep grade via switchbacks, reaching the first of a dozen lakes cradled in Toboggan Lake Basin at 2.1 miles, over 1,000 feet higher than the trailhead. Cross a stream and climb then drop to another inlet crossing at 2.3 miles. Three more streams are crossed in the next half-mile before the trail weaves around two small lakes to Toboggan Lake at 4.5 miles.

The trail fords Scab Creek then skirts the right side of a boggy marsh, reaching a fork at 5.2 miles. To the right, the path heads south to Divide Lake, one of the larger lakes in the basin. To reach the Highline Trail, bear left at the junction and immediately cross Scab Creek. The path follows the west shore of Little Divide Lake. Fringed by whitebark forest, nice campsites can be found away from that lake's shore for those interested in establishing a fishing base camp.

The trail crosses Little Divide's outlet at 5.8 miles, then swings east towards Lightning Lake at 6.6 miles. It continues east on an easy, undulating course through scattered pine and spruce forest and open meadows studded with boulders to wide, shallow South Fork Boulder Creek at 8.5 miles.

Wade the creek and continue walking east, keeping right at 8.8 miles where a trail to your left leads to Dream Lake at 2.3 miles and Bob Lake beyond it. Both offer good fishing but rather poor camping options, as the terrain is open and unprotected.

Splash through South Fork tributaries at 8.9 and 9.0 miles. Two-tenths of a mile further a trail to your right angles southwest towards Monroe Lake; continue straight. Pass a spur trail .4 miles further and begin climbing towards the high point of 10,120 feet at 10.8 miles. Nice views of Raid, Ambush and Mount Geikie peaks are enjoyed due east.

Drop off the rise to an intersection with the Highline Trail at 11.3 miles.

Scarlet Gilia is one of many abundant wildflowers seen along the trail.

Elkhart Park Entrance

Mistake Lake

Trails
Long Lake
Island lake
Titcomb Basin
Titcomb Falls
Fremont Cut-off
Fremont Peak
Wall Lake
Pole Creek Lakes

Administrative Forest Service Office
Pinedale Ranger District
P.O. Box 220
Pinedale, Wyoming 82941
307-367-4326

Nearest Town
Pinedale (pop. 1,200+). Full range of services available, including lodging, gas, groceries, backpacking supplies, fishing licenses and maps. A district office for Bridger-Teton National Forest is located at 210 W. Pine Street. The Chamber of Commerce is at 35 S. Tyler (367-2242). Special attractions include the Museum of the Mountain Men and Faler's General Store, which has a huge collection of trophy heads scattered throughout the store.

Driving Directions
Turn onto paved Fremont Lake Road, located near Faler's at the east end of Pinedale. In 3.3 miles the road forks, with the left branch leading to Fremont Lake. Stay right to continue to Elkhart Park. Pass a right turn-off to Half Moon Lake at 7.2 miles, another right turn-off to a small ski area at 10.4 miles. The road climbs high above Fremont Lake before reaching a summer visitor's center at 14.9 miles. Elkhart Park is just beyond it. Trails to Island Lake, Titcomb Basin and Pole Creek Lake depart from this large parking area, which has pit toilets and a water spigot. To reach Trails End Campground and the Pine Creek Canyon Trailhead, drive .3 miles further. The hike to Long Lake starts here.

Area Campgrounds
Three Forest Service campgrounds are located off the trailhead access road described above. Large Fremont Lake Campground, with 54 sites, is about seven miles from Pinedale. This popular recreation site offers a picnic area, drinking water, restrooms and a boat launch ramp. Half Moon Campground, reached by taking the turn-off to Half Moon Lake, is roughly 10 miles from town. Visitors are alerted that Half Moon does not have drinking water; be sure to fill your jugs and water bottles in town. Trails End Campground at the end of the road is the

furthest from Pinedale, but closest to the trailhead. With only eight sites, this campground often fills early. Tent sites are also available at Lakeside Lodge on Fremont Lake, reached off the access road. In Pinedale you can camp at Campground of Wyoming.

Showers
Campground of Wyoming sells showers to non-campers.

Hiking towards Dinwoody Pass

20 Long Lake

Distance: 2.3 miles
Elevation gain: Negligible
Elevation loss: 1,405 feet
Max. elevation: 9,280 feet
Topo maps:
   Fremont Lake North, Bridger Lakes
   Earthwalk: Northern
Fish:
  Long Lake: Cutthroat,
  Rainbow, Grayling
  Upper Long Lake: Rainbow,
  Grayling

^^^

Stretching east-west for over a mile, Long Lake lies on the floor of a narrow canyon. Views of Fremont Lake, Faler Creek's frothy tumble down a deep ravine, and an array of wildflowers are enjoyed on the short, steep trek to the lake. The trail to Long Lake is a good late summer/early autumn choice. Most of July and August, however, it is overrun by campers and fishermen staying at Trail's End Campground near its start.

The trail begins at the north end of the campground parking lot where a wood sign lists destinations and mileages along the Pine Creek Canyon Trail.

It descends immediately, crossing Faler Creek at .2 miles before turning north and dropping through fir and pine forest. Views of Fremont Lake unfold a half mile further, where the forest gives way to a jumble of lichen-speckled rock shelves and boulders identified as Point 8875 on the Fremont Lake North topo.

Beyond the rock outcropping the grade noticeably steepens as it nears the deep ravine cut by Faler Creek to your left. The sharp, precipitous switchbacks in this section can be tricky if the trail is wet or muddy.

At 1.6 miles the trail turns away from the creek and heads north, climb-

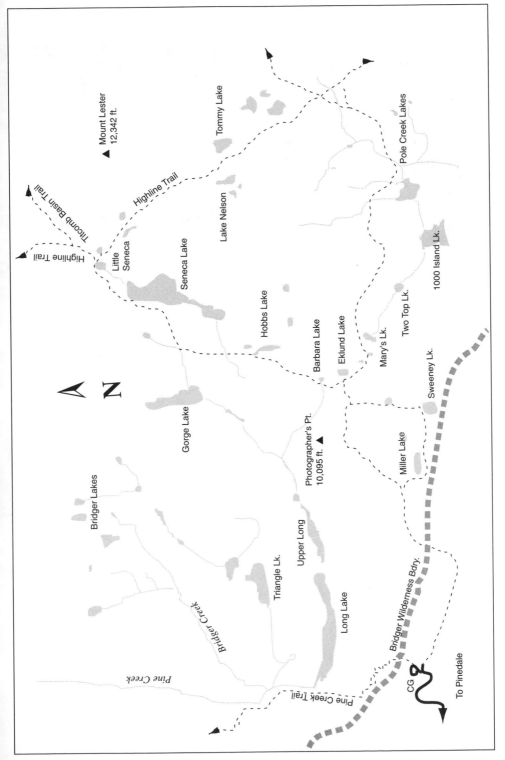

Long Lake is a popular short, but steep hike.

ing a short distance before dropping into dense, mixed forest and leveling out. Here the shady, moist terrain is enriched by a carpet of pine needles. Vines of lavender blue clematis wind up the trees early season, while snowy white Colorado columbine, leafy bluebell, patches of wild strawberry and delicate fairy slippers decorate the forest floor.

Long Lake is reached at 2.3 miles. The forested and talus slopes of the lower canyon drop sharply to its north and south shores, making further travel around the lake problematic. Avid sportsmen occasionally pack in an inflatable raft so they can easily fish both Long and Upper Long. It is possible to reach the lake's north side by walking .4 miles beyond its west end, crossing the outlet, and doubling back. The rocky, brushy terrain from there to Upper Long Lake makes it questionable if it's worth the effort, and the outlet can not always be negotiated safely.

Continuing north on the Pine Creek trail, ambitious hikers can steeply climb via switchbacks 1,400 feet up the west side of Pine Creek Canyon to the Crow's Nest, an aptly named vantage point that yields bird's eye views of the surrounding terrain. After gaining the canyon's rim, Pine Creek Trail traverses north across the bench, passing Glimpse, Prospector, Little Trapper, Trapper, Trail, Neil, Gottfried, Heart and Borum lakes before intersecting the Highline Trail at the southern end of Summit Lake.

21 Island Lake

Distance: 11.7 miles
Elevation gain: 1,840 feet
Elevation loss: 840 feet
Max. elevation: 10,640 feet
Topo map: Bridger Lakes
        Earthwalk: Northern
Fish:
  Eklund: Rainbow
  Barbara: Cutthroat
  Hobbs: Rainbow
  Seneca: Rainbow
  Little Seneca: Rainbow
  Island: Rainbow, Cutthroat

∧∧∧

With Fremont Peak as its backdrop, sparkling Island Lake is an attractive destination. Unfortunately—or fortunately, depending on your point of view—it lies at the portals of Titcomb Basin, an exquisite cirque of glaciated peaks that attracts hundreds of climbers and hikers each summer. Camping around the lake is so crowded that parties have been known to perch on nearby rocks and watch you tear down your tent so they can occupy your site the moment after you hit the trail. Hiking northeast another mile or so towards pretty, secluded Indian Basin is a nicer alternative.

Snippets of trail slip through corners of both Fremont Lake and Fayette Lake topos; the only map realistically needed for this long hike is Bridger Lakes. From the south parking area trailhead (sign reads "Pole Creek Trail", etc.) begin a gradual ascent up Faler Creek drainage through towering lodgepole pine that preclude views of the range. Stay left at 1.4 miles where a trail forks right to Surveyor Park, walking on nearly level ground through pleasant lodgepole pine and spruce to open Miller Park and an unsigned junction to Miller/Sweeney Lakes at 3.1 miles. Stay left here, enjoying fields of silvery lupine early season and an impressive line of distant peaks to the north as you climb through scattered conifers to a small overlook at 4.3 miles. Here 10,095 foot Photographer's Point dominates the foreground of a panorama of jagged peaks, deep blue lakes and canyons reached miles down the trail. It is a nice turn-around or lunch spot for those seeking a day excursion.

Hike left (E) past another junction with the Miller/Sweeney Lakes Trail at 5.1 miles to the Seneca Lake Trail junction near Eklund Lake .2 miles further.

Bear left here and steadily drop to the outlet crossing of pocket-sized Barbara Lake at 5.7 miles. The trail skirts the lake's west shore then switchbacks down to a grassy meadow, passes a small pond, and climbs to Hobbs Lake at 6.5 miles. While the trail closely hugs the west side of this pretty lake, fine camping opportunities exist away from its eastern shore.

Beyond the lake the trail crosses Seneca Lake's outlet stream—which can be quite brisk and powerful early season—before dropping to several small ponds and bearing right, climbing steeply up a lightly forested draw to an overlook of Seneca Lake at 8.5 miles. Massive 12,342 foot Mount Lester rises above Seneca's mile-and-a-half length.

The trail drops north down a bluff to the west shore, occasionally submerged when the lake level is high.

There are few camping spots for those wanting to drop their packs. Beyond Seneca, the trail intersects the sketchy path to Lost Lake (abandoned by the Forest Service) at 9.3 miles.

Stay right here. Pass a small pond, soon walking near the base of an impressive rock wall around Little Seneca Lake to the Highline Trail junction at 10.1 miles. Turn left (N) here and ascend 200 feet to a junction with the Indian Pass Trail at 10.4 miles.

Bear right at this junction, soon hopping a tributary as you climb a gentle grade to an overlook of Island Lake, Fremont Peak and Titcomb Basin at 11.2 miles.

A steep 250 foot descent brings you to the lake's southeast end. Pass a small, sandy beach to an obvious inlet decorated with bluebells, paintbrush and monkeyflowers, 11.7 miles from the Elkhart trailhead.

Fremont Peak, the third highest summit in Wyoming, looms above Island Lake.

Island Lake • Titcomb Basin • Fremont Cut-Off

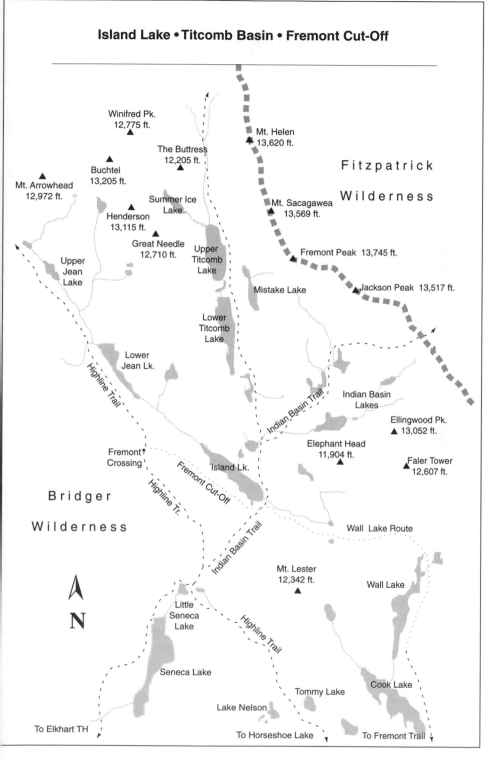

Winifred Pk.
12,775 ft.

The Buttress
12,205 ft.

Mt. Helen
13,620 ft.

Fitzpatrick

Wilderness

Buchtel
13,205 ft.

Mt. Arrowhead
12,972 ft.

Summer Ice
Lake

Mt. Sacagawea
13,569 ft.

Henderson
13,115 ft.

Great Needle
12,710 ft.

Upper
Titcomb
Lake

Fremont Peak 13,745 ft.

Upper
Jean
Lake

Mistake Lake

Jackson Peak 13,517 ft.

Lower
Titcomb
Lake

Lower
Jean Lk.

Highline Trail

Indian Basin Trail

Indian Basin
Lakes

Ellingwood Pk.
▲ 13,052 ft.

Fremont
Crossing

Highline Tr.

Fremont Cut-Off

Island Lk.

Elephant Head
11,904 ft.

Faler Tower
12,607 ft.

Bridger

Wilderness

Indian Basin Trail

Wall Lake Route

Mt. Lester
12,342 ft.

Wall Lake

N

Little
Seneca
Lake

Highline Trail

Seneca Lake

Cook Lake

Tommy Lake

Lake Nelson

To Elkhart TH

To Horseshoe Lake

To Fremont Trail

22 Titcomb Basin

Distance from Island Lake:
    Upper Titcomb Lake: 3.6 miles
    Dinwoody Pass: 5.8 miles
Elevation gain:
    To Upper Titcomb: 250 feet
    To Dinwoody Pass: 2,450 feet
Elevation loss: Negligible
Max. elevation:
    Upper Titcomb: 10,600 feet
    Dinwoody Pass: 12,800 feet
Topo maps:
    Bridger Lakes, Gannet Peak
    Earthwalk: Northern
Fish:
    Mistake Lake: Golden
    Pothole Lake: Golden
    Titcomb Lakes: Golden

∧∧∧

Magnificent Titcomb Basin is bound by glaciated, jagged peaks to the north and east. Its floor cradles Lower and Upper Titcomb Lakes, superb aquamarine bodies of water that deprive their hue from the finely ground rocks and minerals carried in the glacial run-off. Colorful clusters of alpine wildflowers thrive at the foot of huge boulders scattered across the basin.

Winds' pioneers Orrin and Lorraine Bonney correctly called Titcomb "as beautiful a spot as one will find in the Rockies." It is not surprising that the basin is one of the most heavily visited places in the Wind River Range.

The route into the basin was established by climbers in 1936; it has since become a well-worn path.

From the inlet at the eastern end of Island Lake climb north on the trail to the signed Indian Pass junction at .8 miles. Continue straight (N), crossing two tributaries before curving around the east side of Lake 10,548, commonly called Pothole Lake, at 1.6 miles. Beyond it the trail bears west then north along the east side of Lower Titcomb to Upper Titcomb Lake, crossing Mistake Lake's outflow stream at three

Titcomb Basin has been described as one of the prettiest spots in the Rockies.

miles. (To reach that beautiful lake nestled 200 feet above you, ascend either side of the outflow stream. Golden trout were inadvertently stocked in the lake, giving it its name.)

The main trail continues north along the east side of Upper Titcomb Lake to reach its end at 3.6 miles. A use trail parallels the inlet beyond the lake for another mile than disappears in the high meadows. Bear right (E) to ascend obvious snow-covered Dinwoody Pass. Sandwiched between Miriam and Dinwoody peaks, the 12,800 foot pass provides incomparable views of 13,804 foot Gannett Peak, the highest point in Wyoming, and Dinwoody Glacier. It is a major route across the Continental Divide for climbers wanting to scale Gannett from the southeast. Though shorter than other access routes, it suffers the disadvantage of dropping al-most 2,000 feet down Dinwoody Glacier only to climb back up the Gooseneck.

Climbers often set up base camp beyond the upper lake for quick access to other 13,000 foot peaks near the cirque's head, including Mt. Woodrow Wilson, Mt. Helen, and Mt. Sacajawea. Ambitious, experienced hikers can complete a spectacular loop trip by ascending Twins Glacier to 12,240 foot Knapsack Col, dropping west down talus and grass slopes to Peak Lake, and hiking the Shannon Pass Trail to its intersection with the Highline.

Titcomb Basin, lakes and needles are named in honor of Harold and Charles Titcomb, brothers who made the second ascent of Fremont Peak in 1901. Harold was a mine engineer who was employed at the famed Carissa Gold Mine near South Pass.

23 Lower Titcomb Falls

Distance from Island Lake inlet: .7 miles
Elevation gain: Approx. 120 feet
Elevation loss: Approx. 120 feet
Max. elevation: 10,550 feet
Topo map: Bridger Lakes

∧∧∧

Lower Titcomb Falls plunges 40 or so feet into Island Lake. A grassy patch nears its base offers an appealing spot for lunch, reading a book or taking a snooze in the sun. Those wanting to continue into Titcomb Basin can easily walk up the slopes to the right of the falls.

From the inlet at the east end of Island Lake follow the trail to the lake's north side. When it begins heading into Titcomb Basin, stay on a use trail that parallels the lake. Cross a rise where rockfall blocks closer passage. A use trail does wind through the jumble of rock and scrub willow; take this only if you are interested in observing a pika colony that lives in the slide. These industrious little critters are usually hard at work gathering grasses for the long winter ahead. If you choose this route, your approach will likely be heralded by their shrill alarm call. Pikas aside, it is easier to traverse above the slide to an obvious grassy draw that drops to the lake shore. Turn right at the shore, walk a few yards and the pretty waterfall comes into view.

On the moist slopes bordering the falls vivid, deep-rose clusters of Parry's primrose are seen in season, typically

Lower Titcomb Falls

July and August. Its repulsive smell does not match its attractive funnel-form blossoms. While it grows as low as 8,000 feet, it thrives in damp areas above timberline near the edges of melting snowfields, along streambanks, and in moist, cool recesses under overhanging boulders.

24 Fremont Cut-Off

Distance: 1.8 miles
Elevation gain: Approx. 220 feet
Elevation loss: Approx. 320 feet
Max. elevation: 10,470 feet
Topo map: Bridger Lakes (not plotted)
          Earthwalk: Northern (not plotted)
Fish: None

∧∧∧

This abandoned trail is not signed or plotted on the Bridger Lakes map. It is used on occasion by outfitters and area residents who know about it. It offers a much prettier, shorter route to Island Lake from Jean lakes and vice versa.

As you descend the Highline Trail traveling southeast from Upper and Lower Jean lakes towards Little Seneca Lake, look for a small pond to your left just before reaching Fremont Crossing (roughly across from the trail leading to Lost Lake). Walk between the pond and a rock outcropping then head southeast up a grassy draw. You'll soon see a dirt path that leads to a wide but shallow stream crossing. A good trail is visible cutting up the bench on the opposite side. The trail parallels the unnamed body of water a short distance then heads south and east through numerous small knolls on its way to Island Lake. Enroute you pass four beautiful small ponds that offer no fish, but fine camping opportunities away from their shores.

The trail tops a rise above the midpoint of Island's southwest shore, almost directly across from Lower Titcomb Falls. It descends a short distance and joins the trail around the lake.

The unmarked intersection is so faint that if you weren't aware of the Fremont Cut-Off you would miss it. If you are trying to find the cut-off going from Island Lake to Jean Lakes, look for a small pile of rocks about a half mile up the southwest side of the lake. If you pass a pond to your right you've missed it. Backtrack about 10 yards and look again. Sections of this wandering, unofficial trail are easy to follow. Others are quite faint, making it necessary to pay close attention. It is generally easier to track going from Jean Lakes to Island Lake.

25 Fremont Peak

Distance from Island Lake: Approx. 5 miles
Elevation gain: 3,385 feet
Elevation loss: Negligible
Max. elevation: 13,745 feet
Topo maps:
 Bridger Lakes
 Fremont Peak South
 Fremont Peak North
 Gannett Peak

∧∧∧

Fremont Peak is the third highest summit in Wyoming, the second highest in the Wind River Range. At 13,745 feet, its crown is only 25 feet lower than Grand Teton's 13,770 feet summit—the second highest peak in the Cowboy state—and 59 shy of No. 1 Gannett's. Rising abruptly above the east side of Titcomb Basin, it seems improbable that one could scramble to the summit, yet two different "walk-up" routes give non-climbers access to the top. The view of Titcomb Basin and surrounding terrain is worth the effort to get there.

The easier route, for which the elevation and distance of this hike is calculated, is via Indian Basin. From Island Lake's east end follow the trail north to Indian Pass Junction at .8 miles. Bear right (E) and follow that trail to the northwest inlet of Lake 11,008. Leave the trail here, paralleling the left side of the inlet stream as you ascend northwest on open, boulder littered slopes towards a grassy saddle at 12,040 feet, reached 3.3 miles and 1,650 feet above Island Lake. Follow cairns and footprints north of the saddle to reach the summit, another 1,700 feet and 1.7 miles above you.

Alternatively, stay on the trail into Titcomb Basin to the outlet of Mistake Lake, three miles beyond the east end of Island Lake. Ascend the slopes bordering the outlet to Mistake's lakeshore. Ascend the flowered, grassy ledges above and northeast of the lake to the talus slopes and sloping rock slabs near the summit. This is the more difficult of the two walk-up routes, and can be quite tricky in wet or icy conditions.

Neither route should be attempted by those without sufficient cross-country skills and route-finding abilities.

Looking north into Titcomb Basin from Fremont's slopes

Did Fremont climb
Fremont Peak?

∧∧∧

Did John C. Fremont climb the peak that bears his name? Yes — or no, depending on who you believe.

Fremont was the son of Jean Charles Fremont, a Frenchmen who had been exiled to America following that country's revolution. Jean Charles fell in love with the wife of his employer, a scandal that forced him and his lover to leave Virginia. They settled in Savannah, Georgia, where John was born in 1813.

His quick wit and mathematical ability landed him a position with the United States Army Topographical Corps in his early 20s; his performance earned him a minor officer's commission in 1838. Still, he was relatively unknown and undistinguished when, in his 28th year, he eloped with 15-year-old Jessie Benton in October of 1841.

It was a bitter pill for U.S. Senator Thomas Hart Benton of Missouri to swallow. An illegitimate officer had absconded with his daughter! The political powerhouse used his influence to send Fremont west—a move that helped cool the social tittering and simultaneously promote his goal of western expansion. Fremont was selected to head a mapping survey of the territories. He was specifically charged with finding a wagon route to South Pass and recommending appropriate sites for army outposts. It was the first of five expeditions he would lead.

In the spring of 1842, the hitherto obscure lieutenant began his western journey. He met famed mountain men Kit Carson on a steamer bound for St. Louis and promptly hired him as a guide. Others versed in mountain exploration were added as the entourage headed west. In retrospect, retaining skilled help was one of Fremont's best decisions; he had little outdoor savvy himself. Author Don Pitcher noted in *Wyoming Handbook* that many of the "Great Pathfinder's" ventures—"such as floating through the wild waters of Fremont Canyon...or crossing the Rockies in the dead of winter —were downright stupid, and his guides tried to stop him."

What his guides encouraged the summer of 1842 was scaling "the highest peak of the Rocky Mountains,"a statement Fremont penned in his subsequent report to Congress. The false plum generated great enthusiasm, and the assigned task of finding a wagon route was temporarily forgotten. Fremont reached Island Lake, which he named, on August 14th. Members of the expedition made an unsuccessful attempt to climb "the highest peak" that day. Carson did reach the summit of neighboring Jackson Peak in an effort to see if he could find a route up Fremont. That first ascent of 13,517 foot Jackson was not mentioned in his autobiography. Carson apparently did not consider it significant.

The following day Fremont, Charles Preuss, Clement Lambert, Johnny Janisse, a man named Descoteaux or deCoteau, and Basil Lajeunesse attempted to climb the peak again, this time approaching it via "a defile of the most rugged mountains," presumably either Titcomb or Indian Basin. Their attempt was successful, and the crew planted an American flag on the summit. Fremont called the mountain Snow Peak, and wrote in his report that, "the whole scene had one striking feature, which was that of terrible convulsion. Parallel to its length, the ridge was split into chasms and fissures..."

He estimated the peak's elevation at 13,570 feet, wrote a general description, and noted its latitude. The peak was later named Fremont in his honor. The late Orrin Bonney believed the party ascended not Fremont, but Mt. Woodrow Wilson at the north end of Titcomb Basin. In his 1977 *Field Book to the Wind River Range*, Bonney argues that the references to snow and glaciers, surrounding terrain and latitude all point to Woodrow as the peak that was ascended. Other historians, however, hold to the belief that the party scaled the peak that carries Fremont's name.

Interestingly, Fremont himself may not have reached either summit. He suffered from altitude sickness and had little tolerance for higher elevations. Lajeunesse, one of the scouts in the party, is on record stating, " Fremont never ascended the peak."

John C. Fremont

The debate may never be ended with certainty. The fall of 1844 Fremont, ignoring the advice of his guides, attempted a boat journey down a canyon 30 miles southwest of Casper that now bears his name. Author D. Ray Wilson recounted the results in *Wyoming: An Historical Tour Guide*:

"His boat broke apart on the rocky canyon wall, nearly costing the lives of his entire party. Most of his notes, covering two years of exploration in the West, were lost in this accident."

26 Wall Lake

Distance from Island Lake:
    To Wall's north inlet: 2.4 miles
    To Cook Lake 10,170: 4.4 miles
Elevation gain: 900 feet
Elevation loss: 1,170 feet
Max. elevation: 11,180 feet
Topo maps:
    Bridger Lakes, Fremont Peak South
    Earthwalk: Northern
Fish:
    Wall: Golden
    Cook Lakes: Brook, Golden

∧∧∧

Massive rock walls soar almost 2,000 feet above the west shore of mile-and-a-half long Wall Lake. Their precipitous drop precludes travel along that shore, but friendlier ledges and hillside contours to the east allow hikers to explore this incredible lake and basin north of Cook Lakes. The trail to Wall is not plotted on topo maps or officially maintained but is easy to locate on the ground. Follow the large inlet flowing into the east end of Island Lake upstream. The grade of the initially steep trail eases as you ascend to two small lakes at one mile. Elephant Head Peak is prominent to your left (N) while Mt. Lester dominates the view to your right. Walk up the right side of the broad, open saddle. Its 11,180 foot crest is reached 1.8 miles above Island Lake.

Angle left off the saddle and descend snowfields towards the open, sloping meadows below, gradually bearing right towards a small pond near the northern end of Wall Lake at 2.2 miles. Walk due south from the pond and carefully cross the swift stream between Lake 10,488 and Wall. Climb a short distance above the lake and contour around its east shore, staying high to avoid "cliffing" out. At 3.7 miles you'll pass a small pond. Angle left (SE) and climb then drop down a series of rock ledges several hundred feet to a stream. Follow it downstream until you pick up a trail that leads south to Cook Lake 10,170. The trail crosses a stream flowing into that lake at 4.4 miles.

27 Pole Creek Lakes

Distance: 8.8 miles
Elevation gain: 1,040 feet
Elevation loss: 640 feet
Max. elevation: 10,400 feet
Topo maps:
    Bridger Lakes
    Earthwalk: Northern
Fish:
    Miller: Brook
    Middle Sweeney: Golden
    Sweeney: Cutthroat, Golden
    Eklund: Rainbow
    Pole Creek and lakes: Brook, Cutthroat

∧∧∧

Of the 1,600 plus lakes in the Winds, Pole Creek Lakes are not scenic standouts. The ho-hum bodies of water lack the alpine beauty of others. They do, however, have three things to recommend: at the junction above Eklund almost everyone goes to Titcomb basin, providing relative solitude; Pole Creek and neighboring lakes boast good fishing; and a wealth of trails in the area offer many fine extended trip options. Small sections of trail are plotted on the Fremont Lake South and Fayette quadrangles. The only topo realistically needed for this hike is Bridger Lakes.

From the south parking area trailhead (sign reads "Pole Creek Trail", etc.) begin a gradual ascent up Faler Creek drainage through towering lodgepole pine that preclude views of the range. Stay left at 1.4 miles where a trail forks right to Surveyor Park, walking on nearly level ground through pleasant lodgepole pine and spruce to open Miller Park and an unsigned junction to Miller/Sweeney Lakes at 3.1 miles. Bear left here, enjoying both fields of silvery lupine and an impressive line of distant peaks to the north as you climb through scattered conifers to a small overlook at 4.3 miles. Here 10,095 foot Photographer's Point dominates the foreground of a panorama of jagged peaks, deep blue lakes and canyons. It is a nice turn-around or lunch spot for those seeking a day excursion.

Hike left (E) past another junction with the Miller/Sweeney Lakes Trail at

5.1 miles to the Seneca Lake Trail junction near Eklund Lake .2 miles further. Turn right here. The trail stays right of Eklund Lake's west then southern shore before ascending a small, wooded draw and weaving between two unnamed pools nestled in wildflower-specked meadows. Beyond the tarns it curves east, passing yet another small tarn before reaching rock-bound Mary's Lake at 6.1 miles.

Continuing east past that pretty body of water, the trail descends a set of switchbacks then drops more gradually down an open drainage studded with granite boulders to narrow Mosquito Lake at 6.9 miles. It bends south beyond the end of the lake, crosses a tributary, then bears east through forested terrain dotted with small ponds to a crossing of Monument Creek at eight miles.

Here the trail heads southeast down a drainage and crosses a tributary at 8.6 miles. Pole Creek Lake lies directly to your left (SW). The junction with the Highline Trail is reached .2 miles further.

To continue to Cook Lakes, take the left fork, ford Pole Creek, and head southeast for 1.6 miles to the inlet of Cook Lake 10,143 at 10.4 miles. Hike north to reach Cook Lake 10,170 and Wall Lake beyond. There is a maze of trails in the area. Consult your topo map carefully.

∧

Big Sandy Entrance

Warbonnet & The Warriors

Trails
Big Sandy Lake
Clear and Deep Lakes
Cirque of the Towers

Administrative Forest Service Office
Pinedale Ranger District
P.O. Box 220
Pinedale, Wyoming 82941

Nearest Town
Boulder (pop. 70) or Farson (pop. 300). Limited services. Lodging, gas, small store at both locations. Backpacking supplies, maps, etc. available at Pinedale, 12 miles NW of Boulder on U.S. 187/191 or at Rock Springs, 36 miles SE of Farson on U.S. 187/191.

Driving Directions
From Boulder: Turn east onto Wyoming Highway 353 and drive on mostly paved road past signed turn-offs to Boulder Lake and Scab Creek Access to Big Sandy Junction, 19.3 miles from U.S. 187/191 **(Jct. 1).** Turn left and drive nine miles on dirt road to an intersection with Muddy Speedway **(Jct. 2).** Turn left here and drive 7.4 miles to Big Sandy Entrance **(Jct. 3)**, marked by a sign that reads "Dutch Joe Guard Station 3, etc.". Turn left and drive past the Bridger-Teton National Forest Boundary and turn-offs to Dutch Joe, Sedgwick Meadows and Big Sandy Lodge before reaching the campground and parking area, 10.5 miles beyond the entrance turn-off and 46.2 miles from the town of Boulder.
From Farson: Drive 30 miles north of Farson on U.S. 187/191 to a signed turn-off to Big Sandy. Turn right onto the dirt road and follow it approximately eight miles to **(Jct. 1)**, identified above. Go straight at this junction and follow the rest of the directions from the Boulder access.

Big Sandy can also be reached from Farson by driving two miles east on Wyoming Highway 28 to a signed dirt road to Big Sandy on your left. This road heads north approximately 40 miles to **(Jct. 2).** Turn right at this junction and follow the directions to Big Sandy.

Area Campgrounds
Forest Service campground at Big Sandy. Pit toilets, picnic tables, no water. Ox-Yoke Campground near town of Boulder also has tent sites.

Showers
Ox-Yoke sells showers to non-campers.

Big Sandy Lake • Clear and Deep Lakes

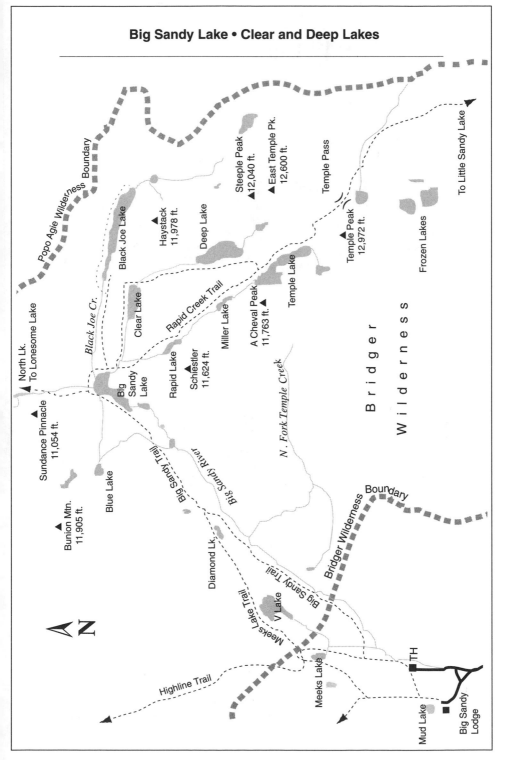

Popo Agie Wilderness Boundary

Steeple Peak ▲12,040 ft.

▲ East Temple Pk. 12,600 ft.

Temple Pass

To Little Sandy Lake

Black Joe Lake

Haystack 11,978 ft. ▲

Deep Lake

▲ Temple Peak 12,972 ft.

Frozen Lakes

North Lk. To Lonesome Lake ▲

Black Joe Cr.

Clear Lake

Rapid Creek Trail

Miller Lake

A Cheval Peak 11,763 ft. ▲

Temple Lake

B r i d g e r

Sundance Pinnacle 11,054 ft. ▲

Big Sandy Lake

Rapid Lake

Schlestler 11,624 ft.

N. Fork Temple Creek

W i l d e r n e s s

Bunion Mtn. 11,905 ft. ▲

Blue Lake

Big Sandy Trail

Big Sandy River

Diamond Lk.

Bridger Wilderness Boundary

Meeks Lake Trail

V Lake

Big Sandy Trail

Highline Trail

Meeks Lake

TH

Mud Lake

Big Sandy Lodge

N

28 Big Sandy Lake

Distance: 5.8 miles
Elevation gain: 780 feet
Elevation loss: 120 feet
Max. elevation: 9,740 feet
Topo maps:
    Big Sandy Opening, Temple Peak
    Earthwalk: Southern
Fish:
    Meeks: Brook
    V Lake: Rainbow
    Big Sandy: Brook, Cutthroat

∧∧∧

The Big Sandy Entrance is second only to Elkhart Park in the number of visitors it attracts. Climbers and backpackers are drawn by the shortest route to Cirque of the Towers and spectacular terrain around Clear and Deep Lakes. Fishermen enjoy easy access to half a dozen lakes and streams stocked with monster trout. The result is a dusty trail so wide in spots that it looks like a jeep road. Expect to see lots of people on this popular hike. The best time to go to avoid crowds is after Labor Day when the kids are back in school and many people have packed away their gear until next July.

The signed trail starts north of the parking area. The well-used path stays left of Big Sandy River and skirts several flowered meadows to reach a signed junction with Meeks Lake Trail at .6 miles. The right fork follows the river to Big Sandy Lake, an alternative route that reaches its north end in 5.4 miles. Though shorter, it is not as scenic. Stay left at the junction and begin a steady climb through lodgepole forest to a crossing of Meeks Lake Creek at one mile. Keep right at 1.5 miles where a trail to the left connects with the Highline. Gently ascend then drop to V Lake at 1.9 miles. The trail circles V's north shore before bearing northeast and cutting through a boggy area. Look for red-violet elephant's head, a distinctive, well-named wildflower whose blooms mimic an elephant's profile, complete with upturned trunk. A favorite snack of both deer and elk, the flower thrives in wet, sunny areas.

Wood posts supplement the indistinct path through the marsh until you

The best view of Big Sandy Lake is above it as you climb to Big Sandy Pass.

reach conifer forest and an obvious trail at 3.1 miles. Diamond Lake lies just ahead. The trail parallels Diamond's north shore, then hops two streams in quick succession at 3.4 and 3.5 miles before intersecting the main Big Sandy Trail at 3.7 miles.

Bear left and continue an easy ascent through scattered spruce and pine forest and small meadows. Hop three small tributaries enroute to the crest of a rise that opens up views of the river valley and the upper scree slopes of 12,416 foot Big Sandy Mountain. The trail reaches the southwest end of the lake at five miles, paralleling its west shore to a rocky crossing of Lost Creek .6 miles further. (The creek leads to little-visited Blue Lake, which offers both good fishing and nice places to camp away from its shore).

Continue around the lake to a trail junction at 5.8 miles. The path to the Cirque and Arrowhead Lake heads left (N), while the trail to the right goes to Black Joe, Clear, Deep, and Temple lakes.

Big Sandy was the name of a Pony Express station and post office near present-day Farson. The west slopes of Big Sandy Mountain were first hiked in 1933 by Finis Mitchell. A much nicer walk-up is the nearby peak that bears his name. Access the southern slope of 12,482 foot Mitchell Peak by continuing on the trail to the Cirque past the junction until you reach a crossing of North Fork Creek. Leave the trail here, or near the north end of Shaft Lake, and pick a route to the top.

29 Clear and Deep Lakes

Distance from Big Sandy Lake:
  Clear Lake 1.1 miles
  Deep Lake: 2.6 miles
Elevation gain: 840 feet
Elevation loss: Negligible
Max. elevation: 10,520 feet
Topo map: Temple Peak
  Earthwalk: Southern
Fish:
  Clear: Brook
  Deep: Brook
  Temple, Rapid and Miller Lakes: Brook
  Black Joe: Cutthroat

∧∧∧

Clear and Deep Lakes lie on the floor of a high basin bound by massive 11,978 foot Haystack Mountain and 12,590 foot East Temple Peak to the east, 11,624 foot Schiestler Mountain and 12,972 foot Temple Peak to the west. Temple Pass connects east and west at the head of the basin. A seldom-used, steep trail drops southeast off the pass to the headwaters of Little Sandy Creek.

Glaciers still cling below sheer Temple Peak in this austerely beautiful alpine basin. Climbers frequently set up base camp near Deep Lake to provide easy access to challenging climbing routes on Haystack's mile-long west slope. Though striking, the exposed upper basin is often windy. Most backpackers opt to camp near Clear Lake 500 feet below.

From the trail junction at the north end of Big Sandy Lake, hike east through an open park to a crossing of North Fork Creek at .1 miles. Black Joe Creek is crossed at .2 miles near its confluence with an unnamed stream to the northeast. There are logs and easy crossing spots in the vicinity. Scout around and you'll find them.

Beyond this double crossing the trail stays left of a meadow as it begins bearing south towards a junction with Black Joe Trail at .4 miles. That trail climbs 500 feet up wooded slopes to Black Joe Lake a mile further.

Stay right at the intersection and continue hiking at the edge of the often wet meadow for .2 miles to an unmarked junction. Here a faint trail heads right (SW) to Rapid Lake. Bear left and soon begin ascending through scattered

12,590 ft. East Temple Peak soars above the rocky basin that cradles Deep Lake.

trees and rock slabs to Clear Lake, reaching its western end at 1.1 miles. The trail stays left of this long lake as it heads north towards striking Haystack Mountain in front of you. Cross the lake's inlet at 1.8 miles and follow it upstream through shrub willow, sloping rock slabs, and ledges to Deep Lake's north end at 2.6 miles.

Those with sharp eyes can often pick out climbers on Haystack, which has more established routes than any other Wind River Peak. The first known ascent was of the mountain's south ridge in 1961 by Bruce Monroe and John Hudson. With challenging routes on Haystack, East Temple and Temple Peak, the basin draws almost as many climbers as Circque of the Towers, and perhaps more than Titcomb Basin.

To reach Temple Pass, continue southwest towards a small saddle that drops to an unsigned intersection with the Temple Lake/Rapid Creek Trail at 3.4 miles. Turn left here and follow Temple's east shore to slopes rising above its end. The trail climbs south then east to the pass, 1.2 miles beyond the junction. A nice loop can be made by turning right at the Temple Lake junction and walking northwest pass Temple, Miller and Rapid Lakes back to the Clear Lake Junction at two miles. Consult your map.

Temple Peak was used as a topographic station by Hayden survey in 1877. It was first climbed by survey members George Chittenden, Frederick Endlich, Charles Howes and Edward Clymer the same year.

30 Cirque of the Towers

Distance:
>   From Big Sandy Trailhead: 8.6 miles
>   From Big Sandy Lake: 2.8 miles

Elevation gain:
>   From Big Sandy Trailhead: 2,120 ft
>   From Big Sandy Lake: 1,340 feet

Elevation loss:
>   From Big Sandy Trailhead: Approx. 1,000 feet
>   From Big Sandy Lake: 880 feet

Max. elevation: 10,780 feet

Topo maps:
>   Big Sandy Opening, Temple Peak, Lizard Head
>   Earthwalk: Southern

Fish:
>   Meeks: Brook
>   V Lake: Rainbow
>   Big Sandy: Brook, Cutthroat
>   North: Brook
>   Lonesome: Cutthroat
>   None in Shaft or Arrowhead

ΛΛΛ

Cirque of the Towers is a spectacular semi-circle of jagged peaks, lush meadows and snow-fed lakes that attracts thousands of backpackers and climbers every summer. Originally called both Dad's Toothpicks and Washakie Needles, it has been known as "The Cirque" since 1941, when climber Orrin Bonney applied that name in an article for *Appalachia* magazine. Bonney and brothers Frank and Notsie Garnick from Rock Springs made numerous first ascents in the area in the 40s. The attendant publicity fueled exploration of the surrounding peaks. Mountaineering clubs from across the country flocked to the basin in the 1950s, when many of the routes were established.

A memorable six or seven day, 35-mile loop hike can be made by following the inlet stream on the northwest corner of Lonesome Lake up to Texas Pass, then descending the steep, rocky trail to Texas, Barren, Billy and Shadow Lakes. Walk west on the Shadow Lake Trail to its intersection with the Highline. Turn south here and walk back to Big Sandy Entrance. Because the route/trail down Texas Pass to the west side of the Cirque is quite precipitous—and can hold snow well into August—this trip is best left for experienced backpackers.

Lonesome Lake

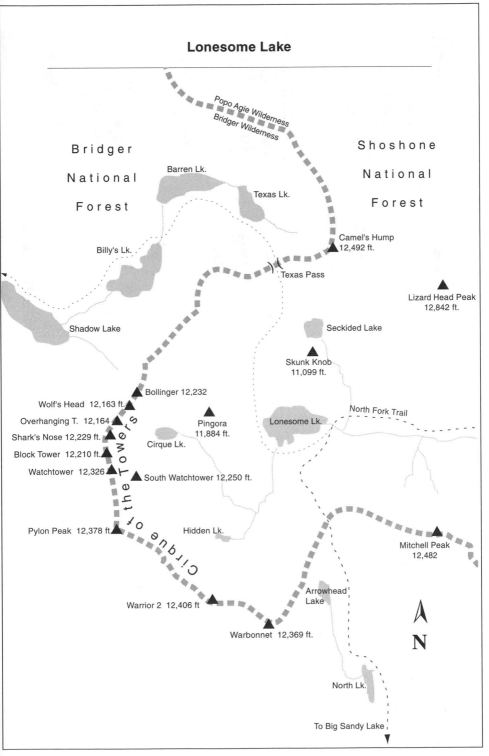

Popo Agie Wilderness
Bridger Wilderness

Bridger

National

Forest

Barren Lk.

Texas Lk.

Billy's Lk.

Camel's Hump
12,492 ft.

Shoshone

National

Forest

Texas Pass

Lizard Head Peak
12,842 ft.

Shadow Lake

Seckided Lake

Skunk Knob
11,099 ft.

Bollinger 12,232

Wolf's Head 12,163 ft.

Overhanging T. 12,164

Shark's Nose 12,229 ft.

Block Tower 12,210 ft.

Watchtower 12,326

Pingora
11,884 ft.

Cirque Lk.

South Watchtower 12,250 ft.

Lonesome Lk.

North Fork Trail

Cirque of the Towers

Pylon Peak 12,378 ft.

Hidden Lk.

Mitchell Peak
12,482

Warrior 2 12,406 ft

Warbonnet 12,369 ft.

Arrowhead
Lake

N

North Lk.

To Big Sandy Lake

Arrowhead Lake, seen above the trail to Cirque of the Towers

The trail to the Cirque and Lonesome Lake via Big Sandy Pass, incorrectly identified as Jackass Pass on the Lizard Head topo map, is an up-and-down slog. It climbs only to drop and climb again on its way to the pass—and even then climbs above its low point before descending. Rough and rocky, it is ill-suited for stock parties.

The first 5.8 miles of trail are described in hike no. 28 to Big Sandy Lake. At the signed junction at the north end of lake, bear left (N) and begin ascending the signed trail to Lonesome Lake. Steep switchbacks cut through rocky terrain shaded by whitebark pine. The gradient eases at .7 miles as it crosses a flowered meadow and skips over North Fork Creek.

The steep climb then resumes, traveling above the creek and Shaft Lake before dropping to skirt its west end.

Beyond the lake it once again bears north and begins climbing through small meadows and rocky terrain. Cairns left of the trail mark a route to Arrowhead Lake. It is possible to walk through a jumble of large boulders that ring its west shore and climb to a pass west of Big Sandy that drops down to Lonesome Lake. While this shorter route eliminates some of the up-and-down quirks of the trail, scrambling through the boulders can be quite arduous with a heavy pack. The route is neither quicker or easier in terms of effort.

Stay on the main trail and continue climbing and seemingly randomly dropping on a winding path that reaches the pass at 2.2 miles. From here it zigzags down 600 feet to the outlet of Lonesome Lake at 2.8 miles.

Sweetwater Gap
Entrance

Trails
Little Sandy Lake
Tayo Park via Sweetwater Gap
Ice and Deep Creek Lakes

Administrative Forest Service Office
Pinedale Ranger District
210 W. Pine Street
Box 220
Pinedale, Wyoming 82941
307-367-4326

Nearest Town
Lander, Boulder or Farson (pop. 300+). Full-services are available at Lander. Boulder has a small store, hotel, bar and gas station. Farson offers gas and great ice-cream cones, but not much else.

Driving Directions
From Lander
From the stoplight near McDonalds, drive south out of Lander on U.S. 287 for 8.5 miles to a signed junction with Wyoming Highway 28. Stay on Hwy. 28 past South Pass to a crossing of the Sweetwater River. Less than a mile beyond that, 43 miles from Lander, you'll see a signed turn-off to Sweetwater Gap Ranch and Big Sandy Opening to your right. Turn north onto this dirt road and set your odometer. Drive 15 miles to an intersection marked by a sign that reads: White Acorn Ranch - 4, Sweetwater Gap Ranch - 7, Sweetwater Camp - 8, Sweetwater Guard Station - 8. Turn right. Continue straight past a junction at 18.3 miles to a junction where a sign reads: Sweetwater Gap Ranch - 2, Sweetwater Guard Station - 3, Sweetwater Camp - 2. Turn left here. In 2.5 miles, the road ends in a T where a sign reads "Sweetwater Wilderness Entrance 6", etc.. Park off-road here or turn right to reach the campground in one mile and park there. If you have a high-clearance vehicle, you can turn left onto a very rough road that passes a jeep trail in one mile and reaches the trailhead in another .8 miles, a total of 68 miles from Lander, 25 miles from the Hwy. 28 turn-off.

From Farson
Turn east on Wyo. Hwy. 28 and drive 33.5 miles to a signed turn-off to Sweetwater Gap Ranch and Big Sandy Opening. From there, follow the directions given above.

From Boulder
Turn east onto Wyo. Highway 353 and drive 19.3 miles on a mostly paved road to Big Sandy Junction. Turn left here and drive nine miles to another junction. Turn left and drive five more miles to a junction with the Muddy Ridge Road. Stay

right here and drive 2.4 miles to the signed Big Sandy turn-off, a total of 16.4 miles from Big Sandy Junction. Stay right at the turn-off and drive 5.6 miles to another junction. Here, the right fork leads to Farson. Stay left. Stay left again at another junction at 10.3 miles. Follow directional signs to Sweetwater Guard Station until you come to the "Sweetwater Wilderness Entrance 6" sign. Park off-road here or turn right to reach the campground in one mile and park there. If you have a high-clearance vehicle, you can turn left onto a very rough road that passes a jeep trail in one mile and reaches the trailhead in another .8 miles.

Area Campgrounds

Most of the camping opportunities are located near Lander. Sinks Canyon State Park above town has two fee campgrounds: Sawmill and Popo Agie. The Forest Service also operates a fee campground with 11 sites in Sinks Canyon. Free camping is available at Lander City Park at 405 Fremont Street; flush toilets and drinking water are available. Area commerical campgrounds include K-Bar Ranch Campground, 10 miles SE of Lander on U.S. 287, and Ox-Yoke Campground in Boulder. There is no water at the Sweetwater Campground near the trailhead.

Showers

Ox-Yoke Campground offers showers to non-campers. K-Bar Ranch Campground 10 miles SE of Lander on U.S. 287 also sells showers to non-campers.

∧

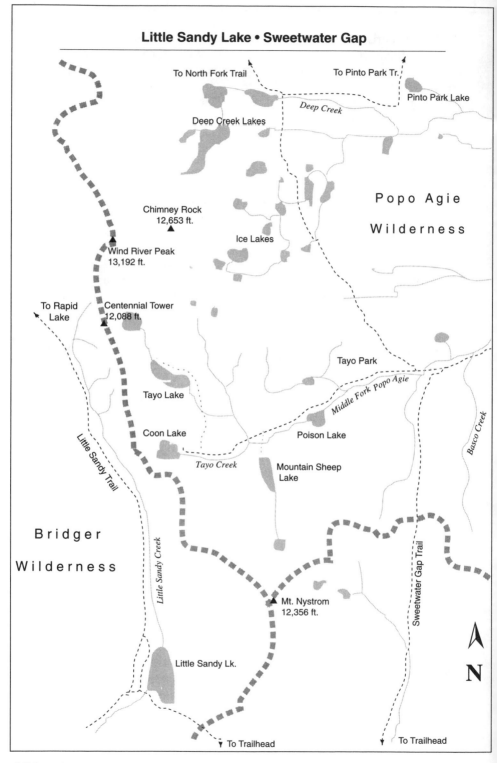

Little Sandy Lake • Sweetwater Gap

To North Fork Trail

To Pinto Park Tr.

Pinto Park Lake

Deep Creek

Deep Creek Lakes

P o p o   A g i e

W i l d e r n e s s

Chimney Rock
12,653 ft.
▲

Ice Lakes

▲ Wind River Peak
13,192 ft.

To Rapid
Lake

Centennial Tower
12,088 ft.
▲

Tayo Park

Middle Fork Popo Agie

Basco Creek

Tayo Lake

Coon Lake

Poison Lake

Little Sandy Trail

Tayo Creek

Mountain Sheep
Lake

B r i d g e r

W i l d e r n e s s

Little Sandy Creek

Sweetwater Gap Trail

▲ Mt. Nystrom
12,356 ft.

Little Sandy Lk.

N

To Trailhead

To Trailhead

31 Little Sandy Lake

Distance: 4.1 miles
Elevation gain: 1,360 feet
Elevation loss: 720 feet
Max. elevation: 10,160 feet
Topo maps:
    Sweetwater Needles, Sweetwater Gap
    Earthwalk: Southern
Fish: Cutthroat, Grayling

^^^

Pretty, rarely-visited Little Sandy Lake lies at the bottom of a scree bowl lined by conifers. Though it gets scant use the trail is generally in good condition; its undulating course provides ample exercise despite its comparatively short distance. Short, that is, if you can drive all the way to the trailhead. Low-clearance vehicles cannot safely negotiate the last half to three-quarter mile of the rough entrance road.

From the trailhead the path climbs through lodgepole pine forest, staying just inside treeline as it skirts marshy Larsen Creek basin to the right. After crossing a tributary at .3 miles the trail becomes indistinct. Head north towards a wooden post. There, it gains firmer ground and becomes clearer as it again ascends through lodgepole forest burned in a 1988 forest fire that consumed over 3,400 acres. Jump a tributary of Larsen Creek at .8 miles, another at 1.2 miles, and climb to the top of a small ridge. Here, the 12,103 foot south summit of Mt. Nystrom rises north

above the trees. The peak was named in 1877 by a member of the Hayden Survey in honor of his fiancee's family. Finis Mitchell scrambled up the slopes facing you in 1922, claiming "first ascent" honors. He climbed the steeper, more challenging 12,356 foot north summit 30 years later.

The trail drops steeply off the ridge, crossing Larsen Creek at 1.6 miles then contouring north above it and jumping an intermittent tributary at two miles. Beyond the tributary the trail climbs steadily up the creek valley, reaching a 10,160 foot saddle at 3.1 miles. This is the high point of the hike. It demarcates the Continental Divide, identified on the Sweetwater Needles topo map.

The trail drops off the saddle in several steep switchbacks, shortly reaching a good vantage point of both Little Sandy Lake to the north and the craggy unnamed peaks west of the lake. After crossing a tributary, it continues its steep descent to the southwest "finger" near the lake's outlet. Here the remnants of a rock dam built by the Civilian Conservation Corps in the 1930s spans the creek. A small log cabin that housed the workers stood several yards north of the creek.

A trail junction is reached by following the outlet .2 miles south. Little Sandy Creek Trail climbs north to Frozen Lakes and Temple Peak saddle before dropping to Temple, Miller and Deep lakes. Those wishing to continue on this trail will need the Temple Peak topo. It is 5.8 miles to North Frozen Lake, 6.2 miles to the saddle. Temple Lake lies 800 feet below the saddle, its south end seven miles from the junction with Little Sandy Creek Trail.

The trail heading south from the junction ends at a 4WD jeep road that leads to the Emigrant Trail or, through a series of complicated turns, the Boulder Entrance. Have good Forest Service travel maps if you plan to exit here or you will get lost.

∧

32 Tayo Park via Sweetwater Gap

Distance: 8.1 miles
Elevation gain: 1,540 feet
Elevation loss: 690 feet
Max. elevation: 10,327 feet
Topo maps:
    Sweetwater Needles, Sweetwater Gap
    Earthwalk: Southern
Fish:
    Rainbow, Brook, Cutthroat

∧∧∧

Located near the confluence of Tayo Creek and the Middle Fork of the Popo Agie River, Tayo Park is a great place to set up base camp and explore neighboring Deep Creek and Ice lakes to the northwest, Poison, Coon, and Tayo lakes to the west. It can be reached by walking 9.3 miles from the Middle Fork trailhead in Sinks Canyon or by ascending the Sweetwater Trail and dropping into the park from Sweetwater Gap, the option described below.

From the signed Sweetwater trailhead walk north several yards to a register and marked trail junction. The left branch leads to Little Sandy Lake, hike no. 31. Go right. The Gap trail drops to Larsen Creek at .1 mile then climbs through lodgepole forest burned in a 1988 fire. Lodgepole seedlings are now sprouting, and lupine thrive on land enriched by nutrients returned to the soil

Mt. Nystrom dominates the western skyline at Sweetwater Gap.

by the blaze. The trail leaves the charred trees at one mile, soon reaching the signed Bridger Wilderness boundary. Open meadows here offer flat, easy walking and nice views of Mt. Nystrom's scree saddle to your left (W).

Pass a small pond at 1.4 miles and continue walking northeast through grassy meadows. Hop a small tributary of Sweetwater Creek at two miles. A half mile further the trail climbs a wooded hill before dropping to a marshy area and crossing another tributary at three miles. The valley begins to narrow beyond this as the trail ascends a series of small drainages. A broad but shallow tributary spills across it at 4.4 miles. Columbine and bluebells thrive at the crossing, making this a beautiful place to rest or eat lunch.

After crossing the Sweetwater yet again at 4.7 miles the trail climbs a draw shaded by limber and whitebark pine then levels out and skirts the right side of a large meadow framed by Nystrom's 12,004 foot summit. At the north end of the meadow it re-enters the spruce and pine forest, crosses the creek, and makes the final, gentle ascent to Sweetwater Gap at 6.1 miles. This broad, north-south saddle is a passageway between Nystrom to the west and Roaring Fork Mountain to the east. It was used as a horse trail extensively in the late 1880s by early settlers wanting to get from Lander to the west side of the range. The trail is one of the oldest in the Winds.

A sign marking the Gap is gone but its post still remains. The trail drops due north off the saddle, descending steeply to a signed crossing of the Middle Fork at 7.1 miles. At 7.5 miles a roaring sound announces the presence of a powerful waterfall on your left, unseen from the trail. Look for a steep spur path off the main thoroughfare: it is worth the short diversion to see the falls. Tayo Park is reached at 8.1 miles. This large, open expanse offers numerous places to camp. Elk are often spotted in the vicinity at dawn and dusk.

∧

33 Poison & Coon Lakes

Distance from Tayo Park (see hike no. 32):
    Poison Lake: 1.7 miles
    Mountain Sheep Lake: 3 miles
    Coon Lake: 3.7 miles
Elevation gain:
    Poison Lake: 367 feet
    Mountain Sheep: 520 feet
    Coon Lake: 854 feet
Elevation loss: Negligible
Max. elevation: 10, 354 feet
Topo map: Sweetwater Gap
    Earthwalk: Southern
Fish:
    Cutthroat, Golden in all.
    Poison also has Rainbow and Brook. Tayo has no fish.

∧ ∧ ∧

Glacier-polished peaks, permanent snowfields and a willow-filled basin studded with lichen-covered rocks surround beautiful Coon Lake, the highest of a trio described in this hike. Good fishing and nice views of 13,192 foot Wind River Peak, the highest summit at the southern end of the range, add to the hike's appeal.

The popular trail is not plotted on the 1953 Sweetwater Gap topo, and is shown incorrectly on the widely-distributed Earthwalk Press' map of the southern Winds. The well-worn path stays on the right (N) side of Tayo Creek, not the south side as drawn on the map. While the walking is not difficult, those who walk up the south side must cross the creek near its outlet to Poison Lake, a dicey proposition when flows are high.

To reach the lakes follow the Middle Fork Trail through Tayo Park until you see a wide, muddy spot on the far side of the Popo Agie River, east of where Tayo Creek flows into it. Cross here and begin climbing steeply up a wooded hillside to Salt Creek Park at .5 miles. A signed junction identifies the turn-off to Ice and Deep Creek lakes to your right. Stay left, hop a tributary, and gently ascend through pleasant limber pine forest right of the creek.

Cross an outlet stream from an unseen lake 250 feet above you at 1.3 miles and continue walking west .4 miles to the east end Poison Lake. The trail follows Poison's north side then swings into the trees beyond the end of the lake to avoid soggy terrain near meandering Tayo Creek.

Half a mile beyond Poison's westernmost finger, Mountain Sheep Lake's outlet stream flows into Tayo. This is easily missed from the trail. When you think you're half mile beyond Poison leave the trail and walk left (S) across a grassy meadow, ford Tayo, and look for the outlet. Ascend its left side to reach the lake, a narrow body of water surrounded by 200 foot rock walls.

If Coon Lake is your destination stay on the main trail beyond Poison Lake. Just before you cross Tayo Creek at 2.7 miles you'll pass an old Forest Service sign that reads "Coon Lake - 1". This is in poor shape and may no longer be in place. Cross the creek and walk left. (A sketchy trail to Tayo Lake turns right after the crossing. Marked by cairns, this steep trail/route climbs approximately 600 feet in its 1.2 miles course to that lake.)

The first .4 mile of trail beyond the crossing switchbacks steeply up a small draw. It then ascends more gradually to the lake, crossing and re-crossing the creek numerous times. Careful rock hopping on the final section will keep your feet dry.

An unnamed peak west of Coon Lake marks the boundary between Shoshone and Bridger Teton National Forests.

34 Ice & Deep Creek Lakes

Distance from Tayo Park (Hike No. 32):
   Boot Lake: 3.5 miles
   Deep Creek Jct.: 5 miles
   Pinto Park Trail: 6.6 miles
Elevation gain:
   Boot Lake: 1,400 feet
   Deep Creek: 1,620 feet
   Pinto Park: 1,740 feet
Elevation loss:
   Boot Lake: 1,100 feet
   Deep Creek: 1,340 feet
   Pinto Park: 1,590 feet
Max. elevation: 10,980 feet
Topo maps:
   Sweetwater Gap, Dickinson Park
   Earthwalk: Southern
Fish:
   None in Chief, Warbonnet, Boulder, Little Walled,
      Walled, Middle and Upper Deep Creek lakes.
   Brook: Boot, Jug, Pinto Park, Heart, Lower and Upper Baer,
      East and West Echo lakes.
   Golden: Lower Deep Creek Lake

ᐱᐱᐱ

Vertical glacier-carved cirques and bowls ring the north and east flanks of majestic Wind River Peak. Their floors are smattered with a collection of sapphire jewels known as Ice and Deep Creek Lakes. Lying between 10,400 - 11,200 feet, the snow-fed gems thaw late and freeze early. They are commonly ice free for only three weeks between late July and mid-August. The harsh but beautiful world of rock, snow and ice is softened by tenacious alpine wildflowers and colorful lichen clinging to granite boulders strewn across the landscape. A fair number of backpackers and fishermen visit the area, but if you walk west of the trail and climb the drainages to Boulder, Walled, Cliff or

The upper reaches of Ice Lake Basin, as seen from the trail to Coon Lake.

other surrounding lakes, you probably won't see anyone else.

The first .5 miles of trail is described in the write-up to Poison and Coon lakes. Turn right at the signed junction and begin ascending a steep, wooded drainage. Pass a swampy pond at 1.1 mile and continue climbing to a small saddle at 10,600 feet, 1.6 miles and 920 feet above Tayo Park. Drop north off the saddle and contour to the left of a small pond before climbing 520 feet up a series of steep switchbacks to a second saddle at 2.2 miles. At 10,980 feet, it is the high point of the hike. Looking south, massive Roaring Fork Mountain rises to the left (SE). The skyline dips at Sweetwater Gap then climbs up the ramparts of rugged Mt. Nystrom to your right (SW).

Dropping .2 miles north off the saddle opens up a panoramic view of Ice Lake basin below. Walled, Boulder,

Warrior and Timberline lakes lie to the west; Boot and Jug are due north.

The trail continues its northerly descent to 10,440 foot Boot Lake, crossing the inlet between it and Chief Lake at 3.5 miles. Here a use trail turns sharply right around the south side of Boot before heading north towards Jug. The main trail continues past Boot Lake's western shore, jumping Cliff Lake's outlet stream at four miles. Deep Creek is crossed at 4.4 miles and again at 4.9.

The trail forks .1 miles further at an unsigned junction. The path to the right heads east along Deep Creek then turns north, intersecting Pinto Park Trail in 2.4 miles. The more interesting option is the trail to your left, which heads west then north past West and East Echo and Upper and Lower Baer lakes before intersecting the Pinto Park Trail at the 6.6 mile mark.

Dickinson Park Entrance

Trail to High Meadow

Trails
Smith, Middle and Cathedral Lake
High Meadow and Cliff Lakes
Lonesome Lake
Bears Ears Trail

Administrative Forest Service District
Lander Ranger District
600 North Highway 287
Lander, Wyoming 82520
307-332-5460

Nearest Town
Fort Washakie. Limited services. Gas, groceries, fishing licenses available. Lodging, backpacking supplies, maps available in Lander, 16 miles SE on U.S. 287. Attractions include a visit to the Shoshone Cultural Center in the Bureau of Indian Affairs compound, the Sacajawea Cemetery and the Shoshone Episcopal Mission.

Driving Instructions
Sixteen miles north of Lander on U.S. 287, or about a mile south of the Texaco Station in Fort Washakie, turn west onto Trout Creek Road near Hines General Store. The pavement ends in five miles. Continue on the narrow dirt and gravel road, soon beginning a long series of switchbacks up Bald Mountain to an intersection with Moccasin Lake Road at 19 miles. Stay left, and enter Shoshone National Forest at 19.4 miles. Cross a cattle guard near Allen's ranch at 20.2 miles. A right turn-off at 20.6 miles leads to public corrals and the trailhead for Bears Ears Trail and the hike to Grave Lake. For other hikes in this section, continue straight and pass Dickinson Creek Campground to your right at 22.0 miles. The parking area is .7 miles further.

Area Campgrounds
Camping at Dickinson Creek is free. There are pit toilets, grills and picnic tables but no water. Make sure you fill up at Fort Washakie or Lander if you plan to camp here. Camping is also available at Ray Lake, half-way between Fort Washakie and Lander on U.S. 287.

Showers:
Ray Lake Campground offers showers.

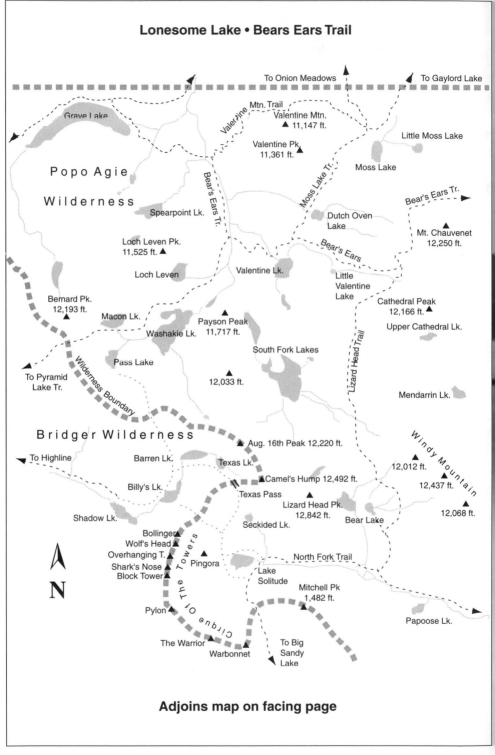

Lonesome Lake • Bears Ears Trail

To Onion Meadows

To Gaylord Lake

Grave Lake

Valentine Mtn. Trail

Valentine Mtn.
▲ 11,147 ft.

Little Moss Lake

Valentine Pk.
11,361 ft.

P o p o A g i e

W i l d e r n e s s

Moss Lake

Bear's Ears Tr.

Bear's Ears Tr.

Moss Lake Tr.

Spearpoint Lk.

Dutch Oven
Lake

Mt. Chauvenet
12,250 ft. ▲

Loch Leven Pk.
11,525 ft. ▲

Bear's Ears

Loch Leven

Valentine Lk.

Little
Valentine
Lake

Cathedral Peak
12,166 ft. ▲

Bernard Pk.
12,193 ft.
▲

Macon Lk.

Payson Peak
11,717 ft.

Upper Cathedral Lk.

Washakie Lk.

South Fork Lakes

Lizard Head Trail

Pass Lake

To Pyramid
Lake Tr.

Wilderness Boundary

▲ 12,033 ft.

Mendarrin Lk.

B r i d g e r W i l d e r n e s s

Windy Mountain

▲ Aug. 16th Peak 12,220 ft.

To Highline

Barren Lk.

Texas Lk.

12,012 ft. ▲

12,437 ft.

Billy's Lk.

▲Camel's Hump 12,492 ft.

Texas Pass

Lizard Head Pk.
12,842 ft.

12,068 ft.

Shadow Lk.

Seckided Lk.

Bear Lake

Bollinger
Wolf's Head
Overhanging T.
Shark's Nose
Block Tower

Of The Towers

North Fork Trail

Pingora

Lake
Solitude

Mitchell Pk
1,482 ft. ▲

Pylon ▲

Cirque Of

Papoose Lk.

N

The Warrior

Warbonnet

To Big
Sandy
Lake

Adjoins map on facing page

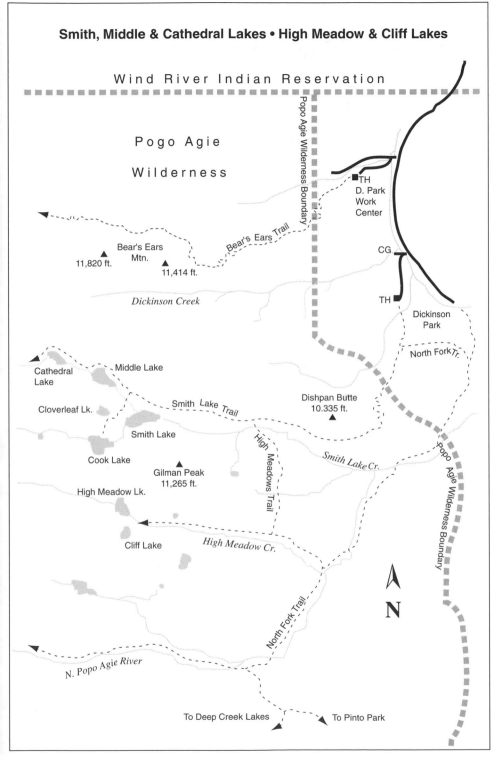

Smith, Middle & Cathedral Lakes • High Meadow & Cliff Lakes

Wind River Indian Reservation

Pogo Agie Wilderness

Popo Agie Wilderness Boundary

TH
D. Park
Work
Center

Bear's Ears Trail

Bear's Ears Mtn.
11,820 ft.
11,414 ft.

CG

Dickinson Creek

TH

Dickinson Park

North Fork Tr.

Cathedral Lake

Middle Lake

Cloverleaf Lk.

Smith Lake Trail

Dishpan Butte
10.335 ft.

Smith Lake

High Meadows Trail

Popo Agie Wilderness Boundary

Cook Lake

Gilman Peak
11,265 ft.

Smith Lake Cr.

High Meadow Lk.

Cliff Lake

High Meadow Cr.

N

North Fork Trail

N. Popo Agie River

To Deep Creek Lakes

To Pinto Park

35 Smith, Middle & Cathedral Lakes

Distance:
   Smith Lake: 5.6 miles
   Middle Lake: 6.2 miles
   Cathedral Lake: 6.8 miles
   Cook Lake: 7 miles
Elevation gain:
   Smith: 880 feet
   Middle: 1,040 feet
   Cathedral: 1,260 feet
   Cook: 1,260 feet
Elevation loss: 560 feet
Max. elevation: 10,120 feet
Topo maps:
   Dickinson Park, Lizard Head
   Earthwalk: Southern
Fish:
   Smith, Middle Cathedral: Brook, Mackinaw
   Cook, Cloverleaf: Brook
   None in Upper Cathedral

∧∧∧

Like High Meadow and Cliff lakes, Middle and Cathedral lakes lie at the foot of sheer rock walls carved thousands of years ago by receding glaciers. Distinctive 12,326 foot Cathedral Peak provides a stunning backdrop to the upper lakes. With over a half dozen lakes dotting this beautiful basin, wonderful camping spots and good fishing, those with time will not regret extending their stay in this corner of the Winds.

Park at the Dickinson trailhead and head for the wood information sign and trail register. The trail begins by immediately crossing the long, plank bridge that spans marshy Twin Park. Turn right off the bridge and climb a rutted hillside to the signed junction at .3 miles.

Bear right onto the Smith Lake Trail and walk gradually uphill through lodgepole forest to a small knoll. The trail then drops to an overlook that provides splendid views of snow-covered Mount Chevro and the North Fork Popo Agie River Canyon.

Continuing its moderately steep descent, the trail jogs west and crosses a small tributary at 2.8 miles before rounding rocky Dishpan Butte, denuded in a 1952 forest fire. It stays to the right of marshy terrain created by Smith Lake Creek, crossing another tributary just before reaching the signed cut-off trail to High Meadows and Sanford Park at 4.4 miles. Stay right here. The almost level trail gently ascends through coni-

Cathedral Peak reflected in the still waters of Middle Lake.

fer, lodgepole and spruce forest. Smith Lake is glimpsed through the trees shortly before reaching it at 5.6 miles. Many fine campsites can be found in the forest away from that lake's shore.

One hundred and sixty feet higher and .4 miles further is the signed junction to Cook Lake. Those with time will enjoy the rewarding walk beyond Cook to 10,383 foot Mendarrin Lake at the base of a rugged, craggy bowl hung with permanent snowfields and laced with alpine flowers.

To continue to Middle Lake stay on the main trail; the lake's eastern end is reached at 6.2 miles. The trail wraps around Middle's north shore on its westward course to Cathedral Lake at 6.8 miles. Cairns mark a route up the right side of Cathedral's inlet to Upper Cathedral Lake, 8.1 miles from the trailhead.

In recent years, black bears have haunted the basin, becoming quite skillful in obtaining food not properly hung. Backpackers should make an extra effort to follow all bear guidelines to avoid a confrontation.

36 High Meadow & Cliff Lakes

Distance: 8.4 miles
Elevation gain: 1,110 feet
Elevation loss: 520 feet
Max. elevation: 9,950 feet
Topo Maps:
    Dickinson Park, Lizard Head
    Earthwalk: Southern
Fish: Cutthroat

∧∧∧

High Meadow and Cliff lakes rest below a glacial outcropping of Windy Mountain. The massif's long eastern flank is a series of deeply cut glacial cirques and bowls that harbor dozens of lakes and tarns on their floor. The beautiful landscape attracts day hikers, fishermen and backpackers. By backtracking .8 miles from High Meadow Lake to Lake 9,845, it is possible to follow that lake's inlet to a high saddle and drop northwest to Cook, Middle and Cathedral lakes, a nice loop option for an extended trip.

High Meadow and Cliff can be reached via the North Fork Trail. The option described below follows the Smith Lake Trail to the High Meadows cutoff, chosen for its slightly shorter distance, moderate grade, and easier stream crossings.

The first half of this hike is described in the write-up for Smith, Middle and Cathedral Lakes, hike no. 35. At the signed cut-off trail to High Meadows at 4.4 miles, turn left, cross a stream, and head southeast through mixed forest of spruce, conifer and lodgepole pine. The trail follows an undulating course to an unsigned junction at 6.4 miles. The left fork eventually intersects the North Fork Trail. Turn right and skirt the north side of a large meadow. The trail disappears in grass but is obvious once you re-enter the woods; continue on the course you think it should take and you'll find it.

Hop a small tributary at 6.8 miles and slog through several mucky stretches before entering an area littered with downed trees. Pay close attention here or you will lose the trail. Ascend slightly to another tributary at 7.8 miles. Gradually drop to a small unnamed lake to your left and a split in the trail at 8.4 miles. Cliff Lake lies directly west .1 mile further. High Meadows, the more scenic of the two, is reached by walking right (NW) a quarter-mile further.

37 Lonesome Lake

Distance: 13.2 miles
Elevation gain: 2,000 feet
Elevation loss: 1,220 feet
Max. elevation: 10,190 feet
Topo Maps:
Dickinson Park, Lizard Head
Earthwalk: Southern
Fish: Cutthroat

∧ ∧ ∧

Hikers and climbers alike flock to renowned Cirque of the Towers, a spectacular semicircle of sheer pinnacles and peaks that is one of the most visited places in the range. Beautiful Lonesome Lake lies at the entrance of this enchanting place. Camping is prohibited in the immediate vicinity, but you should have no trouble finding a nice spot in the surrounding meadows. Expect lots of company: Lonesome Lake is no longer true to its name.

There are two main trails to the lake. The shorter, more heavily traveled route is described in the write-up to Cirque of the Towers, Hike no. 30. The long trail detailed below gets comparatively little use. Four crossings of the North Fork Popo Agie River—two potentially dangerous—deter many hikers until late season when flows have subsided. Even then, many North Fork hikers take Smith Lake Trail to Sanford Park to avoid the first two fords. Check on current river conditions at the Lander Ranger District before attempting this trip.

To access the North Fork Trail, from the Dickinson parking area walk across the plank bridge spanning marshy Twin Park. Turn right off the bridge and hike to a signed trail junction at .3 miles. Turn left here onto the North Fork Trail. The good trail traverses lodgepole forest to an unsigned junction at 1.4 miles. Head right and begin a gradual then steep drop down a series of switchbacks that occasionally provide views of an unnamed, glaciated peak to the southwest. Cross and re-cross two tributaries before reaching a sage-covered bench and the signed cutoff to Shoshone Lake at three miles. Continue straight at this junction, gradually climbing through magnificent stands of red-barked pine to the first river crossing at four miles. Climb up the southeast side of the valley then contour down to a second crossing at 4.9 miles. Be careful; in

Spectacular Cirque of the Towers frames the skyline above Lonesome Lake.

high water, this crossing can be tricky.

Beyond the crossing the trail stays right of grassy Sanford Park, passes a signed junction to High Meadows at 5.6 miles, and jumps two tributaries in quick succession on its way to a third crossing of the North Fork Popo Agie River at seven miles. This is a dangerous ford at high water; it may not be safe to attempt without ropes through July. If you don't feel comfortable, do not cross. Look for a rocky use trail on the same side of the river and follow it for 1.4 miles, at which point the trail recrosses the river. (If you cannot cross, you will miss the signed junction on the south side of the river to the Pinto Park Trail at 7.2 miles, a trip planning consideration).

Beyond the fourth crossing the trail hops a tributary and continues its gradual climb west. Vertical mountain walls and interesting pinnacles come into view as the valley narrows. Cross a tributary at 10 miles, a second at 10.2, and yet another at 11 miles. Shortly pass a shallow pond at the foot of spectacular 12,488 foot Dog Tooth Peak to your left (SW). Here the trail veers right towards prominent Lizard Head Peak. Pass the signed junction to Lizard Head Trail on your right at 11.8 miles.

The trail skirts the right side of the meadows, crosses two tributaries and gently climbs then drops to the eastern end of Lonesome Lake, 13.2 miles from the trailhead.

To protect the resource, camping and fires are prohibited within a half-miles of Lonesome Lake's shores. With numerous streams and marshy areas in the vicinity, mosquitos are almost as legendary as the stunning rock blocks and spires before you. Come prepared.

38 Bears Ears Trail to Valentine and Washakie Lakes

Distance:
> Valentine Lake: 10.5 miles
> Washakie Lake: 13.2 miles

Elevation gain:
> Valentine Lake: 2,680 feet
> Washakie Lake: 3,080 feet

Elevation loss:
> Valentine Lake: 1,600 feet
> Washakie Lake: 2,020 feet

Max. elevation: 11,920 feet

Topo maps:
> Dickinson Park, Lizard Head
> Earthwalk: Southern

Fish:
> Valentine Lake: Cutthroat, Golden
> Washakie: Cutthroat, Golden
> Loch Leven: Rainbow, Brown
> Macon: Brook
> Pass Lake: None

∧∧∧

The Bears Ears Trail is long and unforgiving, climbing up only to drop back down. Sheltered campsites with water are not available before reaching Valentine Lake, over 10 miles in. Those challenges aside, it is one of the more rewarding trips in the range. Horse packers and hardy backpackers savor superb views of the southern Winds, great fishing and increasingly rare solitude, plus excellent opportunities for cross-country rambling. Above treeline for most of its course, continuous sweeping views of the range are enjoyed almost from the onset. A week or more in this beautiful section of the range is highly recommended.

From the trailhead the signed trail heads west past Ranger Creek and soon begins gradually climbing the first of many switchbacks through lodgepole, then fir and pine forest, on its way to 11,000 foot Adams Pass at 3.8 miles. Enroute the trail hops a tributary at 1.8

miles; nice views of Funnel Lake below you to the right (N) are enjoyed a half-mile further.

The trail drops west off the pass and crosses a tributary of Sand Creek at 4.8 miles. This is the best place to view the distinctive rock "ears" that give the trail its name. The twin pinnacles of 11,820 foot Bears Ears Mountain can be reached by ascending the left side of the tributary to a small saddle to the southeast. From here, it is a scramble to the top of either "ear."

Shortly after crossing the tributary the trail fords the main branch of icy Sand Creek—sandwiched between two permanent snowfields—and resumes climbing. At 6.8 miles it bears south around Mt. Chauvenet's western flank and climbs 200 feet to the high point of the hike. The sweeping display of peaks from this hike's zenith is dominated on the northern horizon by 12,767 foot Roberts Mountain. West to east are Mt. Hooker, Tower Peak, Mt. Lander and Musembeah, while Cathedral Peak holds prominent court to the south. For perhaps the most striking 360 degree panorama in the Winds, hike up the open slopes of 12,250 foot Mt. Chauvenet to your left (W). The peak was named by members of the Hayden Survey in 1877 in honor of topographer Louis Chauvenet. It was first climbed 13 years later by William "Billy" Owen of Grand Teton fame.

From its high point the trail begins a gradual then steeper descent via switchbacks to a wide saddle and the signed junction with Lizard Head Trail at 7.9 miles. Turn right (W) here and walk down the narrow alpine valley cut by Valentine Creek. Pass a use trail to Little Valentine Lake at nine miles. Continue descending to a signed junction with Moss Lake Trail at 10.3 miles. Dutch Oven Lake and Moss Lake can be reached by turning right here. To reach Valentine stay left; its northwestern outlet is gained at 10.5 miles. A use trail around that lake's west shore leads to Upper Valentine Lake, .6 miles further and 145 feet above Valentine.

To continue to Washakie, descend long switchbacks beyond Valentine Lake through flowered Valentine Meadows and Ranger Park to a crossing of South Fork Little Wind River at 11.6 miles. Be careful here: the current can be quite strong, and the river knee-deep in high water.

Several hundred yards past the crossing the trail splits. The right branch leads to Grave Lake (see hike no. 39). Bear left and shortly cross a tributary as you head south past the steep walls of Big Chief Mountain on the right. Cross Loch Leven Creek at 12.2 miles and walk southwest through scattered pine and scrub willow to the north shore of Washakie Lake, 13.2 miles from the trailhead. The trail follows the west side of Washakie then climbs northwest to Macon Lake at 14.1 miles. Washakie Pass lies another .6 miles further. That 11,611 foot divide is part of an Indian trail discovered by members of the Hayden Survey in 1878.

It is possible to descend the west side of Washakie Pass to a junction with the Pyramid Lake Trail. By turning right here and heading north over Hailey Pass one can loop back to the Bears Ears Trail, an ambitious but superb five or six day backpacking trip. Consult the Mount Bonneville topo.

39 Grave Lake

Distance: 14.2 miles via the
    Bears Ears Trail
Elevation gain: 3,120 feet
Elevation loss: 2,220 feet
Max. elevation: 11,920 feet
Topo maps:
    Dickinson Park, Lizard Head
    Earthwalk: Southern
Fish: Cutthroat, Mackinaw

∧∧∧

An Indian grave near its north shore gives this beautiful lake its name. The long, boomerang shaped body of water lies serenely at the base of vertical-walled Grave Dome (identified as Pilot's Knob on the topo), Musembeah

Mt. Hooker and Grave Dome frame the shores of Grave Lake.

Peak (incorrectly labeled Petroleum Peak) and an unnamed 11,249 foot summit to the north. The massive, sheer walls of 12,504 Mt. Hooker and pointed 12,330 Tower Peak rise to the west, while to the south massive 12,468 foot Dike Mountain and an unnamed massif completes the horseshoe of rock blocks, peaks and spires that surround the lake.

A visit to this exquisite place and exploration of the surrounding area is worth the long hike in. Grave Lake can be reached from Big Sandy Entrance via Hailey Pass or from Bears Ears, the option described below.

The first 11.6 miles of trail is detailed in the write-up to Valentine Lake, hike no. 38. After crossing South Fork Little Wind River—which may be too hazardous to attempt until late July— bear right and head downstream on level trail that winds through scrub willow and scattered conifers, reaching a signed junction with Moss Lake Trail in one mile. Stay left here and soon cross a tributary. The trail follows it a short distance upstream, passing a pretty cascade as it begins its steady climb through limber pine.

Skirt a small pond at 13.2 miles and drop via switchbacks to a another tributary crossing at 13.4 miles. The path travels northwest across a grassy basin to a footbridge near the eastern end of the lake, 14.2 miles from the trailhead. It continues around Grave's north shore to a signed junction. The right branch leads to pretty Baptiste Lake on the border of the Wind River Indian Reservation. You need a permit to walk beyond its outlet.

The left fork climbs to Hailey Pass. By descending first the Hailey Pass Trail then the Pyramid Lake Trail to its intersection with the Washakie Trail, ambitious, fit hikers can complete a lengthy but rewarding loop.

Alternately, shuttling a car in advance allows backpackers to exit at Big Sandy via the Pyramid Lake then Highline trails.

∧

Sinks Canyon
Loop Road
Entrance

A glacial erratic on the way to Popo Agie Falls

Trails
Popo Agie Falls
Christina Lake
Silas Canyon
Twin Lakes
Stough Creek Basin

Administrative Forest Service District Office
Lander Ranger District
600 North Highway 287
Lander, Wyoming 82520
307-332-5460

Nearest Town
Lander (pop. 7,000+). Full range of services available, including lodging, gas, groceries, backpacking supplies, fishing licenses and maps. The Chamber of Commerce is in an old train station at 160 N. First St. (332-3892). Attractions include the Pioneer Museum and Sinks Canyon State Park, where the Middle Fork of the Popo Agie (pronounced PO-PO-shuh) nose-dives into a cave and re-emerges a half-mile downstream as a large spring.

Driving Directions
 Follow signs in downtown Lander to Sinks Canyon and Wyoming Highway 131. From this intersection, it is 5.8 miles to the entrance of Sinks Canyon State Park. Pass the signed "Rise" (where the Middle Fork re-appears), a visitor's center, and state-run Sawmill and Popo Agie campgrounds before entering Shoshone National Forest at 8.1 miles. Sinks Canyon Campground is reached .3 miles further. Cross a one-lane bridge and park near Bruce picnic area to access the signed Middle Fork Trailhead, 9.7 miles from Sinks Canyon Road. This is the starting point for the hike to Pogo Agie Falls. For other hikes in this section, drive past the parking lot and begin climbing a long, steep, dirt road up Fossil Hill. Pass Forest Service Road 352 at 14.7 miles and climb to Frye Lake Reservoir at 15.9 miles. The road forks at 17.3 miles.

To reach Christina Lake and Silas Lakes
Stay left at the fork. Drive straight pass an unmarked fork to the right at 18.1 miles, another to the left at 19 miles. Pass a signed intersection with Forest Service Road 370 at 21.9 miles to reach Fiddlers Lake Campground at 23 miles. Drive past the campground to Christina Lake Trailhead at 23.4 miles. This is not well-signed. The small trailhead parking area is on the right. The turn-off sign is nailed to a tree on the left side of the road. Watch for it.

To reach Stough Creek Basin and Twin Lakes

Turn right at the fork towards Worthen Meadows Reservoir. Pass Worthen Meadows Campground on your right at 19.6 miles and the signed trailhead to Stough Creek on your left at 19.8 miles. The parking lot is reached .2 miles further. Pit toilets and water are available. The trail to Twin Lakes begins off the parking lot at the Sheep Bridge Trailhead. Walk back up the road to the Stough Creek Trailhead to begin that hike.

Area Campgrounds

There are five Forest Service fee campgrounds in the vicinity. Sinks Canyon Campground, Fiddler Lake Campground, and Worthen Meadows Campground are passed at various points on the access to hikes in this section (see above). The Forest Service also maintains campgrounds at Little Popo Agie Creek and Louis Lake, located off the loop road beyond the Christina Lake Trailhead. Sawmill and Popo Agie campgrounds are fee areas in Sinks Canyon State Park. You may camp for free at Lander City Park at 405 Fremont Street. Flush toilets and drinking water are available. Commercial campgrounds in the area include Ray Lake Campground, eight miles NW of Lander on U.S. 287; Rocky Acres Campground, 4.5 miles NW of Lander, also on U.S. 287; and K-Bar Ranch Campground, 10 miles SE of town on U.S. 287.

Showers

Ray Lake and K-Bar Ranch campgrounds both sell showers to non-campers.

40 Popo Agie Falls

Distance: 1.5 miles
Elevation gain: 600 feet
Elevation loss: Negligible
Max. elevation: 7,720 feet
Topo maps:
    Fossil Hill, Cony Mountain
Fish:
    Rainbow, Brook, Cutthroat

∧∧∧

Popo Agie Falls (pronounced PO-PO-shuh) is actually a succession of falls tumbling a total of 200 vertical feet; the largest drop is 60 feet. The popular feature marks the head of Sinks Canyon. Its gentle ascent, scenic canyon, and interesting glacial erratics—combined with easy access and short walking distance —make this the most heavily used trail in the area. An early or late start will reduce the number of people you encounter on the trail.

Beyond the falls the Middle Fork Trail leads into the heart of the range and offers several options for extended trips. One tantalizing possibility is completing a loop hike by leaving the Middle Fork Trail at Three Forks Park, hiking north on the Pinto Park Trail to its intersection with the Deep Creek Cut-off. The cut-off leads to the heart of the beautiful, high alpine basin cradling Deep Creek Lakes before intersecting Ice Lakes trail. By traveling south on Ice Lakes to the Middle Fork trail, east on Stough Creek Basin Trail,

then north to Sheep Bridge Trail, you eventually intersect the Middle Fork Trail to return to your vehicle.

To hike to the falls, park in the large lot just beyond the Bruce Picnic Area. Walk across the bridge to the signed Middle Fork Trailhead on your left. The trail stays right of the Middle Fork of the Popo Agie River as it begins gradually climbing through aspen and forested hillsides sprinkled with wildflowers. As it gains elevation it cuts across open, sage-covered terrain that can be quite hot in mid-summer.

Numerous overlooks provide good places to rest and view the river as you ascend. A large rock outcropping directly in front of you at 1.2 miles heralds the steepest portion of the trail. As you approach the boulders it swings sharply right and climbs three switchbacks to a marked intersection. The Middle Fork Trail to your right continues into the range. The trail to the falls goes left and crosses a wooden bridge over a small stream, reaching the

Popo Agie Falls drops a total of 200 feet over a series of plunges.

broad head of the canyon in a matter of minutes. This is interesting terrain studded with large glacial erratics and broken rock formations. From here you can see the upper section of Popo Agie Falls to your left (W). Continue on the trail to the first set of wooden benches at 1.4 miles. A prettier view of the falls can be reached by crossing two more bridges to a second set of wooden benches at trail's end.

41 Christina Lake

Distance: 4.3 miles
Elevation gain: 531 feet
Elevation loss: 90 feet
Max. elevation: 9,942 feet
Topo maps:
    Cony Mountain, Christina Lake
Fish:
    Gustave Lake: Mackinaw, Brook
    Christina Lake: Mackinaw, Brook
    Atlantic Lake:Brook

∧∧∧

Like Twin Lakes, the main attraction of the hike to Christina Lake is easy access to good fishing rather than striking mountain scenery. There are, however, nice views of a wall of unnamed 11,500 foot peaks and an interesting earthen dam at the east end of the lake that is fun to explore. From Christina

Christina Lake can be reached by trail or by a jeep road.

Lake it is possible to hike northwest to Atlantic Lake and the head of rugged, rarely visited Atlantic Canyon beyond.

If you aren't on horseback be prepared to get muddy feet . Fiddler, Silas and Atlantic creeks saturate the floor of Little Popo Agie Basin. Horse hooves turn the moist ground into fairly spectacular bogs on sections of trail.

The trailhead has been moved since the 1953 Cony and Christina Lake topos were plotted. Instead of beginning at Fiddler Lake Campground, the trail heads due west from the parking area south of the lake, passes a pair of stagnant pools, then crosses Fiddler Creek at .3 miles. From here it follows the course plotted on the topo.

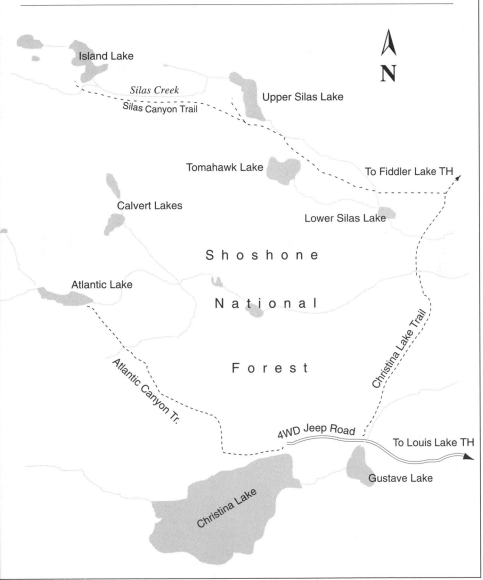

After crossing the creek the trail bears southwest and gains 200 feet before gradually dropping and crossing three tributaries of Silas Creek between one and 1.2 miles. It climbs again to a signed junction with the trail to Lower Silas, Tomahawk and Upper Silas Lakes (see hike no. 42) at 1.6 miles. Stay left here and gradually ascend through forest carpeted with whortleberry and lupine.

Young willows and boggy ground mark the approach of the outflow from Lower Silas Lake at two miles. Cross a log over the creek and walk through open meadows bound on the west by a wall of unnamed 11,500 - 11,800 foot peaks, often snow-capped through July. At 2.3 miles you cross Atlantic Creek. Walk through a short stretch of lodge-pole pine before entering a large park. At its end a wooden post marks an unsigned trail junction. The path to your left becomes indistinct in about half a mile: it is the old southern trail from Fiddler Lake to Christina Lake shown on the 1953 topo.

Go right at the junction. After skirting the park the trail enters the forest. From here to Gustave Lake at 3.8 miles it is often quite boggy. The eastern end of Christina Lake lies .5 miles beyond Gustave. The "trail" between the lakes is a wide, rocky 4WD swath, the end of a jeep trail that starts at Louis Lake.

The earth and rock dam at the eastern end of Christina was built to help supply water for gold mining operations near South Pass at the turn of the century.

∧

42 Silas Canyon

Distance:
   Lower Silas: 2.4 miles
   Tomahawk Lake: 3.0 miles
   Upper Silas Lake: 3.4 miles
   Head of Silas Canyon: 5.6
Elevation gain:
   Lower Silas: 310 feet
   Tomahawk Lake: 670 feet
   Upper Silas Lake: 710 feet
Elevation loss: Approx. 90 feet
Max. elevation: 11,280 feet
Topo Maps:
   Cony Mountain,
   Christina Lake
   (Trail not plotted)

Fish:
   Lower Silas: Brook
   Tomahawk: Cutthroat
   Upper Silas: Brook

∧∧∧

Relatively short distances and easy walking to Lower Silas, Tomahawk and Upper Silas lakes make this hike a popular one for families, fishermen and community groups. Less visited but far more spectacular is Silas Canyon, west of Upper Silas. The striking glacier-carved canyon holds half a dozen crystalline lakes and is worth exploring.

Mishapen lodgepole cover sections of forest floor along Silas Canyon Trail.

The first 1.6 miles of trail is described in the Christina Lake hike, no. 41. At the signed junction turn right and climb through a section of dead timber before contouring along a small ridge to Silas Creek at 2.2 miles. Deformed lodgepole pine is common along this section of the trail. When lodgepole are infested by bacteria, viruses, insects or disease, they form protective layers around the injured area and twist out of their normal ramrod-straight form. At different times the grotesquely shaped wood has been highly prized for its decorative value. Prime examples of its use can be seen in the atrium lobby at Old Faithful Inn in Yellowstone National Park, and at the Cowboy Bar in Jackson Hole.

To reach Lower Silas do not cross the creek. Turn left (S) off the main trail onto a spur path to the lake, which lies .2 miles further. Tomahawk Lake is gained by crossing the creek and continuing northwest on the main trail to the signed turn-off at 2.8 miles, a nice walk through open parks and pine forest. Like Lower Silas, it is .2 from the main trail to the lake. Upper Silas Lake is another .6 miles beyond the turn-off to Tomahawk.

To enter the canyon, walk to Upper Silas' northwest corner and pick up a use trail heading west. The trail parallels then crosses Silas creek and ascends a series of plateaus on the south side of the canyon. It is 2.2 miles and 1,170 feet higher from Upper Silas' inlet to Island lake at the head of the canyon. Those with solid climbing ability and equipment can scale the sheer 600 foot walls surrounding that lake, drop northeast into Stough Creek Basin, and walk out to Worthen Meadows on the Stough Creek Trail (hike no. 43).

43 Twin Lakes

Distance:
   Sheep Bridge: 2.1 miles
   East Twin: 3.7 miles
   West Twin: 4.1 miles
Elevation gain: Approx. 725 feet
Elevation loss: Approx. 585 feet
Max. elevation: 9,080 feet
Topo map: Cony Mountain
Fish: Brook (both lakes)

∧∧∧

The hike to Twin Lakes isn't particularly scenic. Surrounding terrain lacks the sweeping vistas and rugged alpine beauty of higher ground, and the shallow lakes' marshy shorelines are better suited for hatching mosquitoes than camping. The lure of this trail—which is neither signed nor plotted on the 1953 topo map—is three-fold: it's snow-free relatively early in the season, the lakes have good fishing, and there is just enough up-and-down to justify eating the candy bar in your pack.

The hike begins at the Sheep Bridge trailhead on the north side of the parking lot. Cross a bridge over the Roaring Fork a short distance past the trail sign and begin a moderate climb through Aspen groves, gaining enough elevation to get good views of Worthen Reservoir below you to your right.

After 15 minutes of climbing the trail levels then drops almost 600 feet through lodgepole pine forest to Middle Fork Popo Agie River at 2.1 miles, identified by a wood sign. Here the trail swings right and reaches the Sheep Bridge in a few minutes, an interesting

short diversion. The bridge was constructed by the Forest Service in 1926 as part of a "stock highway" that linked grazing land near Shoshone Lake and Dickinson Park with Beaver Creek. For those with the time and inclination, turning left after crossing the bridge and walking about 15 minutes will bring you to an impressive series of beaver dams right of the trail.

To continue to Twin Lakes do not cross the bridge. Backtrack to the river sign and head left (w) on a use trail that parallels the south side of the Middle Fork. The distinct path turns south in roughly half a mile and begins following the lakes' outflow up a steep, rocky drainage, gaining almost 600 feet in under a mile.

Pass a small pond at 3.4 miles and climb more gradually to East Twin Lake at 3.7 miles. West Twin Lake is another .4 miles further west.

The lakes are not named on the old topo map. Do not confuse them with named "Twin Lakes" due north, accessed by Pete's Lake Trail. East and West Twin Lakes are known locally as

The hike to placid Twin Lakes is a good early season choice.

"Buzz" lakes. In July it is tempting to think this is for the distinctive whine of blood-sucking mosquitoes, but the nickname is for an early Lander resident, "Buzz" Darlington, who stocked the lakes years ago.

It is possible to follow the inlet stream from West Twin to the point where it is crossed by the Stough Creek Basin Trail. Turn left (S) here to reach that ruggedly beautiful alpine basin, described below.

∧

44 Stough Creek Basin

Distance: 6.4 miles
Elevation gain: 1,900 feet
Elevation loss: 440 feet
Max. elevation: 10,560 feet
Topo maps:
    Cony Mountain
    Sweetwater Gap
Fish:
    Cutthroat, Brook

Stough Creek Basin is the epitome of beautiful alpine landscape. Over a dozen clear lakes dot the floor of a rugged amphitheater carved by receding glaciers. In its six-plus mile course the trail climbs from lush meadows to the rocky landscape near treeline. It is just long enough to discourage casual day hikers; the basin is primarily visited by backpackers and fishermen.

Stough Creek Trail is not plotted on the 1953 Cony Mountain topo but clearly exists on the ground. Park at Worthen Meadows and walk .3 miles back up the entrance road to the signed trailhead (mileage for the hike begins at this point). The first half-mile of the hike is on a wide, double-track path, remnants of an old jeep road that ran from Frye Lake to Roaring Fork Lake before Worthen Meadows Reservoir was created.

Roaring Fork Lake is reached at .6 miles. A use trail created by fishermen heads right (S) around the east side of the lake. Follow this for about 20 yards, looking through the trees to your left for an obvious stock crossing of the lake's wide, shallow outlet.

Leave the use trail here and ford the outlet. The trail to the basin continues on the other side, marked by a wood Forest Service sign that reads "Stough Creek Lakes - 5."

Climb gradually but steadily through trees, gaining roughly 380 feet before crossing a creek at 1.2 miles and heading west through wet meadow spanned by long plank bridges. It is common to see cattle grazing in this vicinity, a vsiaul reminder to treat your water.

At 1.8 miles, the trail leaves the marshy terrain and begins a 1,120 feet climb to a open saddle at 3.2 miles, following a small stream that peters out 300 feet below the high point. The 10,560 foot saddle is a good place to rest and enjoy the view. Snowy 13,400 foot Wind River Peak to the southwest stands out on the peak-filled horizon.

Descending the left side of the saddle, the trail contours around a hillside then drops through a conifer forest and crosses a branch of Stough Creek at 4.3 miles. After a short climb and drop it levels out and skirts three small ponds to your left. Just beyond the last pond you come to a signed junction at 5.2 miles. Although the sign says it is two miles to Stough Creek Lakes, the shore of Big Stough is only 1.2 miles further. Turn left and cross the bridge—where there is a great view of the 11,546 foot scree sub-summit of Roaring Fork Mountain—and steadily climb through limber pine. The grade lessens shortly before reaching Big Stough at 6.4 miles. To continue into the basin turn right (S) at the lake shore. It is over two miles from Big Stough Lake to the uppermost lake, 550 feet higher.

The basin is named after Charlie Stough, a Lander cattleman who served in the state legislature from 1896-1900. He was Fremont County Sheriff both before and after his political term. In 1894 he transported Butch Cassidy to Laramie by buckboard to serve time in the state pen for stealing horses. Stough is best known, however, for capturing a man named Keefer who had murdered a sheepherder east of town. Keefer was apprehended in 1903 near the Montana border and brought back to Lander. A jury found him guilty and he was subsequently hanged. It was the first legal hanging in Fremont County.

Twin Lakes • Stough Creek Basin

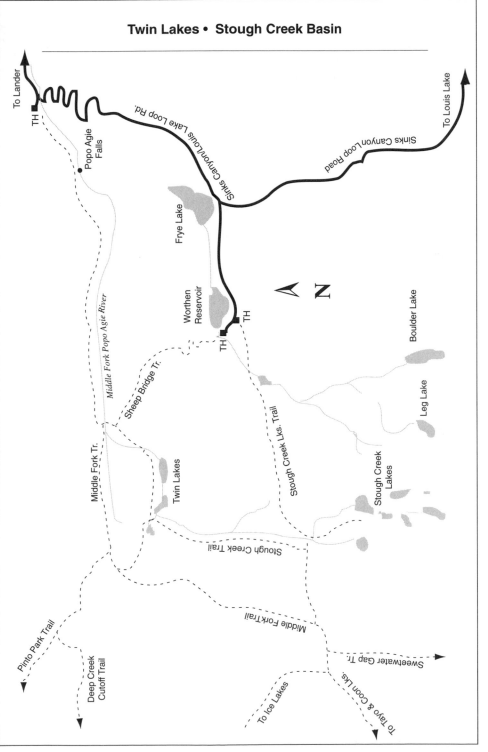

Notes

The Highline Trail

Wells Creek flowing into the Green

The Highline Trail

The Highline Trail traverses the length of the Wind River Range. It begins near South Pass City and travels northwest for over 80 miles to Union Pass near Dubois. The spectacular high country trail stays near or above timberline on the western side of the Continental Divide, passing beautiful alpine lakes, glaciers, and jagged peaks. Because jeep and other access roads cross both ends of the Highline, most backpackers opt to hike the portion between Green River Lakes and Big Sandy Opening—the section outlined in the following pages.

For ease of description the trail has been broken into segments that correspond with major trail junctions with the Highline. This should help backcountry users plan trips that cover only segments of the lengthy route.

∧

Squaretop Mountain reflected in Lower Green River Lake.

45 Green River Lakes to Summit Lake

Distance: 15.8 miles
Elevation gain: 2,790 feet
Elevation loss: 460 feet
Max. elevation: 10,362 feet
Topo maps:
    Green River Lakes, Squaretop Mtn., Gannett Peak
    Earthwalk: Northern
Fish:
    Lower Green: Mackinaw, Grayling, Whitefish
    Upper Green: Mackinaw
    Summit: Cutthroat

∧∧∧

Over half of the long hike to Summit Lake is easy walking through level lodgepole, fir and spruce forest bordering Lower and Upper Green River Lakes. Superb views of Squaretop Mountain, tumbling streams and open parks characterize the first eight miles. Significant climbing begins near the south end of Three Forks Park. Here the trail switchbacks up almost 1,000 feet to Trail Creek Park before continuing to climb at a more moderate grade to the lake, reached 15.8 miles from the start. Above treeline and often windy, Summit is not an ideal place to camp. Trail Creek Park—with plentiful water and nice views of the east side of Green River Canyon—is a better choice.

The trail begins at Green River Lakes parking area. Walk to the obvious trailhead sign and turn left. Follow the well-worn path around the northern end of Lower Green River Lake and cross a bridge over the outlet at .4 miles.

On the other side of the bridge turn right at the signed junction and begin a pleasant, rolling walk along the lake's eastern shore. The trail cuts through open grasslands and sage hillsides that can be quite hot in July and August. Small, scattered aspen groves and sparse cottonwoods add to the scenery but provide little shade. An early morning start is rewarded not only with cooler temperatures, but often mirror reflections of Squaretop Mountain in the still waters of Lower Green River Lake. This granite monolith—one of the most photographed landmarks in Wyoming—dominates the skyline as you bear southeast around the lake.

At two miles the trail splits at a signed junction. Bear right and descend to a bridged crossing of Clear Creek. The trail stays just inside treeline as it skirts the east side of a large meadow. At three miles you reach a signed trail junction to Porcupine Pass. Stay left and

Exposed Summit Lake is viewed as you drop off Green River Pass.

continue hiking southeast toward Upper Green River Lake. Climb then drop down a rock outcropping near that lake's shore and walk three-quarters of a mile to its end.

Beyond the upper lake the trail stays left of meandering Green River, following it upstream towards Squaretop Mountain ahead of you. Hop an intermittent stream at 5.6 miles. Elbow and Pixley creeks (bridged) are crossed in quick succession in another 1.2 miles, marking the entrance to Beaver Park. This is a popular place to camp, particularly if you are interested in exploring Granite Lake and Squaretop Mountain (hike no. 46).

The south end of Beaver Park is reached at 8.4 miles. Cross a log bridge over the Green and hike southeast through lodgepole and spruce to a bridged crossing of Martin Creek at 9 miles. Ford the Green twice in the next

.2 miles before entering Three Forks Park, a large meadow that turns tawny gold by late August.

Stay to the right (W) side of the park to its end at 10.4 miles. Begin a gradual then steeper switchbacking ascent to a crossing of Clark Creek at 11.4 miles. Ascend more gradually through Trail Creek Park to a signed junction with the New Fork Trail at 12.8 miles.

To continue to Summit Lake stay left (S) and hike through scattered stands of towering spruce. In three-quarters of a mile a trail to the left leads to Vista Pass. Stay right and continue to climb, reaching treeline around 14 miles. The broad, grassy bowl ahead of you is Green River Pass, the high point of this hike at 10,362 feet. Trail Creek is crossed twice before reaching it's crest. The trail drops to Summit Lake, reached at 15.8 miles.

Highline: Green River Lakes to Summit Lake

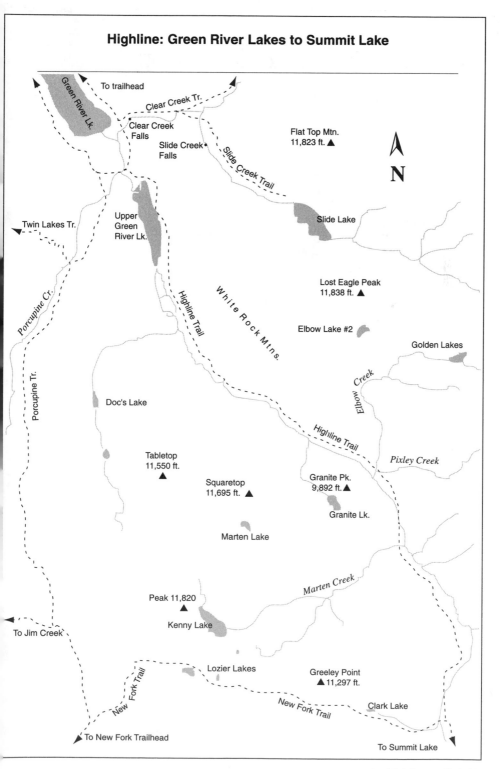

46 Granite Lake & Squaretop Mountain

Distance:
> **Green River to Granite Lake: 9**
> **Beaver Park to Granite Lake: 1.2**
> **Beaver Park to Squaretop: 3.2**

Elevation gain:
> **Beaver Park to Granite Lake: 1,247 feet**
> **Beaver Park to Squaretop: 3,695 feet**

Elevation loss: Negligible
Max. elevation: 11,695 feet
Topo maps: Squaretop Mountain
> **Earthwalk: Northern**

Fish: Brook, Cutthroat

∧∧∧

Those intent on doing the Highline Trail often bypass a hidden treasure above the beaten path—quiet Granite Lake. This small body of water is hugged by Squaretop Mountain to the west and Granite Peak to the northeast. Good camping spots away from the lake and easy walk-up routes on both Squaretop and Granite Peak reward those willing to leave the trail and carry their packs up the slopes above Beaver Park. Establishing a base camp at the park and day hiking to the lake is also an option.

Follow directions to Beaver Park given in the write-up to Summit Lake, hike no. 45. Immediately after crossing Elbow and Pixley Creeks wade across shallow Green River and begin angling south then west up the slopes on the right side of the park. There is a steep game/human trail that is easy to follow, although it is just as easy to walk off-trail up the slopes to the lake. The Earthwalk Press maps shows a trail to Granite Lake angling up the slopes immediately after crossing the bridge at the south end of Beaver Park. Both Bonney's Field Guide and Finis Mitchell's Wind River Trails mention this old trail, formerly marked with a wood sign. The trail fell out of use after a 1953 fire near Martin Creek made traveling up the slope difficult. The sign to the abandoned trail is no longer there.

From the lake the route up Squaretop is evident (but easy to lose on the way down!) Walk around its right (E) side, cross the outlet and head south past a section of cliff bands. Begin ascending south then west to a high plateau .6 miles south of the 11,695 foot summit. Walk right (NW) to reach the top. The magnificent view encompasses Green River Lakes, Gannett and other high peaks at the north end of the range. Surveying the panorama of jagged alpine peaks it seems ironic that blocky Squaretop is the most photographed mountain in the Winds.

The monolith has drawn climbers for many years. The first ascent of the southeast side was made by William "Rocky Mountain Bill" Stroud sometime before 1921. That was the year a second party failed in its attempt of the west face.

Many parties put up different routes on the peak in the succeeding decades. In 1958, Teton guides Bill Byrd and Dave Dingman, and climbing friend Roland Watt, successfully scaled the 2,000 foot northeast wall. The precipitous west face was not successfully climbed until 1974 by Jeff and Greg Lowe and Kent Christensen.

The sheer northeast face of Squaretop is a difficult climb, but experienced, skilled hikers can scramble up its southeast flank.

47 Summit Lake to Little Seneca

Distance: 10.8 miles
Elevation gain: 1,560 feet
Elevation loss: 1,480 feet
Max. elevation: 11,050 feet
Topo maps:
   Gannett Peak, Bridger Lakes
   Earthwalk: Northern
Fish:
   Elbow Lake: Golden
   Jean Lakes: Cutthroat
   Little Seneca: Rainbow
   Pass Lake: Cutthroat

∧∧∧

Summit Lake to Little Seneca is my favorite section of the Highline Trail. Sparkling blue lakes reflect the snow-covered, rocky peaks that rise above them. Almost entirely above treeline, every mile offers panoramic views of nearby 12,000 and 13,000 foot peaks. Alpine wildflowers bloom with impunity as the snow recedes from the rocky basin floors, and spectacular side trips to Peak Lake and Titcomb Basin are within reach.

There are three trail junctions within .2 miles on the west side of Summit Lake. The first, marked by cairns, heads west to Palmer Lake and eventually the New Fork Entrance. The second goes to Trapper Lake. Take the third, which is furthest left, to continue on the Highline.

This dirt and rock path soon splits. The left fork is a use trail around the lake. Stay right to descend to a crossing of Pine Creek at .6 miles, which can

be fast and a foot or so deep at high water. Climb above the creek, bearing left at one mile where a newer section of the Highline, not plotted on the 1968 Bridger Lakes topo map, drops to a log bridge spanning the narrow divide through which Elbow Creek flows. Stay left again at 1.3 miles where the lightly-used trail to Sauerkraut and Bridger Lakes heads south. Pass Lake is right of the trail as you climb a knoll and enter the beautiful, high valley that cradles the 10,455 ft. tarn. Cross the lake's outflow, and wind through the base of a large rockslide before a wide but relatively shallow crossing of Elbow Creek. Beyond, the trail begins a steady 500 climb up a rocky draw sporadically shaded by whitebark pine and spruce toward the high rocky basin that cradles Elbow Lake. There are numerous nice but exposed places to set up camp near its north end, allowing you to enjoy the alpenglow on 12,232 ft. Mt. Oeneis and

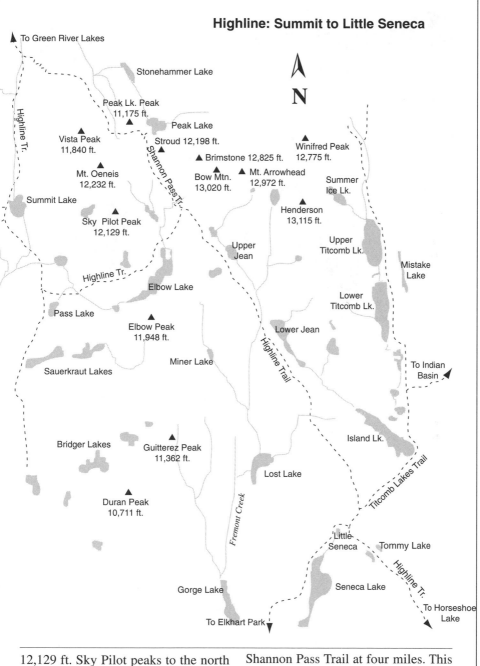

To Green River Lakes

Stonehammer Lake

Highline Tr.

Peak Lk. Peak
11,175 ft.

Peak Lake

N

Vista Peak
11,840 ft.

Stroud 12,198 ft.

Shannon Pass Tr.

Winifred Peak
12,775 ft.

Brimstone 12,825 ft.

Mt. Oeneis
12,232 ft.

Bow Mtn.
13,020 ft.

Mt. Arrowhead
12,972 ft.

Summer
Ice Lk.

Summit Lake

Sky Pilot Peak
12,129 ft.

Henderson
13,115 ft.

Upper
Titcomb Lk.

Upper
Jean

Mistake
Lake

Highline Tr.

Elbow Lake

Lower
Titcomb Lk.

Pass Lake

Elbow Peak
11,948 ft.

Lower Jean

Highline Trail

Miner Lake

To Indian
Basin

Sauerkraut Lakes

Bridger Lakes

Guitterez Peak
11,362 ft.

Island Lk.

Lost Lake

Titcomb Lakes Trail

Duran Peak
10,711 ft.

Fremont Creek

Little
Seneca

Tommy Lake

Gorge Lake

Seneca Lake

Highline Tr.

To Elkhart Park

To Horseshoe
Lake

12,129 ft. Sky Pilot peaks to the north and 11,948 foot Elbow Peak south of the lake. Hop a stream at 3.9 miles and walk uphill to a signed junction with the Shannon Pass Trail at four miles. This leads north to Peak Lake in 1.6 miles (see hike no. 48.) Stay right here and climb southeast up open slopes to an

Bow Mountain, left, rises above Upper Jean Lake. To the right is Mt. Arrowhead.

11,060 foot saddle that provides a pleasing overlook of 13,020 foot Bow Mountain and 12,972 foot Mount Arrowhead to the north, 13,115 foot Henderson Peak and the Titcomb Needles due east. These massive peaks and spires rise thousands of feet above 10,799 foot Upper Jean Lake.

The trail drops 200 feet off the pass, skirting the west side of Lake 10,935, before reaching Upper Jean's west shore at 5.7 miles. The trail then climbs above the lake before following a gradual downhill course towards Lower Jean Lake. At 6.6 miles a large cascade tumbles into Fremont Creek to your left. It competes for attention with the mucky mess of trail that crosses and recrosses Fremont before reaching the inflow to Lower Jean at seven miles.

Here the trail seems to disappear. Rock-hop the inflow and walk right around the steep outcrop in front of you and you'll pick it up again.

The trail stays above the lake, gradually dropping towards Fremont Crossing. At 8.6 miles a faint trail to the right leads to Lost Lake. I highly recommend leaving the trail here and walking left (E) towards the Fremont Cut-off Trail (see hike no. 25.).

To continue on the Highline walk past Lost Creek junction to bridged Fremont Crossing at 8.7 miles. Shortly cross a tributary and follow an undulating course to yet another tributary crossing at 9.7 miles. Beyond a small lake to your left the trail bears south and climbs a draw. The Indian Pass Trail intersection is reached at 10.4 miles. Stay right, cross a small saddle, and descend 200 feet to a signed junction with the Seneca Lake Trail at 10.8 miles.

48 Peak Lake & Stroud Peak

Distance from Highline Trail
   via Shannon Pass: 1.6 miles
Elevation gain: 280 feet
Elevation loss: 580 feet
Max. elevation: 11,120 feet
Topo map: Gannett Peak
   Earthwalk: Northern
Fish: Golden

∧∧∧

Peak Lake is a deep green jewel ringed by towering mountains. A path to Stonehammer Lake due north, or a rigorous two mile hike east to Knapsack Col for a bird's eye view of Titcomb Basin, are attractive extensions of this worthwhile side trip.

The hike begins at the Shannon Pass Trail intersection with the Highline. Turn northwest onto the trail, cross a stream and begin climbing towards the 11,120 foot pass. It's crest is reached in .8 miles, just after hiking past two snow-fed lakes. The pass marks the divide between 12,232 foot Mount Oeneis to your left and 12,198 foot Stroud Peak to the right. A short scramble up Stroud provides one of the best views from a walk-up peak in the Winds. It can be accessed from Peak Lake by walking towards the obvious saddle east of the summit, or by ascending Stroud's grassy southeast slopes beginning near the Highline junction.

Beyond a second pair of lakes the trail begins a switchbacking drop over rocky slopes to a spur path at 1.4 miles.

This heads left (W) a short distance to Dale Lake. Stay right and continue descending to the outlet of Peak Lake at 1.6 miles.

Shannon Pass is named in honor of

Peak Lake is a worthwhile side-trip.

Harmon Shannon, a District Ranger who helped build many of the trails and routes around the Upper Green. Stroud Peak immortalizes William "Rocky Mountain Bill" Stroud, a kind but peculiar Rock Springs man known for perpetually wearing a suit and hat—regardless of the activity. He spent his leisure time in the mountains, taking photographs to give to friends.

∧

---

49 Little Seneca to Horseshoe Lake

Distance: 14.1 miles
Elevation gain: 960 feet
Elevation loss: 1,910 feet
Max. elevation: 11,120 feet
Topo maps:
　　Bridger Lakes, Fremont Peak South, Horseshoe Lake
　　Earthwalk: Northern & Southern
Fish:
　　Nelson, Tommy: Golden
　　Upper Cook: Golden, Brook
　　Lower Cook: Brook
　　Lower Chain: Cutthroat, Rainbow
　　Middle Chain: Rainbow, Rainbow/Cutthroat hybrid
　　Upper Chain: Rainbow/Cutthroat hybrid
　　Horseshoe: Brook
　　Spruce: Rainbow, Cutthroat
　　Pole Creek # 7 (see fishing map): Brook
　　Pole Creek #8 (see fishing map): Brook, Golden
　　Upper Pole Creek Lake: Brook, Cutthroat
　　Thousand Island Lake: Cutthroat, Brook

∧∧∧

After climbing Lester Pass this portion of the Highline Trail heads generally southeast away from the spine of the range towards the rolling hills and numerous lakes that characterize its middle portion. Beyond Horseshoe Lake it follows a winding, up-and-down route to North Fork Lake. Non-fishermen may want to leave the Highline at Cook Lakes and take the Fremont Trail to North Fork. In addition to being a shorter, pretty route that stays in the

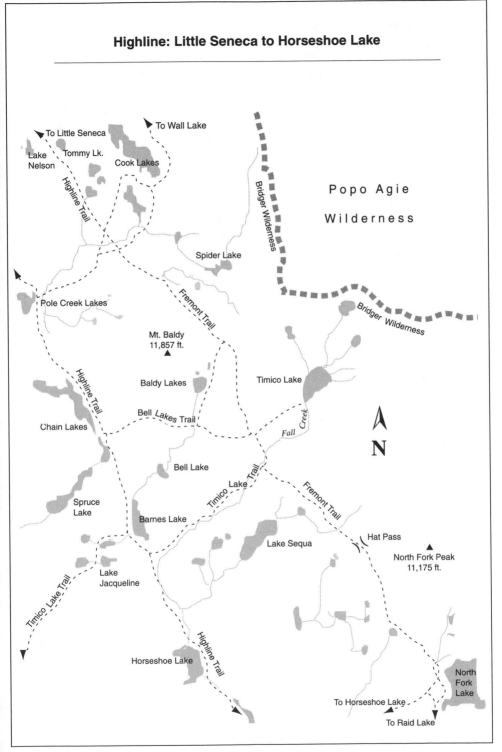

Highline: Little Seneca to Horseshoe Lake

To Little Seneca

To Wall Lake

Lake Nelson

Tommy Lk.

Cook Lakes

Highline Trail

Popo Agie

Wilderness

Bridger Wilderness

Spider Lake

Fremont Trail

Pole Creek Lakes

Bridger Wilderness

Mt. Baldy 11,857 ft.

Baldy Lakes

Timico Lake

Highline Trail

Bell Lakes Trail

Fall Creek

Chain Lakes

N

Bell Lake

Timico Lake Trail

Spruce Lake

Barnes Lake

Fremont Trail

Lake Sequa

Hat Pass

North Fork Peak 11,175 ft.

Timico Lake Trail

Lake Jacqueline

Highline Trail

Horseshoe Lake

To Horseshoe Lake

To Raid Lake

North Fork Lake

high mountains, this option avoids traveling through miles of charred forest burned in the Fayette fire of 1988, a lightning-caused blaze that consumed almost 39,000 acres of forest.

From the signed junction at Little Seneca turn onto the Highline and walk southeast towards Lester Pass, immediately passing an unnamed lake on your left as you climb towards two larger tarns at .6 miles. The trail cuts between the pair of pretty lakes then climbs 500 feet up open, rock-studded slopes to Lester Pass at 1.4 miles. The 11,120 foot divide provides unobstructed views of Island Lake and Titcomb Basin to the north. To the south and east is a panoramic vista of the lower lake country you will be crossing. Resting between Peak 11,550 to the southwest and 12,342 Mount Lester to the northeast, the pass marks the highest point reached on this hike. It and the peak were named for packer Lester Faler. Mt. Lester's first recorded ascent was made it 1930 by eight members of the Colorado Mountain Club, although Orrin and Lorraine Bonney believe it was probably scaled by a Geological Survey crew near the turn of the century.

The trail drops east then south off the divide and passes Tommy Lake at 2.2 miles on its way to a crossing of Cook Lake 10,155's narrow neck a mile further. At 3.8 miles you reach a poorly marked, three trail intersection. The path continuing straight is the Fremont Trail, hike no. 50.

For reasons listed above, this is the trail I recommend taking to North Fork Lake instead of the Highline. The path to your left heads southeast to Cook Lakes 10,143 and 10,170.

To continue on the Highline bear right, hiking south then west past another junction with the Fremont at 4.5 miles; stay right again. Pass a small pond of your left, hop a tributary, then walk past several small tarns in quick succession. The trail enters a short section of pine and spruce before cutting through an open park and following a string of pools. At 5.7 miles, it crosses wide Pole Creek. With depths up to your knees, a noticeable current, and a rocky bottom, extra precaution should be taken when fording the creek.

Reach a signed intersection shortly after the ford. Pole Creek Trail to Elkhart Entrance is on your right. Take the left fork to continue on the Highline. Cross and recross a tributary as the trail heads southwest to Chain lakes.

Hop another tributary at 7.2 miles shortly before reaching the north end of the half-mile long lake chain. The trail stays left of the lakes, crosses an inflow stream at 7.6 miles, and reaches a junction with the Bell Lakes Trail to your left at 8.1 miles. Stay right and continue walking to the end of the lakes.

At 8.7 miles a spur trail to Spruce Lake on your right intersects the Highline. Stay left on the main trail, descending past numerous ponds to the north end of Barnes Lake at 9.2 miles. Beyond, miles of burned forest await. Hike around the west shore of the lake and cross a stream between it and Lake Jacquline at 10.3 miles before climbing and dropping over a small rise to an intersection with the Timico Lake Trail at 10.8 miles. To avoid the heart of the burn, which affords few camping opportunities, some hikers choose to hike northeast on this lightly-used trail to its intersection with the Fremont Trail, bearing right (SE) at the junction to eventually reach North Fork Lake. My preference is to leave the Highline at Cook Lakes, as mentioned earlier.

If you opt to continue on the Highline stay right at the Timico Lake Trail junction and descend, following a stream to a fork in the trail at 11 miles. Here the Highline splits to skirt both sides of an open park. Take either branch; the trails rejoin at 11.8 miles.

At this juncture walk through meadow, staying right of meandering Fall Creek as you drop to the north end of Horseshoe Lake at 12.8 miles. The trail circles the lake to the west, passing several ponds and climbing a knoll above its west shore before dropping to a crossing of the wide creek at 13.8 miles. Here it bears left and soon reaches a junction with the Horseshoe Lake Trail to your right at 14 miles. Continue left another .1 miles to a second junction with the Horseshoe. Bear left here to continue to North Fork Lake, reached in another 5.3 miles. (See hike no. 51).

∧

50 Fremont Trail to North Fork Lake

Distance: 9.8 miles
Elevation gain: 2,040 feet
Elevation loss: 2,100 feet
Max. elevation: 10,048 feet
Topo maps:
    Fremont Peak South, Horseshoe Lake
    Earthwalk: North & South
Fish:
    Baldy Lake: Cutthroat
    Spider Lake: Cutthroat
    Lake 10,450: Brook
    Horseshoe: Brook

∧∧∧

The Fremont Trail offers a more direct route from Pole Creek to North Fork Lake than the Highline. It stays closer to the Continental Divide and high peaks and, unlike its counterpart, most of the rugged up-and-down trail is above treeline. Moreover, it avoids the large section of forest charred by the

1988 Fayette forest fire that Highline hikers encounter along eight or so miles of trail below Barnes Lake to North Fork Lake.

The trail begins at a junction with the Highline Trail south of Cook Lakes (see hike no. 49). Hike southeast at this juncture, crossing Pole Creek at .3 miles and again at .8 miles as you gradually ascend 300 feet to reach a group of small lakes in rocky Bald Mountain Basin at 1.2 miles. While this appealing basin is dotted with almost a dozen small ponds and lakes, only three are stocked with fish. Cross-country rambling through the basin, however, will likely provide pleasing places to camp without company.

The trail continues its predominantly southern ascent across the basin through open, meadowed slopes and weathered rock slabs to a broad pass at 10,840. Cook and Wall lakes and rugged Titcomb Basin are handsomely showcased on top of the divide.

The trail drops 300 feet off the pass to a junction with the Baldy Lakes Trail to your right at 2.7 miles. With the sheer east face of 11,857 foot Mt. Baldy rising above the alpine floor cradling Baldy Lakes, numerous good camping opportunities are found off this trail, as well.

The Fremont continues straight, ascending 200 feet to a small rise before dropping at a steeper gradient to a crossing of a small inflow stream to Baldy Lake at 3.4 miles. After skirting a small pond it again climbs to a small saddle before descending at a moderate gradient to an intersection with Timico Lake Trail at 4.1 miles. An easy ascent through open terrain brings you to the southeast end of that 10,512 foot lake. Brook trout can be found in Timico's waters.

Continue straight (SE) at the junction, descending almost 200 feet at a moderate gradient to a crossing of Fall Creek at 4.6 miles.

Beyond the ford the trail follows a rolling course through alpine tundra, crossing a tributary of Little Fall Creek at 4.7 miles, Little Fall itself at 5.1, then two more tributaries of that small stream at 5.7 and 6.2 miles. Beyond the last stream crossing it ascends 350 feet at an easy to moderate grade up open, alpine tundra to the crest of 10,848 foot Hat Pass at 6.5 miles. While Peak 11,747 lies only a half-mile to the east, the star of the divide's panorama shines on the distant west and northwest horizons, where dozens of alpine lakes and jagged high peaks command attention.

The stony path steadily drops off the pass at a moderately steep grade, regaining timberline before reaching the eastern shore of small Rambaud Lake at 7.8 miles. After a brief level stretch, the trail descends a wooded draw to the western shore of August Lake at 8.4 miles.

The Fremont Trail intersects Hay Pass Trail at the nine mile mark. Here you enjoy great views of large North Fork Lake, perched at an elevation of 9,754 feet, just ahead. Leave the Fremont at 9.2 miles, bearing right onto the new Highline Trail. Follow the trail above the lake's west shore to an intersection with the North Fork Trail at 9.8 miles. There are a number of confusing trails here. Consult the map so you take the one you want.

51 Horseshoe Lake to Raid Lake
North Fork Lake to Raid

Distance:
   Horseshoe Lake to Raid: 15.4 miles
   North Fork Lake to Raid: 10.1 miles
Elevation gain:
   Horseshoe Lake to Raid: 1,220 feet
   North Fork Lake to Raid: Approx. 690 feet
Elevation loss:
   Horseshoe Lake to Raid: 660 feet
   North Fork Lake to Raid: 380 feet
Max. elevation: 10,050 feet
Topo maps:
   Horseshoe Lake, Halls Mountain, Raid Lake
   Earthwalk: Southern
Fish:
   Horseshoe: Brook
   Lake George: Brook
   Junction: Brook
   Dream: Brook, Cutthroat
   Raid: Brook, Mackinaw
   North Fork: Cutthroat
   Winona: Cutthroat
   Vera: Cutthroat
   Isabella: Cutthroat
   Fall Creek: Brook
   Bob's: Brook
   Firehole Lakes (Wilderness, Lake 9584 & Lake Susan): Cutthroat

∧∧∧

The Highline Trail from Horseshoe to Raid Lake passes a dozen lakes, with twice that number nearby. There are few sustained climbs or drops. This section is a gentle, undulating walk through scattered forest, open slopes, meadows and—as you will discover—bogs and marshes. The lakes, forests and meadows offer a different kind of beauty and serenity than that found in the high peaks. The large number of trails intersecting this section of the Highline provide access to pretty alpine basins to the east and offer enticing loop possibilities.

There are, however, two drawbacks to this section of the Highline. First, you may see domestic sheep, particularly on the stretch from Junction to Raid Lake. These sweaters-on-the-hoof pollute the lakes and streams and leave an unbelievable amount of slippery poop in their wake. If you don't welcome encountering what domestic sheep leave behind, sounds of their bleating and the barking of herd dogs, check for approximate herd locations at the district Forest Service office before you plan a Highline trip. The helpful staff can often suggest a good alternative.

The second drawback is walking through a large burn area between Horseshoe and North Fork lakes, the legacy of a massive lightning-caused forest fire that originated near Fayette Lake in 1988 and consumed almost 39,000 acres before burning itself out near timberline.

I generally recommend taking the Fremont Trail from Cook Lakes to North Fork Lake to avoid both drawbacks. However, if you chose this portion of the Highline, you will likely have sparse company. The fishing is fair to good, and you'll see first-hand how landscapes regenerate following a massive blaze. Lodgepole seedlings are now an inch in diameter, in keeping with normal growth rates for this elevation. The carpet of wildflowers is quite lush,

thriving on numerous streams and rich nutrients returned to the soil after the fire. True to its name, the deep pink blossoms of fireweed are especially noticeable. The plant provides significant forage for both elk and deer. Its leaves, petals and roots were all used by different Indian tribes and pioneers throughout the west for food.

Because trail users will be traveling the Highline from both Horseshoe Lake and North Fork Lake, the description below is broken into segments.

Horseshoe Lake to North Fork Lake

From its intersection with Horseshoe Lake Trail at the south end of Horseshoe Lake, the Highline ascends a draw to narrow Lake George, paralleling its shores before trending south and reaching a junction with the North Fork Trail at 1.1 miles.

Bear left to continue on the Highline. The trail immediately loops around a small bog to a crossing of Lake George's inlet at 1.6 miles. It then bears northeast past a number of ponds as it gradually climbs a small draw, hops an intermittent stream at its head, and turns east a quarter-mile before reaching 9,961 foot Edmund Lake.

Splash through Edmund's outlet at 2.9 miles. Don't get obsessed with keeping your feet dry: the trail crosses streams six times in the next mile as it descends to 9,658 foot Mac's Lake and the junction with the Lake Ethel Trail just beyond.

The Highline Trail bears left (NE) at the junction and gradually ascends a close draw—passing three large ponds enroute—before climbing a small rise at the top of the draw and reaching a

Highline: Horseshoe Lake to Raid Lake • North Fork Lake to Raid

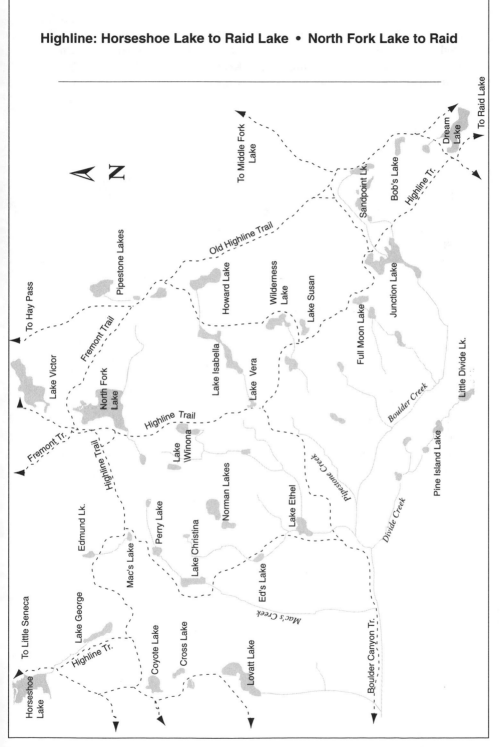

signed trail intersection at five miles. The trail to the left leads to North Fork Boulder Canyon and Hay Pass. Hike right through soggy terrain around the west end of large North Fork Lake to a crossing of its neck at 5.3 miles.

North Fork Lake to Raid Lake

From the ford the Highline Travel travels south to 9,688 foot Lake Winona, crossing an inlet to the lake at 6.1 miles. It stays left of the lake and, thankfully, only jumps one stream in its way to tiny Lake Vera and a signed intersection with Boulder Canyon Trail at 7.4 miles. Bear left here on a newly constructed trail to Firehole Lakes. Cross the inlet to Lake 9,584 at 8.4 miles, another stream at 8.8 miles.

Walk past a spur trail to your left that winds between Firehole Lakes and continue south to a crossing of Lake Susan's outlet at 9.1 miles. Here the trail climbs a rise then drops steeply down through lodgepole forest to Full Moon Lake at 10 miles. The path loops northeast in a broad semi-circle to avoid a large bog. At the top of the loop a trail continues northeast up Hall Creek towards beautiful Hall Lake, a great destination if you have the time.

As the Highline loops back it stays to the left of Full Moon and passes a pond before reaching Junction Lake at 10.8 miles. Bear right around Junction's north end and cross its inlet just before reaching an intersection with the Middle Fork Boulder Creek Trail at 11.2 miles. Keep right here and immediately hop a stream. Cross and recross Junction Lake outlet streams at 11.8 miles and slog through a boggy area before beginning a gradual climb to Dream Lake's outlet at 12.8 miles, passing a turn-off to Rainbow Lake enroute. Begin climbing again to an intersection at 13.8 miles, the high point of the hike. This bisecting trail travels northeast to southwest, connecting Scab Creek Trail to the Fremont Trail.

Continue straight (SE) at the junction. The trail drops to cross a shallow arm of Raid Lake at 14.2 miles. It follows the arm a short distance then heads left (E) to a stream crossing at 15 miles. The intersection with Scab Creek Trail is reached .4 miles further.

Raid Lake and Raid Peak to the east are both named in commemoration of a 1903 sheep massacre. Escalating conflict between cattle ranchers and sheepmen over range and grazing rights boiled over that summer. Cattlemen rode out to the docile sheep and slaughtered over 1,200 animals. Warned that hostile cowmen were on the way, sheepman Ora Hailey moved his herd east over a divide and escaped harm. The divide was subsequently named Hailey Pass in his honor.

∧

52 Raid Lake to Big Sandy Entrance

Distance: 14 miles
Elevation gain: 1,130 feet
Elevation loss: 2,090 feet
Max. elevation: 10,522 feet
Topo maps:
    Raid Lake, Mount Bonneville, Big Sandy Opening
    Earthwalk: Southern
Fish:
    Cross Lake: Brook, Golden
    N.F. Silver Creek: Brook
    Marms: Brook
    Dad's Lake: Brook, Cutthroat
    Mirror Lake: Brook, Rainbow
    Meeks Lake: Brook

∧∧∧

The hike from Raid Lake to Big Sandy Opening leaves the heart of the Wind River Range. The first 5.6 miles, through a valley bound by high peaks to the northeast, is strikingly scenic. At that mile mark, however, the trail turns south and leaves the high country and its grand peaks behind on its way to Big Sandy Opening. Those with time and energy are well-rewarded by continuing east to the Shadow Lake Trail, crossing Texas Pass, and dropping down to Lonesome Lake and Cirque of the Towers. Ascend Big Sandy Pass above the lake and drop down Big Sandy Trail to reach the opening.

From the junction of Scab Creek and Highline trails south of Raid Lake, hike left (SE) up a gentle grade to an intersection with the Silver Lake Trail at .4 miles. Bear left here and walk another .5 miles to a split in the Highline. The right fork bears southeast pass Upper Silver Lakes to a junction labeled "Highline Trail" on the Mount Bonneville map. It descends the canyon cut by East Fork River to Poston Meadows, climbs a rise, then drops southeast past Boulter and Twin Lakes to Big Sandy—an alternative route to that entrance.

The option described here stays left at the split and climbs to a junction with the Fremont Trail at two miles. Stay

Highline: Raid Lake to Big Sandy

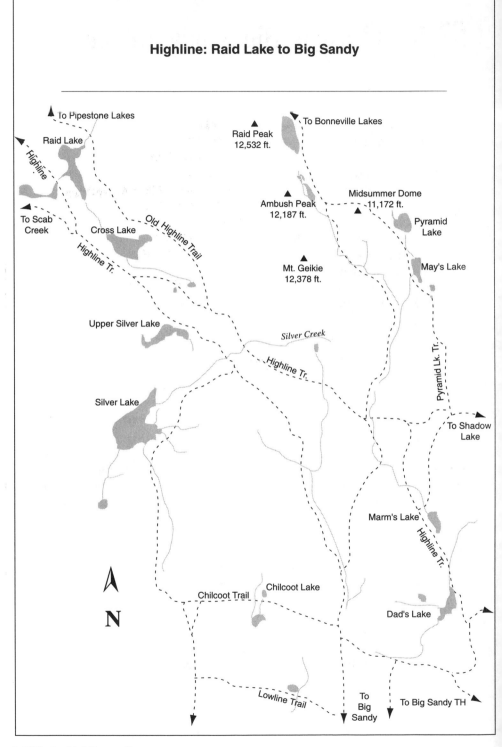

To Pipestone Lakes

Raid Lake

Highline

To Scab Creek

Cross Lake

Old Highline Trail

Highline Tr.

Raid Peak
12,532 ft.

To Bonneville Lakes

Ambush Peak
12,187 ft.

Midsummer Dome
11,172 ft.

Pyramid Lake

Mt. Geikie
12,378 ft.

May's Lake

Upper Silver Lake

Silver Creek

Highline Tr.

Pyramid Lk. Tr.

Silver Lake

To Shadow Lake

Marm's Lake

Highline Tr.

N

Chilcoot Trail

Chilcoot Lake

Dad's Lake

Lowline Trail

To Big Sandy

To Big Sandy TH

right and descend to a crossing of North Fork Silver Creek at 2.5 miles before climbing to an outlet stream of an unnamed lake on your left at 2.8 miles.

The trail hops the stream and continues ascending through open forest to a broad, open hilltop, the high point of the hike at 10,522 feet. The rise provides excellent views of the surrounding country. Mount Geikie is prominent to the north, Mount Washakie and the west side of the Cirque to the east.

The trail heads towards the peaks on its way to a junction with East Fork River Trail at five miles. Stay left here and hop two tributaries in quick succession as you climb southeast to yet another trail junction at 5.6 miles. Bear left to go to Shadow Lake. To reach Big Sandy Entrance, turn right (S) and contour around a hill before climbing a rise and dropping into a wooded canyon. The trail passes an unnamed lake to the right at 6.4 miles.; the west side of Marms Lake is reached .7 miles further. Beyond Marms the trail crosses its outlet stream at eight miles and bears left to the east side of Dad's Lake, .reached in .2 miles. Hop a stream flowing into Dad's at 8.4 miles and continue past a cairn to your left. (The cairn marks the route to Donald Lake.)

The trail stays right of small Mirror Lake a half mile further on its way to Fish Park, bisecting the .6 mile long marshy area before reaching firmer ground. Stay straight where two junctions lead right to Francis Lake and begin dropping through patches of meadow and pine forest to a fork in the trail at 12.4 miles. Both trails lead to Big Sandy. The left fork, described here, is the shorter option. It heads east to a junction with the Meeks Lake Trail, then turns right and drops through the trees to a crossing of Meeks Creek at 12.8 miles. Winding through meadows and trees, the good path crosses Meeks two more times before reaching Big Sandy at 14 miles.

Big Sandy was the name of a Pony Express Station and post office near Farson. The station was torched by Indians in 1862, six months after the Pony Express had become defunct.

Those planning on finishing the Highline Trail at Big Sandy may be interested in staying at Big Sandy Lodge not far from the campground. The lodge was built in 1929; its large lounge is decorated with trophy heads and two stone fireplaces. For information, write Big Sandy Lodge at Box 223, Boulder, Wyoming, 82923.

∧

Highline Notes

Other Hikes

AlpineLakes

Over 600 miles of trail and innumerable routes criss-cross the Wind River range. This guide does not cover all of them. Low-lying trails and those that traverse sheep country were excluded by personal preference. Others were left out because of space considerations and the desire to leave areas for you to discover on your own. This section outlines some of the possibilities. A brief description, trail/route length and maps you will need are provided to help get you started.

Simpson Lake Trail
Distance:
    4.4 miles from Whiskey Mtn. Jct.
Topo maps:
    Simpson Lake
    Earthwalk: Northern
Drop down the west side of Whiskey Mountain on the Whiskey Mtn. Trail (see hike no. 9) to its junction with the Simpson Lake Trail. Turn left (SW) and hike through forest to the large lake. A trail on the east side of Simpson leads south to Sandra Lake.

•

Porcupine/New Fork Trail
Distance: 17.3 miles
Topo maps:
    Green River Lakes
    Squaretop Mtn.
    Earthwalk: Northern
From the southwest end of Lower Green River Lakes the Porcupine Trail climbs through forest and high meadows to 10,680 foot Porcupine Pass, then descends to a junction with the Clark Creek Trail. A nice loop can be made by following that trail east to the Highline and hiking back to Green River Lakes.Those that exit at New Fork Park should plan a car shuttle in advance.

Hidden and Thompson Lakes
Distance from New Fork Trail:
    1.1 miles to Lake 11,130
Topo map: Squaretop Mtn
    Earthwalk: Northern
Leave Clark Creek Trail at a small saddle near Greeley Point (13.3 miles from New Fork Entrance, or 2.5 miles above Trail Creek Park) and walk southwest cross-country to a beautiful group of alpine lakes at the base of a small cirque, 1.1 miles and 200 feet above the saddle.

•

Doubletop Mountain Trail
Distance: 12.7 miles
Topo maps:
    Squaretop Mountain
    Fremont Lakes North
    New Fork Lakes
    Earthwalk: Northern
This open trail provides nice views of the range on its way to Summit Lake. From the New Fork Entrance, follow the New Fork/Porcupine Trail to its junction with the Lowline Trail at two miles. Turn right and walk to a junction with the Doubletop Mountain Trail. Climb northeast past Rainbow Lake and Doubletop Mountain to an intersection with the Palmer Lake Trail. Doubletop

Trail continues east past Cutthroat and No Name Lakes to an intersection with the Highline near Summit Lake.

•

Pine Creek Canyon Trail
Distance: 13.2 miles
Topo maps:
   Fremont Lake North
   Squaretop Mountain
   Gannett Peak
   Earthwalk: Northern
From Trail's End Campground at Elkhart Park, this trail drops 2,000 feet to Long Lake than climbs to Crow's Nest Lookout at 5.3 miles on the west side of Pine Creek Canyon. It continues north past Glimpse, Trapper, Gottfried and Borum lakes, climbs to a saddle, then drops to the Highline near Summit Lake.

•

Hay Pass and Alpine Lakes
Distance:
   10.8 miles from North
   Fork Lake to Lake 10,163
Topo maps:
   Horseshoe Lake
   Fremont Peak South
   Earthwalk: Southern
From the northwest corner of North Fork Lake, Hay Pass Trail follows the west shore of Lake Victor then travels north to the head of North Fork Boulder Canyon, crosses Hay Pass, and descends to Dennis, Golden and Upper Golden Lakes in the Fitzpatrick Wilderness. It then climbs a small pass between Douglas and Quintet Peak and descends to Camp Lake.

From that lake's northwest end, use trails lead to Snowbridge Lake and a chain of lakes to the west. The beautiful, lightly-visited basin is bound by jagged pinnacles and Brown Cliffs to the east, glaciers to the west. It is one of the wildest, most remote regions of the Winds.

•

Timico Lake
Distance:
   Via Timico Lake Trail Jct.
   with Highline: 3.1 miles
   Via Bell Lakes Trail Jct.
   with Highline: 3.6 miles
Topo maps:
   Horseshoe Lake
   Earthwalk: Southern
Pretty Timico Lake is reached by either the Bell Lakes Trail, which begins off the Highline Trail near Chain Lakes, or by the Timico Lake Trail from its junction with the Highline south of Barnes Lake. The large lake is surrounded by high rock walls.

•

Europe Canyon
Distance:
   4.7 miles from North Fork Lake
Topo maps:
   Halls Mountain
   Horseshoe Lake
   Earthwalk: Southern
Follow the Fremont Trail from the northwest corner of North Fork Lake east to an unmarked trail at 1.2 miles.

Follow cairns/path NE to the west shore of Valley Lake, round its east end and continue to head up the narrow alpine canyon to a 11,400 foot pass at its head. This marks the boundary of the Wind River Indian Reservation. You need a permit/guide to descent to Milky Lakes below.

Near the entrance of the canyon the trail splits. The right branch leads to Lake 10,542. By staying right again at a second split it is possible to walk cross-country between Lake 10,806 and Medina Mountain to the south, cross the tributary, and head east to Halls Lake.

•

Pyramid Lake
Distance: 12 miles
Topo Maps:
   Big Sandy Opening
   Mount Bonneville
   Earthwalk: Southern
Hike the Highline Trail from Big Sandy Entrance to Marms Lake. Take the right fork at the end of Marms. Stay left at the intersection with Shadow Lake Trail, cross Washakie Creek (walk upstream to an easier crossing if the creek is running high) and walk north, passing a trail to Washakie Pass and another junction to Hailey Pass before reaching the lake. Head west cross-country north of Midsummer Dome to reach a pretty string of lakes near the head of East Fork River. The lakes lie beneath Raid, Ambush and Mount Geikie Peaks. Mount Bonneville is to the north.

Lizard Head Trail
Distance: 8.6 miles
Topo Maps:
   Lizard Head Peak
   Earthwalk: Southern
Lizard Head Trail connects the North Fork Trail to the Bears Ears Trail. From its junction with the North Fork east of Lonesome Lake, the trail passes a left turn-off to Bear Lake and climbs to its junction with Bears Ears Trail where that trail turns sharply west and drops to Little Valentine and Valentine Lakes.

•

Middle Fork Trail
Distance: 15.7 miles
Topo maps:
   Cony Mountain
   Sweetwater Gap
   Earthwalk: Southern
The Middle Fork Trail begins near Bruce Picnic Area in Sinks Canyon and ends at Sweetwater Gap. Trails to Shoshone Lake, Pinto Park, Stough Creek Basin, Tayo and Ice Lakes all intersect this thoroughfare.

•

Pinto Park Trail
Distance: 6.7 miles
Topo maps:
   Sweetwater Gap
   Dickinson Park
Pinto Park Trail was built to connect the Middle Fork Popo Agie Trail with the North Fork Trail. It also provides access to stunning Deep Creek and Ice Lakes without the worrisome river crossings of the North Fork Trail.

Fishing

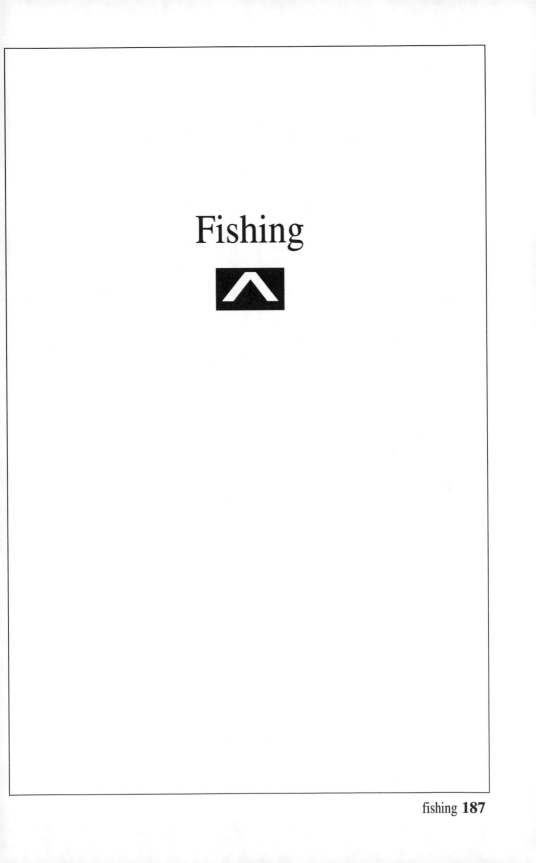

Fishing in Shoshone
&
Bridger Teton National Forests

Some of the best fishing in the west is found in the many lakes and streams in the Wind River Range. Hundreds of lakes and over 800 miles of stream make the range an anglers heaven.

But it has not always been a fisherman's paradise. Historically, most of the lakes and streams in the Winds were devoid of fish. The alpine lakes rest at the base of glacial cirques. Fish in lower lakes found the lakes' steep outflow streams inhospitable to migrate upstream. The first known transplant of fish in the range took place in 1907 when cutthroat were introduced into North Fork Lake. Considerable fish stocking by the U.S. Forest Service, Wyoming Game & Fish and individuals occurred between 1924 and 1935.

Finis Mitchell led the effort.

Mitchell was a toddler when his father moved the family from Missouri to Wyoming in a wagon pulled by mules in 1906. His love affair with the mountains began almost immediately. He learned to climb while accompanying his father on hunting trips, garnering over 30 first ascents. (By his own estimate, he has climbed over 240 Wind River peaks.) The range was his playground, visited whenever he was not working.

Mitchell moved to Rock Springs to accept a job with Union Pacific Railroad on June 4, 1923. Two years later, to the day, he married his beloved wife, Emma. Life was comfortable until the Depression struck. By the spring of 1930, the railroad had laid him off and Mitchell, like thousands of other people, could not find a job. After discussing their options, he and Emma decided to open a fishing camp in the Winds. They pooled their dwindling resources and bought a wall tent, which they set up near Mud Lake. They then borrowed 10 semi-retired horses and used saddles from ranching friends, and spread the word that they were in business. To their own surprise and delight they made several hundred dollars that summer. Clients were charged $1.50 for the horseback ride to camp; guide service was free. Sumptuous meals, concocted by Emma in her dutch oven, were $.50.

But Mitchell knew that fishing had to improve for the business to survive: few lakes in the area contained fish. He began packing in fingerlings acquired from a state hatchery. The fish were transported into the backcountry in five-gallon milk cans strapped to pack horses. The cans were topped by squares of burlap that allowed the water to splash around and aerate itself so the tiny trout wouldn't suffocate. They were released in unspoiled lakes full of things fish like to eat, and grew at an unprecedented rate. Within three years anglers were landing monster trout.

The Mitchells ran their Mud Lake camp for seven years. During that time, Finis estimated he packed in 2.5 million golden, brook, cutthroat, and German brown trout. Over 300 lakes were stocked and named (the state required that he name and record the lakes planted with fish). Fishermen today enjoy the results of his efforts.

Wyoming Game & Fish continues to stock 16 lakes in the range. No new lakes are planned to be stocked. The lakes listed below are stocked by helicopter every two years:

Daphne and Bear: Rainbow
Long: Cutthroat
Trophy, Belford, Lovatt,
Ruff: Brook
Wall, Native, Pyramid, Peak,
Jim Harrower, Stonehammer,
Mistake and Middle Sweeney:
Golden

Licensing

To maintain healthy fish populations in the Winds and throughout the state, fishing is strictly regulated by the Wyoming Game and Fish Commission. A license is required for residents and non-residents older than 14. They may be purchased at sporting goods stores, retail outlets, and Game and Fish offices. Resident; non-resident; tourist one, five and 10 day; resident youth; nonresident tourist youth; and military licenses are available. With the exception of tourist one and five day licenses, sportsmen licensed to fish in Wyoming must also purchase a conservation stamp. The stamp must be signed in ink, and you must have it in your possession while fishing. Stamps are sold in conjunction with licenses at all sales outlets.

Regulations

When you purchase a license, you will be given a pamphlet outlining general fishing regulations. It is your responsibility to know them. A brief summary of general regulations, as listed in Wyoming Game and Fish literature, is printed below. It is unlawful to:

1. Snag fish. Snagging is attempting to catch a fish in such a manner that the fish does not voluntarily take the hook in his mouth.

2. Catch fish by aid of artificial light or lighting device.

3. Catch or destroy fish by using poison, drugs, electrical devices, chemicals, explosives or similar means or substances.

4. Take, wound or destroy fish with a firearm.

5. Seine or trap fish without a valid permit

6. Plant or release live fish or fish eggs without the consent and supervision of the Wyoming Game and Fish Department or its authorized personnel. This does not include fish captured by legal means and released immediately upon capture.

7. Sell, barter, dispose of, abandon or obtain by sale or barter any edible portion of any game fish in this state.
8. Enter, fish or beach a boat upon private land or streambeds without securing the landowner's permission.
9. Take game fish for another person.
10. Transport live fish or live eggs from the water of capture.
11. Tag or mark fish and release them, unless prior approval has been obtained from Wyoming Game and Fish.
12. Use or possess corn while fishing.
13. Unless specified, all fishing is with artificial flies and lures only. Living or dead organisms, natural or prepared food stuffs or chemical attractants may not be used.

General Creel Limits

Fishermen in the Winds are generally after "game fish," whose definition includes all species of trout, whitefish and grayling. During any given day, a person can keep a total of six trout, salmon and grayling in any combination, but only one of the six may be 20 inches or longer. (Fish are measured in a straight line along a flat surface from the tip of the snout to the tip of the tail.) In the same day fishermen are also allowed to keep up to 10 brook trout eight inches or less in length, and up to 50 whitefish. Any fish caught above the creel limit must be immediately released back into water with as little injury as possible. Fish not immediately released, including those kept on stringer or in a container, will be counted in the creel.

Releasing Live Fish

Released fish have the greatest chances of surviving if you take the following precautions suggested by the Game and Fish:
1. Play and land fish as rapidly as possible to reduce exhaustion stress. This is especially critical when water is warm.
2. Keep the fish in the water as much as possible.
3. Do not squeeze the fish or place finger in the gills. A landing net is helpful.
4. Remove hook gently. Rather than pulling the hook out of a deeply hooked fish, cut the leader. The hook will decompose in time.
5. To revive an exhausted fish, hold it gently in an upright position facing upstream and move it slowly back and forth to move water through its gills. Release the fish gently in quiet water after it can hold itself upright.
6. The use of artificial flies or lures is recommended whenever many fish are being caught and released. Survival of released fish is five to 10 times greater when the angler uses artificial rather than natural baits.
7. Anglers may choose to use barbless hooks so fish can be released more easily. Standard hooks can be made barbless by flattening the barb with needle-nose pliers.

Game Fish

Game and Fish has published a pamphlet called "Game Fish of Wyoming" that helps identify what it is you have caught. Coloration by itself is inadequate, since there are wide variations and overlap between species. Ask for the pamphlet when you get your license. Below is a brief description of fish common in the Winds:

Whitefish
Distinguished from trout by larger scales; from grayling by the small, pointed mouth and smaller dorsal fin; and from suckers and chubs by the presence of the adipose fin. (The adipose fin is located on the fish's spine above the tail).

Grayling
This close relative to the trout has a gray to olive green back. Its sides are silvery to light purple, its belly bluish-white. Most distinguishing feature is long, brightly-colored dorsal fin. Its upper margin is green with pink or red spots, and it has alternating gray and rose bands.

Cutthroat Trout
Black spotting is generally concentrated towards the tail; few or no spots on head. Red or orange slash under jaw, no white tips on fins. This is the only species of trout native to Wyoming. Its back and sides are frequently steel gray in color.

Rainbow Trout
Distinguished from cutthroat by a concentration of spots near the head, absence of "cutthroat" slash, and presence of white tips on fins. Rainbow trout typically have a pinkish horizontal streak on their sides. Their backs are greenish-blue, their bellies silvery.

Golden Trout
Black spots strongly concentrated towards tail. Distinguished from cutthroat by white tips on anal and pelvic fins. Distinguished from rainbow by lack of spotting on the front of the body. The species was introduced to the range in 1929. It is called "golden" because of the yellow to deep orange hue of its fins, sides and belly.

Brook Trout
Light spots on dark background. Some red or pink spots with blue halos concentrated on lower half of body. Lower fins and tail have striking white border offset by black. The tail fin is square or only slightly forked.

Brown Trout
Distinguished from cutthroat and rainbow by general lack of spots on the tail and light-colored halos, or rings, around the dark spots. May have some red or orange spots. Distinguished from brook trout by dark spots on a light background versus light spots on a dark background. The tail fin on this species is also square or only slightly forked.

Lake Trout (Mackinaw)
Light-colored spots on a dark background. Distinguished from brook trout by a deep forked tail and absence of red or pink spots. This fish is not as highly colored as other species. Its body is typically gray with light-colored spots

Further Information
For further information on fishing in the Winds contact: Wyoming Game and Fish Department, Information Section, 5400 Bishop Blvd., Cheyenne, Wyoming 82006-0001.

Fishing on Wind River Indian Reservation

Fishing on Wind River Indian Reservation is regulated by the Shoshone and Arapaho Fish and Game Office, headquartered in Fort Washakie. A permit is needed to fish on Indian land. The same permit allows the holder to camp, hike and boat in areas that are open to the public. Seasonal resident and non-resident; one-day resident and non-resident; seven-day resident and non-resident; resident and non-resident youth; and resident and non-resident senior citizen permits are available.

Permits may be purchased at the office, which is open from 8 a.m. to 4 p.m. weekdays, or at retail outlets and campgrounds in the surrounding area. The permit only applies to areas that are open to the general public, determined by the Shoshone and Arapaho Joint Business Council.

Most areas in the interior are closed to fishing and hiking unless you hire an outfitter licensed to operate on the reservation Persons hiring a guide must still purchase a permit.

Licensed Reservation Fishing Outfitters

The outfitters listed below are licensed to operate on the reservation. Rogue outfitters may be fined $10,000 and sentenced to a year in jail.

North Fork Little Wind River Lakes: Raft, Twin, Movo, Wykee, Sonnicant, Heebeecheeche, Kagevah, Solitude, Icy, Polaris and Moraine. Outfitter: Benny Le Beau, Box 717, Fort Washakie, Wyoming, 82514. 307-332-2410

•

Bull Lk. Creek & Wilson Creek Lakes: Wilson Creek Lakes, Lydie, Steamboat, Hatchet, Alpine, Deadman and Paradise. Outfitter: Darwin Griebel, Star Route 2815, Kinnear, Wyoming, 82516.

Washakie Park Lakes: Shoshone, Twenty Lakes and Roberts Lake. Outfitter: Ben Snyder & Arleen LeClair, Box 31, Fort Washakie, Wyoming, 82514. 307-332-9282

•

Moccasin Lake and Mosquito Park Lakes: Moccasin, Marys, Squaw, Hidden and Baptiste. Outfitter: Leo Lajeunese, Box 634, Crowheart, Wyoming, 82512. 307-486-2220

•

Bobs Creek Lakes
Outfitter: Rocky O'Neal, Box 582, Crowheart, Wyoming, 82512. 307-486-2261

•

Kirkland Park Lakes
Outfitter: Will O'Neal, Box 591, Crowheart, Wyoming 82512. 307-486-2230

•

Cold Springs and Dry Creek
Outfitter: Ramona and Ron Givens, Box 601, Crowheart, Wyoming 82512. 307-486-2318

•

Bull Lake/Upper Bull Lake Creek
Outfitter: Darrell Brown and Gary Collins, Box 715, Fort Washakie, Wyoming, 82514. 307-332-6015

•

Wind River Canyon Rafting/Fishing
Outfitter: Pete Calhoun, Box 592, Crowheart, Wyoming 82512. 307-486-2253

General Creel Limits

Fishermen are allowed a daily catch of eight trout (excluding mackinaw), only one of which may be 20 inches or over. They may also catch three mackinaw, only one 24 inches or over. There is no limit on whitefish or brook trout 10 inches and under.

On Bull Lake, Dinwoody Lakes, Dinwoody Creek, Wind River Canyon and Upper and Lower Bull Lake Creek, the daily take drops to five trout and three mackinaw. On Little Bob Lake, creel is limited to two trout, only one 15 inches or over.

Regulations

1. The use of live bait in wilderness lakes is strictly prohibited.
2. Fish may not be harvested by spearing or the use of firearms, poisons, nets, bows, explosives, seines, electrical devices,snagging, chemicals or traps.
3. Anglers are required to either "Release or Kill" fish immediately after catching. Maintaining live fish on stringers or in live wells on watercraft, or any other life sustaining method, is strictly prohibited.
4.   Each and every person on a navigable vessel must have a U.S. Coast Guard approved life jacket. Each person on board must also have a valid fishing permit.

Further Information

For additional information on regulations and obtaining permits on the Wind River Indian Reservation, please write the Tribal Fish and Game Office, Box 217, Fort Washakie, 82514, or call 307-332-7207.

Where to Catch What

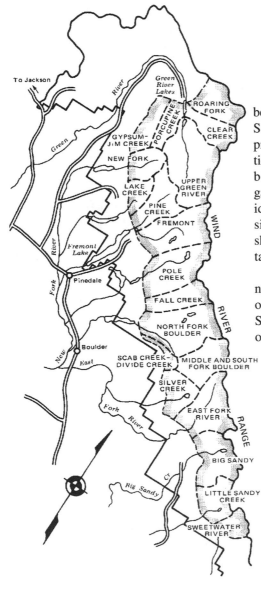

Fishing opportunities have been outlined in the hike write-ups. Since many lakes can be approached from a different direction, or on trails not included in this book, this section "fills in the gaps." The map shown on this page identifies the drainages on the west side of the range. Individual maps show each drainage in greater detail.

While there are no accompanying maps, fishing opportunities on the east side of the range in Shoshone National Forest are also outlined.

Roaring Fork Drainage

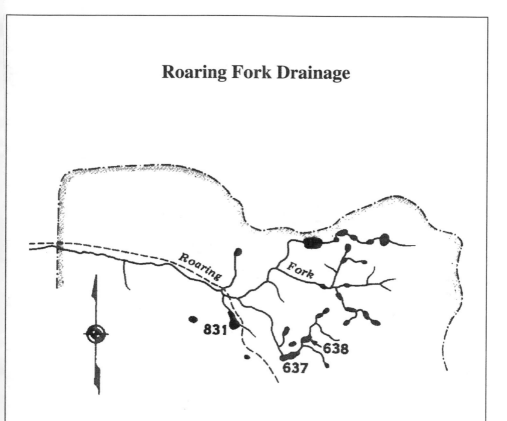

Code	Name	Fish
637	Crescent Lake	Cutthroat
638	Upper Crescent	Cutthroat
831	Native Lake	Rainbow, Golden

Clear Creek Drainage

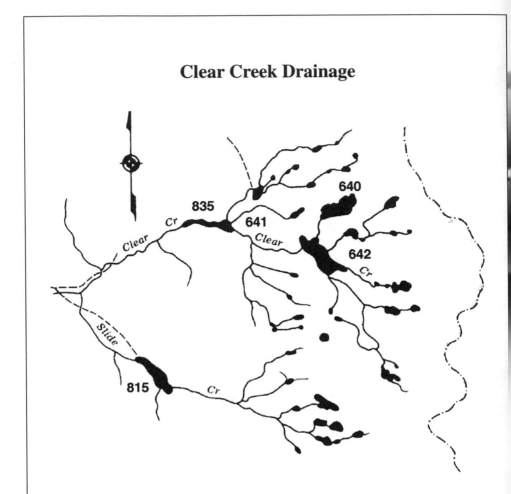

Code	Name	Fish
640	Daphne Lake	Rainbow
641	Faler Lake	Golden
642	Bear Lake	Rainbow
835	Clear Lake	Golden

Porcupine Creek

817 Shirley Lake
Fish .... Cutthroat
818 Twin Lakes (Both)
Fish .... Cutthroat
819 Valaite
Fish .... Cutthroat
820 Gadsby
Fish .... Cutthroat
823 Doc's
Fish .... Brook

Gypsum Creek - Jim Creek

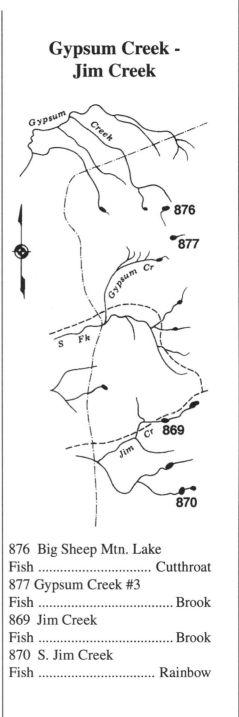

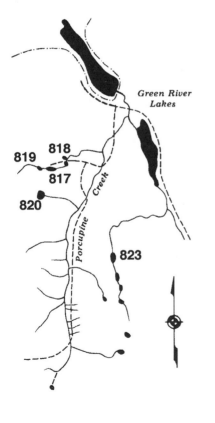

876 Big Sheep Mtn. Lake
Fish .... Cutthroat
877 Gypsum Creek #3
Fish .... Brook
869 Jim Creek
Fish .... Brook
870 S. Jim Creek
Fish .... Rainbow

Upper Green River Drainage

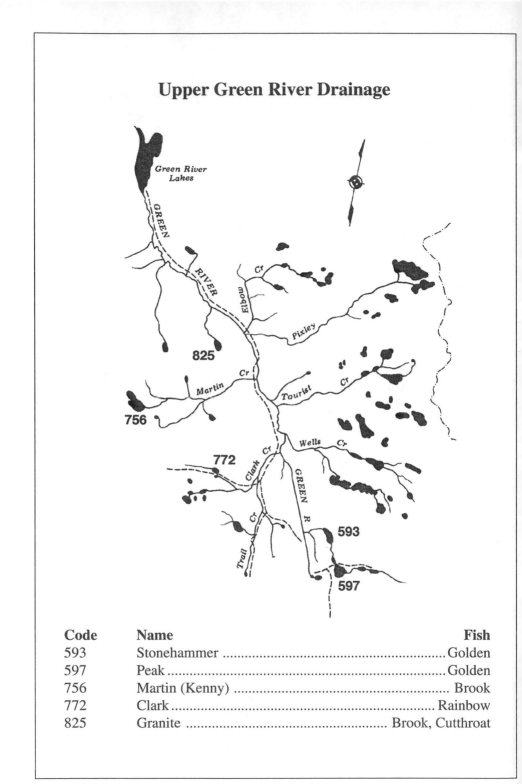

Code	Name	Fish
593	Stonehammer	Golden
597	Peak	Golden
756	Martin (Kenny)	Brook
772	Clark	Rainbow
825	Granite	Brook, Cutthroat

New Fork Drainage

Code	Name	Fish
760	Kenny (Lozier)	Brook
774	Lyn's (Hidden #1)	Brook
775	Thompson (Hidden #2)	Brook
776	Hidden #3	Brook
873	Joe's	Golden

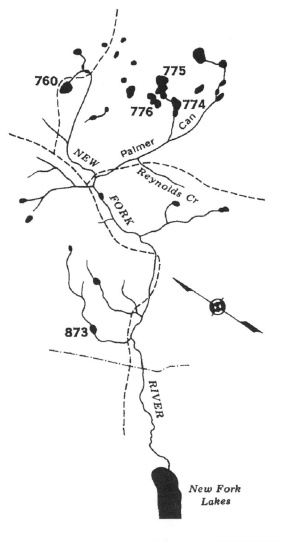

Lake Creek

701 Coyote
Fish ....Grayling
710 Trail
Fish ....Grayling
723 Section Corner
Fish ....Brook, Brown, Grayling
724 Little Trapper
Fish ....Cutthroat
725 Trapper
Fish ....Cuttthroat
787 Penny
Fish .... Brook
795 Palmer
Fish .... Brook
797 Pocahontas
Fish ....Cutthroat
801 Dean
Fish .... Brook
857 Round
Fish .... Brook
858 Lost Camp
Fish .... Brook
861 Rainbow
Fish .... Brook, Rainbow
865 Snake
Fish .... Brook

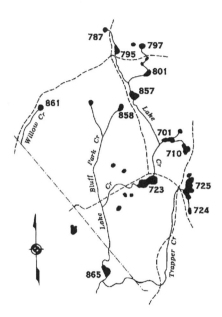

Fall Creek Drainage

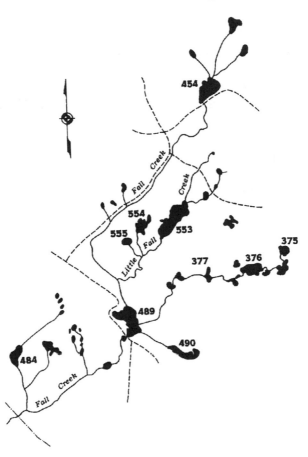

Code	Name	Fish
375	Fall Creek #10	Brook
376	Fall Creek #9	Brook
377	Fall Creek #7	Brook
454	Timico	Brook
484	Surprise	Golden
489	Horseshoe	Brook
490	George	Brook
553	Sequa	Brook
554	Leaville	Brook
555	Sarah Lea	Brook

Pine Creek

Code	Name	Fish
604	Summit	Cutthroat
606	Upper Elbow	Golden
681	Elbow	Golden
686	Lower Twin	Cutthroat, Golden
687	Pass	Cutthroat
691	Upper Twin	Cutthroat, Golden
696	Borum	Cutthroat
704	Heart	Rainbow
706	Gottfried	Cutthroat, Rainbow
707	Neil #2	Cutthroat, Rainbow
709	Neil #1	Cutthroat, Rainbow
712	Sauerkraut #1	Cutthroat
714	Sauerkraut #2	Cutthroat
716	Sauerkraut #3	Cutthroat
747	Glimpse	Brook
749	Prospector	Brook
782	Lower No Name	Cutthroat
783	Upper No Name	Cutthroat
799	Cutthroat	Cutthroat

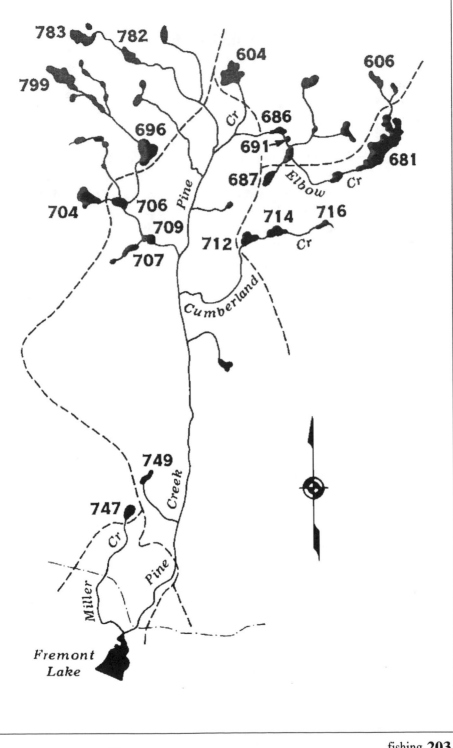

Pole Creek

Code	Name	Fish
476	Baldy Creek #1	Brook
479	Belford	Brook
480	Trophy	Brook
501	Lower Cooks	Brook
502	Don	Brook
503	Peter	Brook, Mackinaw
507	Mary's Creek	Brook
511	Pole Creek #7	Brook
512	Pole Creek #8	Brook, Golden
514	Pole Creek #4	Cutthroat
517	Upper Pole Creek	Brook, Cutthroat
518	Thousand Island	Cutthroat, Brook
520	"J"	Brook
522	Emma	Rainbow, Cutthroat, Brook
524	Upper Chain	Rainbow/Cutthroat Hybrid
526	Middle Chain	Rainbow, Rainbow/Cutthroat Hybrid
531	Baldy	Cutthroat
533	Bell	Cutthroat
539	Lower Chain	Cutthroat, Rainbow
542	Spruce	Rainbow, Cutthroat
545	Junction	Brook, Cutthroat/Rainbow Hybrid
547	Dollar	Brook
548	Sturrey	Brook
549	Karen	Brook
550	Jacquline	Brook, Cutthroat
551	Rodney	Cutthroat, Brown, Brook
552	Barnes	Cutthroat
580	Wall	Golden
583	Nelson	Golden
584	Upper Cooks	Brook, Golden
585	Tommy	Golden

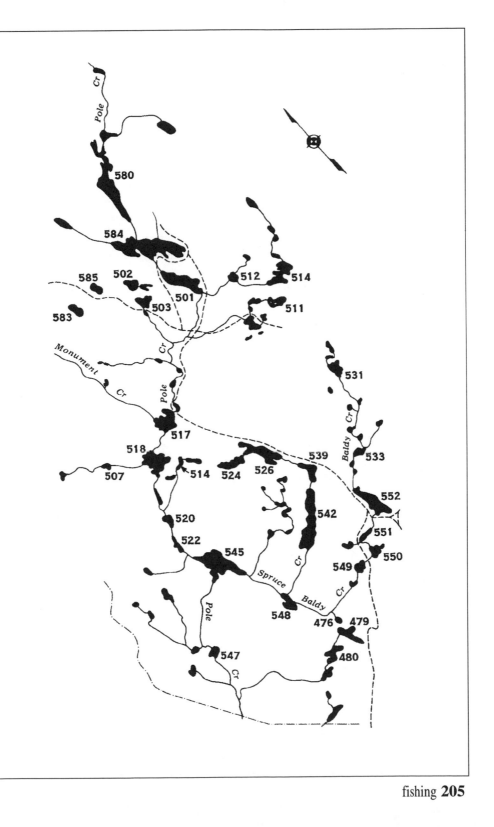

North Fork Boulder Creek

Code	Name	Fish
290	Europe Creek #7	Cutthroat
359	Europe Creek #4	Cutthroat
361	Europe Creek #3	Cutthroat
370	Europe Creek #1	Cutthroat
372	Victor	Cutthroat
386	August	Cutthroat
388	North Fork	Cutthroat
390	Valley	Cutthroat
394	Prue	Cutthroat
396	Upper Pipestone	Cutthroat
397	Lower Pipestone	Cutthroat
398	Howard	Cutthroat
407	Winona	Cutthroat
411	Perry	Brook
413	Christina	Brook
414	Norman	Golden
419	North Fork Creek #3	Cutthroat
422	Isabella	Cutthroat
430	Upper Firehole	Cutthroat
431	Middle Firehole	Cutthroat
432	Lower Firehole	Cutthroat
434	Vera	Cutthroat
437	Ethel	Cutthroat
438	Ed's	Golden
440	Dugway	Rainbow
455	Barber	Cutthroat
456	North Fork #13	Cutthroat
457	North Fork #14	Cutthroat
459	Glacier	Cutthroat
464	Long	Cutthroat
490	Lake George	Brook
494	Coyote	Grayling
495	Cross	Brook, Grayling
496	Lovatt	Golden, Brook
500	Blueberry (Ruff)	Brook, Grayling

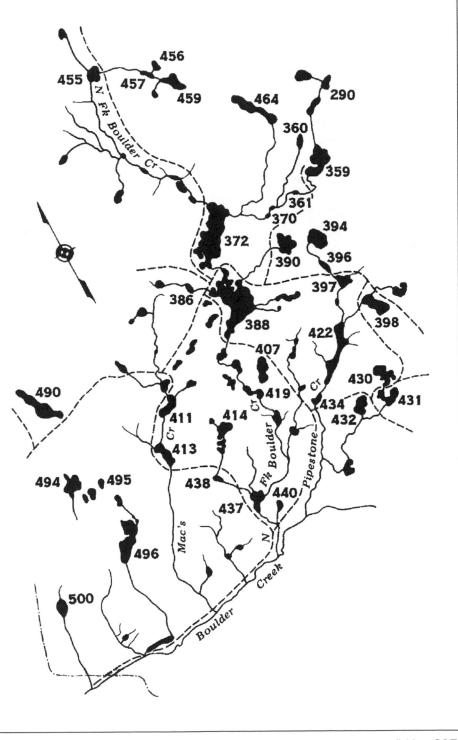

Fremont Creek

Code	Name	Fish
505	Hobbs	Rainbow
506	Eklund	Rainbow
556	Upper Titcomb	Golden
557	Mistake	Golden
558	Lower Titcomb	Golden
560	Lower Jean	Cutthroat
564	Pothole	Golden
570	Island	Rainbow, Cutthroat, Golden
576	Lost	Rainbow, Brook
577	Little Seneca	Rainbow
582	Seneca	Rainbow
607	Upper Jean	Cutthroat
668	Upper Long	Brook, Rainbow, Cutthroat
670	Triangle	Golden
672	Upper Triangle	Golden
674	Lone (Secret)	Brook
675	Long	Cutthroat, Brook, Brown
676	Barbara	Rainbow
677	Miller	Brook
679	Middle Sweeney	Golden
680	Sweeney	Cutthroat, Golden
718	B6	Brook
726	B3	Brook
727	W3	Golden
729	B2	Brook, Golden
730	B4	Brook
731	B5	Brook
738	Gorge	Rainbow, Brook
742	B1	Brook, Golden

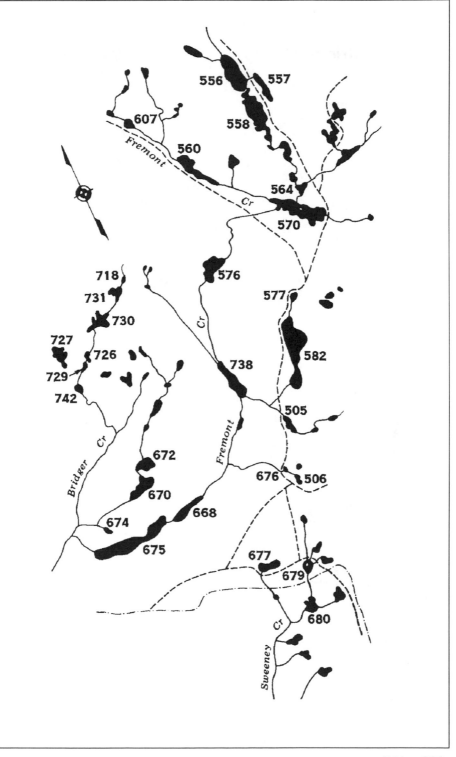

Little Sandy

Sweetwater River
No Lakes

031 Little Sandy
Fish .... Cutthroat, Brook

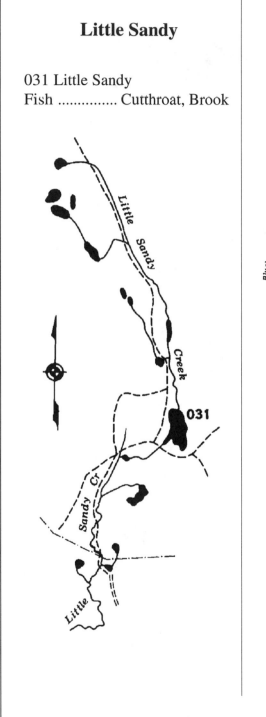

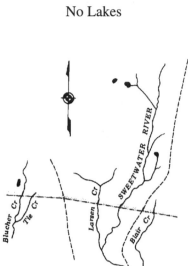

Scab Creek and Divide Creek

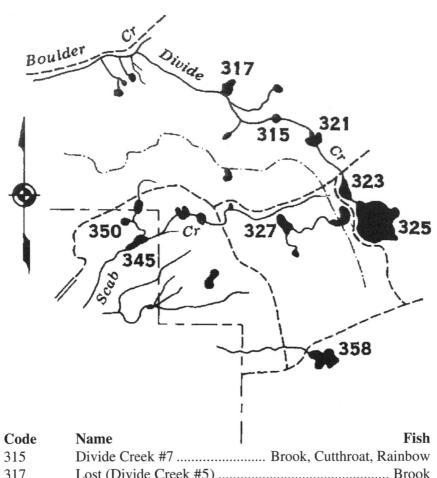

Code	Name	Fish
315	Divide Creek #7	Brook, Cutthroat, Rainbow
317	Lost (Divide Creek #5)	Brook
321	Pine Island	Rainbow, Cutthroat
323	Little Divide	Rainbow, Brook, Cutthroat
325	Divide	Rainbow, Cutthroat, Brook
327	Toboggan #15	Brook
345	Jack's	Cutthroat, Brook
350	Toboggan #3	Brook
358	Scab	Brook

Middle and South Fork Boulder Creek

Code	Name	Fish
149	Bonneville	Golden
155	Dream	Brook, Cutthroat
156	Crescent	Brook
158	South Fork	Brook
159	Raid	Brook, Mackinaw
181	Cross	Brook, Mackinaw
225	Howe	Brook
227	Hall's	Brook
228	Hall's Creek #12	Brook
247	Middle Fork	Brook
251	Hall Creek #4	Brook
257	Middle Fork #2	Brook
258	Middle Fork #3	Brook
265	Dream Creek #3	Rainbow
268	Rainbow	Rainbow
280	Sand Point	Brook
281	Bob's	Brook
283	Sunrise	Cutthroat
288	Jim Harrower	Golden
426	Hall Creek #1	Brook
427	Hall Creek #2	Brook
445	Junction	Brook

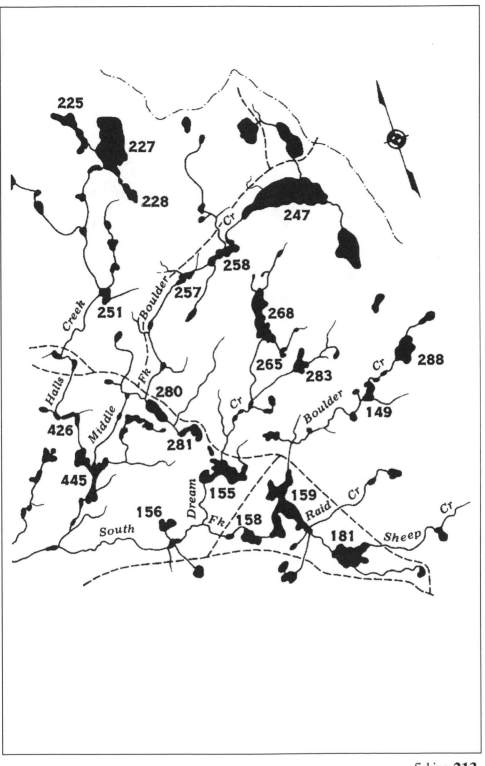

Silver Creek

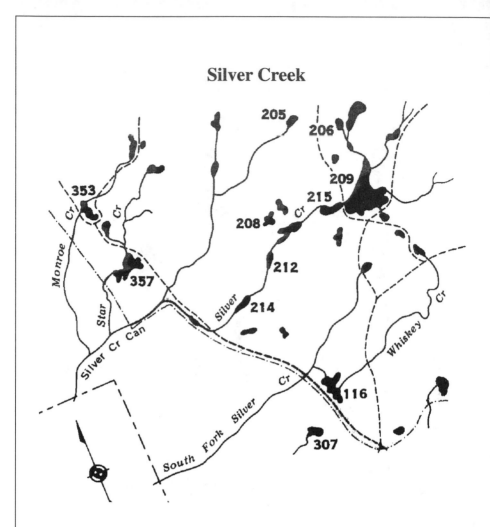

Code	Name	Fish
116	Wolf	Rainbow, Brook
205	Warbonnet	Brook
206	Upper Silver	Brook
208	Indian	Brook
209	Silver	Brook
212	Long Gut	Brook
214	Silver Creek #1	Brook
215	Lower Silver	Brook
307	Cottonwood	Rainbow
353	Monroe	Brook, Cutthroat
357	Star	Brook

Big Sandy

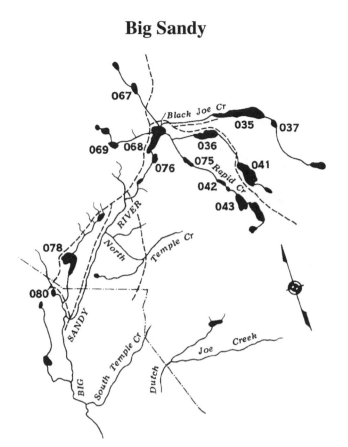

Code	Name	Fish
035	Black Joe	Cutthroat
036	Clear	Brook
037	Black Joe #1	Cutthroat
041	Deep	Brook
042	Miller (Little Temple)	Brook
043	Temple	Brook
067	North	Brook
068	Big Sandy	Brook, Cutthroat
069	Blue	Brook
075	Rapid	Brook
076	Big Sandy #2	Brook
078	V	Rainbow
080	Meeks	Brook

East Fork River

Code	Name	Fish
056	Marm's	Brook
057	Dad's	Brook, Cutthroat
065	Donald	Cutthroat
071	Fish	Brook
072	Mirror	Brook, Rainbow
074	Divide	Brook
086	Pyramid	Golden
087	Maes	Rainbow, Brook, Mackinaw
088	East Fork #5	Golden, Brook
090	Skull	Brook
100	Barren	Brook
108	Shadow	Brook
109	Billy's	Brook
125	Francis	Brook, Cutthroat
127	Poston	Brook
145	Boulter	Cutthroat, Brook
147	East Fork	Golden
157	East Fork #6	Golden

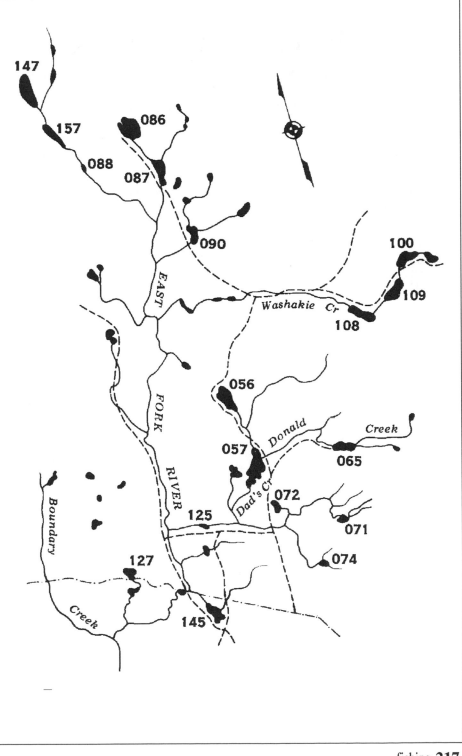

Shoshone Winds Fishing

LITTLE POPO AGIE RIVER DRAINAGE

Lake Name	Fish
Little Popo Agie (Lower)	Brown, Rainbow
Christina	Mackinaw, Brook
Gustave	Mackinaw, Brook
Lower Silas	Brook
Upper Silas	Brook, Cutthroat
Island	Cutthroat
Tomahawk	Cutthroat
Louis Lake	Mackinaw, Rainbow, Splake, Brook
Fiddlers Lake	Rainbow
Atlantic Lake	Brook
Little Atlantic	Brook, Splake
Rock	Brook, Splake

MIDDLE FORK POPO AGIE DRAINAGE

Lake Name	Fish
Middle Fork Popo Agie (Lower)	Brook, Rainbow
Roaring Fork	Brook
Stough	Cutthroat, Brook
Toadstool	Brook
Worthen Meadows Reservoir	Brook, Rainbow

LOWER DEEP CREEK LAKES

Lake Name	Fish
Jug	Golden, Brook
Boot	Golden, Brook
Squirrel	Grayling
Poison	Rainbow, Cutthroat, Golden
Mountain Sheep	Cutthroat/Golden Hybrid
Coon Lake	Cutthroat/Golden Hybrid
Hank	Rainbow

NORTH FORK POPO AGIE RIVER DRAINAGE

Lake Name	Fish
Shoshone Lake	Brook
Dickinson/Sand Creeks	Brook
Funnel Lake	Brook
Bears Ears Lake	Cutthroat
Smith	Brook, Mackinaw
Middle	Brook, Mackinaw
Cathedral	Brook, Mackinaw
Cook	Brook
Cloverleaf	Brook
Phyllis	Brook
Glacier	Brook
High Meadow/Cliff Lakes	Cutthroat
Lonesome Lake	Cutthroat

BROOKS LAKE DRAINAGE

Lake Name	Fish
Brooks Lake Creek	Rainbow, Brook
Wind River Lake	Rainbow
Pelham Lake	Cutthroat, Brook
Brooks Lake	Rainbow, Brook, Mackinaw

JAKEY'S FORK/ TORREY CREEK DRAINAGES

Lake Name	Fish
Simpson	Brook
Soapstone	Brook
Blanket	Brook
Rim	Cutthroat
Sandia	Cutthroat
Pinto	Cutthroat
Lost	Golden
Dyke/Peak	Rainbow
Marion	Brook
Moon	Brook, Mackinaw
Union	Rainbow, Mackinaw
Louise	Brook
Hidden	Rainbow/Cutthroat Hybrid

Ross .... Rainbow/Cutthroat Hybrid
Upper Ross .... Rainbow, Cutthroat
Torrey Creek .... Rainbow, Cutthroat
Trail .... Mackinaw
Ring .... Mackinaw, Brown, Rainbow
Torrey .... Brown, Rainbow, Ling

DINWOODY CREEK DRAINAGE

Lake Name	Fish
Honeymoon Lake	Cutthroat
Star	Splake
Double	Splake, Brook, Cutthroat
Phillips	Brook, Cutthroat
Long	Brook, Cutthroat
Golden	Golden

ADDITIONAL AREAS ACCESSED BY CAR

Big Wind River: Marked access off US. 287 between Togwotee Pass and Dubois. Rainbow, Brown, Cutthroat, Brook.

Boysen Reservoir: U.S. 26 West of Shoshone. Walleye, Perch, Bass, Ling, Brown, Rainbow in 19,000 acre Reservoir.

Lake Cameahwait: West of Boysen Reservoir. Rainbow, Largemouth Bass.

Ocean Lake: 6,100 acre lake off U.S 26, 15 Miles NW of Riverton. Largemouth Bass, Crappie, Bluegill, Yellow Perch, Walleye, Ling.

Appendix

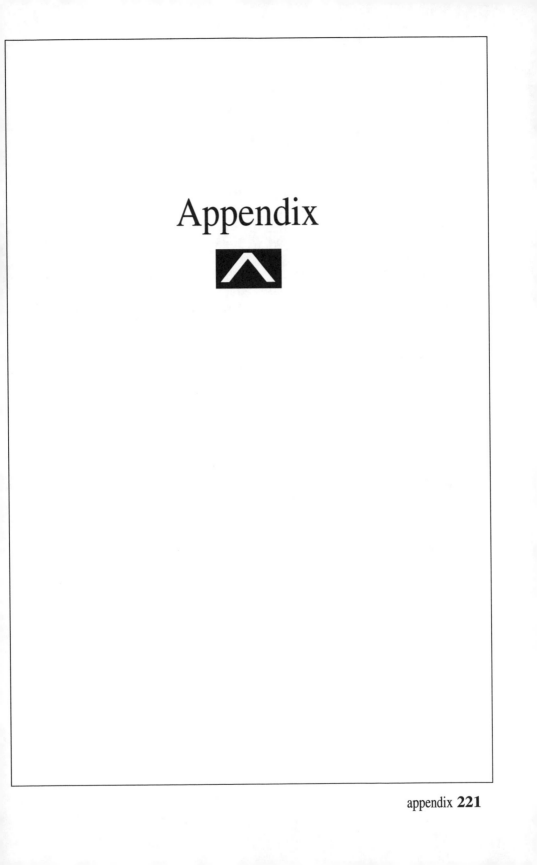

Peak Index By Elevation

Mt. Lander	12,623	Warrior I	12,350
Faler Tower	12,607	Cathedral Peak	12,348
Wolverine Peak	12,602	Mt. Lester	12,342
East Temple Peak	12,600	Tower Peak	12,335
Musembeah	12,593	Big Chief Mtn.	12,335
Mt. Solitude	12,590	Hitching Post Peak	12,314
West Sentinel	12,585	Burch Peak	12,314
Mt. Bonneville	12,570	South Twin Lion	12,305
Three Cirque Needle	12,560	Chess Ridge	12,302
Point 12,560	12,560	Peak 12,301	12,301
Peak 12,551	12,551	Thunder Bolt Pinnacle	12,300
North Cleft Peak	12,548	Lightening Rod Pinnacle	12,300
Windy Mountain	12,539	North Twin Lion	12,300
Raid Peak	12,532	Bear's Tooth	12,294
Mt. Washakie	12,524	Mt. Chauvenet	12,280
Titcomb Needles	12,520	Europe Peak	12,259
Mt. Hooker	12,504	Peak 12,258	12,258
Camel's Hump	12,500	Grave Peak	12,255
Peak 12,495	12,495	Mt. Victor	12,254
Renegade Peak	12,492	South Watchtower	12,250
Atlantic Peak	12,490	North Peak of Musembeah	12,250
Dogtooth Mountain	12,488	Peak 12,248	12,248
Goat Flat	12,488	Ram Flat	12,242
Mitchell Peak	12,482	Roaring Fork Mtn.	12,239
Lost Temple Spire	12,480	Spider Peak	12,234
Peak 12,480	12,480	Mount Oeneis	12,232
Hall's Mountain	12,475	Bollinger Peak	12,232
South Cleft Peak	12,471	Peak 12,229	12,229
Dike Mountain	12,468	Watchtower	12,228
Point 12,450	12,450	Cusp Peak	12,226
North Wind Peak	12,440	The Buttress	12,205
West Atlantic Peak	12,430	August 16th Peak	12,200
Downs Lake Towers	12,428	Buttressed Mtn.	12,200
Big Sandy Mountain	12,416	Stroud Peak	12,198
Warrior II	12,406	Bernard Peak	12,193
Angel Peak	12,402	Douglas Peak	12,191
Nylon Peak	12,398	Ambush Peak	12,187
Pylon Peak	12,378	Torrey Peak	12,181
Mt. Geikie	12,378	Point 12,161	12,161
Warbonnet	12,369	Elephanthead	12,160
Glissade Peak	12,361	Cairn Peak	12,152
Mt. Nystrom	12,356	Peak 12,152	12,152
Pronghorn	12,353	The Monolith	12,150

Walt Bailey Peak	12,150	Vista Peak	11,840
Peak 12,150	12,150	Fourts Horn	11,835
Wolf's Head	12,150	Peak 11,836	11,836
Dragon Head	12,140	Peak 11,820	11,820
Kagevah Peak	12,134	Roaring Fork Mtn.	11,804
Sky Pilot Peak	12,129	Peak 11,765	11,765
Eagle Pinnacle	12,120	A Cheval Peak	11,763
Horseshoe Ridge	12,113	Mt. Heebeecheeche	11,755
Symmetry Tower	12,100	Buffalo Head	11,731
Continental Tower	12,088	Little Sandy Buttresses	11,720
Glover Peak	12,068	Point 11,720	11,720
Runelbick	12,058	Arrow Mountain	11,696
Wykee Peak	12,055	Squaretop Mtn.	11,695
Odyssey Peak	12,053	Triple Divide Peak	11,680
Shark's Nose	12,050	Hobbs Peak	11,663
Block Tower	12,050	Easy Day Peak	11,660
Pinnacle 12,050	12,050	Independent Mtn.	11,653
Round Top Mountain	12,048	Schiestler Mtn.	11,640
Steeple Peak	12,040	Forlorn Pinnacle	11,640
Pyramid Peak	12,030	Mt. Shoshone	11,636
Red Wall Peak	12,000	Big Sheep Mtn.	11,618
Overhanging Tower	12,000	Dinwoody Peak	11,610
		Battleship Mtn.	11,607

11,000 Foot Peaks

		Tabletop	11,550
Haystack	11,978	Peak 11,535	11,535
Sentry Peak	11,938	Medina Mtn.	11,541
The Fortress	11,927	Union Peak	11,491
Mt. Quintet	11,922	Peak 11,486	11,486
Bunion Mtn.	11,905	Prairie Falcon Peak	11,475
Elizabeth Peak	11,901	Mount Chevro	11,396
Pipe Organ	11,900	Valentine Peak	11,361
Hailstorm Pinnacle	11,900	Salt Lick Mountain	11,350
Petroleum Peak	11,900	Laturio Mountain	11,342
Baptiste Lake Tower	11,900	Greeley Point	11,297
Peak 11,900	11,900	Gilman Peak	11,265
Peak 11,894	11,894	The Guardian	11,256
Pingora	11,884	The Monolith	11,252
Osborn Mtn.	11,880	Dome Peak	11,234
Flat Top Mtn.	11,868	North Fork Peak	11,175
Mt. Baldy	11,857	Whiskey Mtn.	11,157
Peak 11,850	11,850	ValentineMtn.	11,147
Hoowagant Pinnacle	11,845	Skunk Knob	11,099
Bear's Ears Mtn.	11,841	Kendall Mtn.	11,091
Lost Eagle Peak	11,840	Sundane Pinnacke	11,054

First Ascents

Listed below are first ascents of well-known peaks in the Wind River Range. Most peaks have numerous routes to their summit, varying greatly in difficulty. The first ascents detailed here reflect the first recorded time an explorer stood on the summit—not necessarily the peak's most challenging route. Climbing enthusiasts can find a complete listing of first ascents via routes on these and many more peaks in Joe Kelsey's comprehensive climbing guide to the range, printed by Chockstone Press in in 1994.

Big Sandy Mountain, 1933
  Finis Mitchell
Block Tower, 1957
  Chambers & Gran
Bob's Towers, 1939
  Robert & Miriam Underhill
Bollinger Peak, 1941
  Clyde, Pitcher,
  Edith & J. Holliday
Bow Mountain, 1939
  Bigclow, Klots & Ladd
Cathedral Peak, 1948
  Finis Mitchell
Desolation Peak, 1930
  Koven
Dinwoody Peak, 1922
  Bent, Jackson,Wyman
Dogtooth Mountain, 1941
  Clyde, Pitcher
  Edith & J. Holliday
Doublet Peak, 1929
  Hall, Henderson & Underhill
East Temple Peak, 1933
  Finis Mitchell
Elizabeth Peak, 1932
  Finis Mitchell
Ellingwood Peak, 1926
  Albert Ellingwood

Elephant Head, 1927
  Feltner & Sprague
Fremont Peak, 1842
  Members of John C. Fremont's
  surveying party
Jackson Peak, 1842
  Kit Carson
G-4, 1931
  Koven & Petzoldt
G-14, 1939
  Alexander Klots
Gannett Peak, 1922
  Arthur Tate & Floyd Stahlnaker
Gjetetind, 1960
  Chris Goetze & Brian Underhill
Grave Lake Dome, 1933
  Finis Mitchell
Guardian (The), 1960
  Chris Goetze & Brian Underhill
Haystack Mountain, 1961
  John Hudson & Bruce Monroe
Knife Point Mountain, 1926
  Ellingwood & Hart
Miriam Peak, 1939
  Robert & Miriam Underhill
Mitchell Peak, 1923
  Finis Mitchell
Mt. Arrowhead, 1931

Gustav & Theodore Koven
Paul Petzoldt
Mt. Bonneville, 1927
W.H. Bolinger, Joe Feltner
L.W. Sprague
Mt. Chauvenet, 1890
William "Billy" Owen
Mt. Febbas, 1920
Arthur Tate
Mt. Geikie, 1890
Willian "Billy" Owen
Mt. Helen, 1924
Blaurock, Buhl, Ellingwood
Mt. Hooker, 1890
William "Billy" Owen
Mt. Koven, 1933
H.H. Bliss, Paul Petzoldt,
Henry Clark Smith
Mt. Lester, 1930
Lewis Perkins party
Mt. Oeneis, 1939
Bigelow, Copeland, Klots,
Ladd
Mt. Sacajawea, 1926
Davis, Ellingwood,
Hart, Warner
Mt. Washakie, 1930
Finis Mitchell
Mt. Woodrow Wilson, 1924
Edgar Doll, Albert Bessine,
Carol Thompson Jones
Overhanging Tower, 1948
Harry King & Ralph Widrig
Pingora Peak, 1940
Orrin Bonney
Frank & Notsie Garnick
Pylon Peak, 1919
Finis Mitchell
Pyramid Peak, 1934
Bradley Gilman party
Ram Flat, 1960
Goetze & Underhill
Ross Mountain, 1960

Goetze & Underhill
Runelbick, 1960
Goetze & Underhill
Shark's Nose, 1949
Bell, Fox & Sargent
Sphinx (The), 1929
K. Henderson & R. Underhill
Squaretop Mountain, before 1921
William Stroud
Stroud Peak, 1929
Gaylord Hall
Charles Lobeck, Ruth Phillips
Temple Peak, 1877
Chittenden, Clymer
Endlich, Charles Howes
Titcomb Needles, 1939
Orrin Bonney
Frank & Notsie Garnick
Robert & Miriam Underhills
Torrey Peak, 1960
Goetze & Underhill
Turret Peak, 1924
Blaurock & Ellingwood
Valentine Mountain, 1948
Finis Mitchell
Warrior I, 1919
Finis Mitchell
Warrior II, 1919
Finis Mitchell
Watch Tower, 1919
Finis Mitchell
West Sentinel, 1920
Arthur Tate
Wind River Peak, 1873
Comstock, Hardy & Putnam
Winifred Peak, 1919
Arthur Tate
Wolf's Head, 1949
Bell, Fox & Sargent
Wolverine Peak, 1936
J. Bowie
Yukon Peak, 1961
Finis Mitchell

Threatened, Endangered & Sensitive Species on Bridger-Teton Wilderness

Wildlife

<u>Endangered</u>

(s)   Gray wolf
(p)   Peregrine Falcon
(s)   Whooping Crane
(p)   Bald Eagle
       Kendall Warm Springs Dace
       Sockeye Salmon
       Chinook Salmon

<u>Threatened</u>

       Utah Prairie Dog
(p)   Grizzly Bear
       Desert Tortoise
       Railroad Valley Springfish
       Lahontan Cutthroat Trout
       Paite Cutthroat Throat
       Mexican Spotted Owl

<u>Proposed</u>

       Southwestern Willow
         Flycatcher

<u>Sensitive</u>

       Spotted Bat
       Western Big-Eared Bat
(p)   Lynx
(p)   Wolverine

(p)   Fisher
(p)   boreal owl
       Flammulated Owl
(p)   Great Grey Owl
(p)   Trumpeter Swan
(p)   Common Loon
(p)   Harlequin Duck
(p)   Northern Goshawk
       White-headed Woodpecker
(p)   Three-toed Woodpecker
       Mountain Quail
       Columbian Sharp-tailed
         Grouse
(p)   Spotted Frog
       Wood River Sculpin
       West slope Cutthroat Trout
(p)   Colorao Cutthroat Trout
       Bonneville Cutthroat Trout
       Fine Spotted Cutthroat
         Trout
       Steelhead Trout
       Bull Trout

(p) = present within Bridger Wilderness
(s) = suspected, but unconfirmed within Bridger Wilderness

Sensitive Plants Found on Pinedale Ranger District, BTNF

Common Name	Habitat Present	Species Present or found	Inside/Outside Wilderness or both
Pink agoseris	Yes	Yes	Both
Sweet-flowered rock jasmine	Yes	No*	
Soft aster	Yes	No*	
Payson's milkvetch	Yes	No*	
Seaside sedge	Yes	No*	
Black and purple sedge	Yes	Yes	Wilderness only
Boreal draba	Yes	Yes	Wilderness only
Rockcress draba	Yes	No*	
Woolley fleabane	Yes	Yes	Both
Narrowleaf goldenweed	Yes	No*	
Payson's bladderpod	Yes	Yes	Outside Wilderness
Naked-stemmed parrya	Yes	Yes	Wilderness only
Creeping twinpod	Yes	No*	
Greeland primrose	Yes	Yes	Wilderness only
Webber's saussurea	Yes	Yes	Wilderness only

* Not known in the prject area but could be inhabitant.
   Habitat is theplace or type or site where a plant or animal naturally
   or normally could live and grow.

Bridger Wilderness Trail Inventory

In its 1995 Bridger Wilderness Action Plan and Implementation Schedule, Bridger-Teton National Forest officials included a mileage inventory of existing trails on the wilderness. Since some recreationists use the Pinedale Ranger District map when doing initial trip planning, the inventory is included here. The trail numbers concur with those printed on the district map.

Trail No.	Trail Name	Number of Miles
1046	Indian Pass	5.7
1086	Crows Nest	5.3
1093	Crossover	1.4
1094	Highline	80.2
1095	Lowline	16.6
1096	Fremont	34.6
1097	Sweetwater Gap	4.7
1098	Little Sandy	15.1
1099	Big Sandy	6.3
1100	Diamond Lake	7.4
1101	Chilcoot	7.4
1102	Boundary Creek	1.2
1104	Fremont Driveway	10
1108	Cottonwood	10.9
1109	Sage Basin	10.4
1110	Scab Creek	11.4
1111	Hailey Pass	6.2
1112	Middle Fork	8
1113	Boulder Canyon	9.1
1114	Europe Canyon	4.7
1115	Hay Pass	7.4
1116	Black Joe	1.5
1117	Timico	8.5
1118	George Lake	4.2
1119	Pole Creek	7.1
1120	Bell Lakes	2.8
1121	Sweeney Creek	5.1
1122	Long Lake	1.5
1123	Seneca Lake	4.9
1124	Baldy Lake	1.6
1125	Shannon Pass	4.6
1127	Willow Lake	5.6
1128	Snake Lake	5
1129	Palmer Lake	7.6

**Abandoned trails that will be removed from future Pinedale Ranger District maps and maintenance schedules.

Visitor Use Statistics
on Bridger Wilderness

Year	RVD
1966	17,368
1967	52,538
1968	58,085
1969	77,976
1970	135,453
1971	151,477
1972	183,344
1973	181,708
1974	196,146
1975	207,790
1976	236, 415
1977	222,350
1978	202,243
1979	200,122
1980	189,158
1981	258,081
1982	242,133
1983	224,072
1984	217,849
1985	213,898
1986	198,442
1987	207,407
1988	220,253
1989	189,795
1990	231,877
1991	255,642
1992	214,646
1993	235,022
1994	243,562

An RVD (Recreational Visitor Day) is defined as one person visiting for 12 hours. Sources used for determining RVD's are: Trailhead registration boxes, group permits, stock permits, and Outfitter/Guide actual use reports.

Source: Bridger Wilderness Action Plan and Implementation Schedule March 1995

Regional Accommodations

Boulder

Boulder Inn Motel 307-537-5626
    Hwy. 191

Dubois

Badlands Bed & Breakfast 307-455-2161
    8 miles E of Hwy. 26/287

Black Bear Country Inn 1-800-873-BEAR
    505 N. Ramshorn
    Local phone 455-2344

Chinook Winds Motel 307-455-2987
    Hwy. 26/287

Dunloggin Bed & Breakfast 307-455-2445
    305 S. First Street

Geyser Creek Bed & Breakfast 307-455-2702
    151 Bald Mountain Road

Jakey's Fork Homestead Bed & Breakfast 307-455-2769
    Fish Hatchery Road

Pinnacle Buttes Lodge 307-455-2506
    W of Dubois on Hwy. 26/287

Red Rock Ranch Motel 307-455-2337
    2 miles E on Hwy. 26/287

Rendezvous Motel 1-800-682-9323
    1349 N. Ramshorn
    Local phone 455-2844

Stagecoach Motor Inn 307-455-2303
    103 E. Ramshorn

Super 8 1-800-800-8000
    1414 Warm Springs Drive
    Local phone 455-3694

Trail's End Motel 307-455-2540
    511 Ramshorn

Twin Pines Lodge & Motel 307-455-2600
    218 Ramshorn

Wind River Motel 307-455-2611
    519 W. Ramshorn

Lander

Blue Spruce Inn Bed & Breakfast 307-332-8253
    677 South Third Street

The Bunkhouse Bed & Breakfast 1-800-582-5262
    2024 Mortimore Lane
    Local phone 332-5624

Country Fare Bed & Breakfast 307-332-5906
   904 Main Street
Downtown Motel 307-332-5220
   568 Main
Edna's Bed & Breakfast 307-332-3175
   53 North Fork Road
Holiday Lodge 1-800-624-1974
   210 McFarlane Drive
   Local phone 332-2511
Horseshoe Motel 307-332-4915
   685 Main
Maverick 307-332-2821
   808 Main Street
Outlaw Bed & Breakfast 307-332-9655
   2415 Squaw Creek Road
Pioneer Court Motel 307-332-2653
   181 N. 6th Street
Pronghorn Motel 1-800-BUD-HOST
   150 E. Main
   Local phone 332-3940
Silver Spur Motel 1-800-922-7831
   1240 Main
   Local phone 332-5189
Western Motel 307-332-4270
   151 N. 9th Street

Pinedale

Branding Iron Bunkhouse Bed & Breakfast 307-367-2146
   141 Ehman Lane
Camp O' of the Pines Motel 307-367-4536
   38 N. Fremont
Chambers House Bed & Breakfast 1-800-567-2168
   111 W. Magnolia Street
Half Moon LodgeMotel 307-367-2851
   46 N. Sublette Avenue
Lakeside Lodge Resort Marina 307-367-2221
   99 FS 111 on Fremont Lake
Log Cabin Motel 307-367-4579
   49 E. Magnolia
Pine Creek Inn 307-367-2191
   650 W. Pine
Pole Creek Ranch Bed & Breakfast 307-367-4433
   244 Pole Creek
Rivera Lodge 307-367-2424
   442 W. Marilyn

Sundance Motel 307-367-4336
    148 E. Pine
Teton Court Motel 307-367-2871
    123 E. Magnolia
Wagon Wheel Motel... 307-367-2871
    407 S. Pine
Window on the Winds Bed & Breakfast 307-367-2395
    10151 Hwy. 191
The ZZZZ Inn 307-367-2121
    327 S. Hwy. 191

Area Outfitters

Cora

Green River Guest Ranch 307-367-2314
Loziers Box R Ranch 307-367-4868

Dubois

CM Ranch 307-455-2331
Early Guest Ranch 1-800-532-4055
Grand Slam Outfitters 307-486-2269
Great Outdoor Adventure Company 307-455-2839
Press Stephens 307-455-2250
Suda Outfitters 307-455-2866
Taylor Outfitters 307-455-2161
Triangle C Ranch 307-455-2225
Washakie Outfitting 307-455-2616

Lander

Allen's Diamond Four Ranch 307-332-2995
Great Divide Tours 1-800-458-1815
Lander Llama Company.. 1-800-582-5262
Rocky Mtn. Horseback Vacations 1-800-408-9149

Pinedale

Boulder Lake Lodge... 307-537-5400
Bridger Wilderness Outfitters 307-367-2268
Green River Outfitters 307-367-2416
Half Moon Guest Ranch 307-367-6373
The Fishing Guide 307-367-4760
O'Kelley Outfitting 307-367-6476
Petersen Outfitting 307-367-6353
Window on the Winds 307-367-2600
Wind River Hiking Consultants 307-367-2560
Wyoming Rails & Trails 307-537-5666

Bibliography

My field observations were double-checked against topographic maps, notes from friends and previously published work. History, geology and wildlife information was drawn from a wide array of sources. Selected references used in compiling this guide are listed below, with thanks to the authors.

Books And Pamphlets

Armstrong, David M. *Rocky Mountain Mammals*. Boulder, Colorado: Colorado Associated University Press, 1987.

Bonney, Orrin H. and Lorraine G. *Field Book: The Wind River Range, Third Revised Edition*. Self-published, 1977.

Brink, Beverly Elaine. *Wyoming, Land of Echoing Canyons*. Flying Diamond Books, 1986.

Brown, Robert Harold. *Wyoming: A Geography*. Boulder, Colorado: Westview Press, 1980.

Burt, William Henry. *A Field Guide to the Mammals*. Boston, Massachusetts: Houghton Mifflin Company, 1964.

Chittenden, Hiriam Martin. *The American Fur Trade of the Far West*. Stanford, California: Academic Reprints, 1954.

Del Monte, H.D. *Early History of Lander, Wyoming and the Wind River Valley*. Lander, Wyoming: Self, 1947.

Hayden, Elizabeth Wied. *From Trappers to Tourists in Jackson Hole*.

Jackson, Wyoming: Grand Teton Natural History Association, 1981.

Kelsey, Joe. *Climbing and Hiking in the Wind River Mountains.*
San Francisco, California: Sierra Club Books, 1980.

Lain, Gayle and Sheryl. *Wyoming, The Proud Land.* Powell, Wyoming:
Polecat Printing, 1968.

Larson, T.A. *Wyoming: A History.* New York, New York: W.W. Norton &
Company, 1984.

Mann, Luther, *Letter to F.H. Head, Superintendent of Indian Affairs,*
House Executive Document 1 - Serial 1326, July, 1867.

Mitchell, Finis. *Wind River Trails.* Salt Lake City, Utah: Wasatch
Publishers, 1975.

Morgan, Dale L. *Jedediah Smith and the Opening of the West.*
Lincoln, Nebraska: University of Nebraska Press, 1967.

Pinkerton, Joan Trego. *Knights of the Broadax.* Caldwell, Idaho:
The Caxton Printers, Inc., 1981.

Pitcher, Don. *Wyoming Handbook, Second Edition.* Chico, California:
Moon Publications, 1993.

Sudduth, Tom and Sanse. *Wyoming Hiking Trails.* Boulder, Colorado:
Pruett Publishing Company, 1978.

Unruh, John D., Jr. *The Plains Across.* Chicago, Illinois: University of
Illinois Press, 1982.

Urbanek, Mae. *Wyoming Place Names.* Missoula, Montana:
Mountain Press Publishing Company, 1988.

U.S. Dept. of Agriculture. *Bridger Wilderness Fishing Lakes.*
Government Document No. 26.16.403, 1979

Whittenburg, Clarice. *Wyoming: Prelude to Statehood.* Cheyenne,
Wyoming: Wyoming Travel Commission & Wyoming State
Department of Education

Wind River Reservation Indian Consultants, *Wind River Reservation:
Yesterday and Today.* 1984.

Wyoming Indian Liaison Committee, Bureau of Indian Affairs, Wyoming
Department of Health and Social Services. *Wind River Indian Needs
Determination Survey Final Report, August 1988.*

Magazine and Newspaper Articles

Bell, Tom. "The Riches That Were Beaver," *Wind River Mountaineer*,
April-June, 1985.

Carlson, Vada F. "Riverton: From Sage to City," *Annals of Wyoming*,
October 1956, Vol. 28, No. 2

Delo, David M. "Early Times, the Wind River Valley," *Wind River
Mountaineer*, October-November, 1985.

Delo, David M. "The Road to Yellowstone," *Wind River Mountaineer*,
April-June, 1986.

Delo, David M. "Settlers Came to the Valley," *Wind River Mountaineer,*
    July-September, 1987.
Dickinson, Norman. "Story of South Pass," *Annals of Wyoming*, Fall 1972,
    Vol. 44, No. 2.
"Historic South Pass," *Wind River Mountaineer*, October-December, 1991.
"History of Old Fort Laramie, Post is Finally Abandoned,"
    Wyoming State Journal, July 2, 1953.
Jost, Loren. "John Charles Fremont — Fremont County's Namesake,"
    Wind River Mountaineer, July-September, 1985.
Lewis, Ila. "The Story of Fort Stambaugh." *Annals of Wyoming*,
    Fall 1972, Vol. 44, No. 2.
Linford, Dee. "Wyoming Stream Names," *Annals of Wyo.*, 1943, Vol. 4
Roundy, Charles. "Origins and Early Development of Dude Ranching in
    Wyoming," *Annals of Wyoming*, Spring 1973, Vol. 45, No. 1.
"Shoshone Now Decorate Graves, Used to Bury Dead in Mountains,"
    Wyoming State Journal, May 28, 1959.
Springer, Agnes Wright. "Sheep Wagon Home on Wheels Originated in
    Wyoming," *Wyoming Stockman Farmer,* December, 1940.
"Story of Atlantic City," *Annals of Wyoming*, Fall 1972, Vol. 44, No. 2
Wolf, James R. "Fremont in the Wind Rivers," *Annals of Wyoming,*
    Fall 1988.

Λ

Further Reading

The history of the early west, Indian Wars, mountaineering, geology, etc., has generated dozens of fascinating books. If your interest was sparked by the brief range introduction at the front of the book, you will enjoy reading the publications listed below.

History

Combs, Barry. *Westward to Promontory: Building the Union Pacific Across the
    Plains and Mountains.* New York, New York: Crown Publishers, 1986.
DeVoto, Bernard. *Across the Wide Missouri,* New York, New York:
    Houghton Mifflin Company, 1947.

Greesley, Gene. *Bankers and Cattlemen.* Lincoln, Nebraska: University of Nebraska Press, 1971.

Haines, Aubrey. *Journal of a Trapper: Osborne Russell.* Lincoln, Nebraska: University of Nebraska Press, 1955.

Homsher, Lola M. *South Pass, 1868. James Chisholm's Journal of the Wyoming Gold Rush.* Lincoln, Nebraska: University of Nebraska Press, 1960.

Larsen, T.A. *Wyoming: A History.* New York, New York: W.W. Norton and Company, 1984.

Lavendar, David. *Westward Vision, the Story of the Oregon Trail.* New York, New York: McGraw-Hill, 1971.

Morgan, Dale. *Jedediah Smith and the Opening of the West.* Indianapolis, Indiana: Bobbs-Merrill, 1953.

Munkres, Robert. *Saleratus and Sagebrush: The Oregon Trail. Through Wyoming.*Cheyenne, Wyoming: Wyoming State Archives and Historical Department, 1974.

Pinkerton, Joan Trego. *Knights of the Broadax.* Caldwell, Idaho: The Caxton Printers, Inc., 1981.

Indians

Howard, Harold. *Sacajawea.* Norman, Oklahoma: University of Oklahoma Press, 1971

Trenholm, Virginia Cole and Maurine Carly. *The Shoshonis, Sentinels of the Rockies.* Norman, Oklahoma: University of Oklahoma Press, 1965.

Trenholm, Virginia. *The Arapahoes, Our People.* Norman, Oklahoma: University of Oklahoma Press, 1970.

Utley, Robert. *The Indian Frontier of the American West 1846-1890.* Albuquerque, New Mexico: University of New Mexico Press, 1984.

Geology

Brown, Robert. *Wyoming: A Geography.* Boulder, Colorado: Westview Press,1980.

McPhee, John. *Rising from the Plains.* New York, New York: Noonday Press, 1986.

Wildlife

Clark, Tim and Mark Stromberg. *Mammals in Wyoming.* Lawrence, Kansas: University of Kansas Museum of Natural History, 1987.

General

Kelsey, Joe. *Wyoming's Wind River Range.* Helena, Montana: American Geographic Publishing, 1988.

Index

NEPAL

Ama Dablam and Tengboche Monastery

Trek the

Himalayas

If you like to hike, you'll love trekking in Nepal. The Kingdom of Nepal is a narrow sliver of land squeezed between burgeoning India to the south and the vast Tibetan plateau to the north. She rises from plain to plain, valley to valley, mountain to mountain — a precipitous staircase that ends at the roof of the world: The Himalayas, "abode of the snows." Eight of the world's 10 highest summits lie within her borders.

For her size and population, Nepal is the least roaded country in the world. To see her, you must travel as her people do — on foot. Mountain Journeys can get you there. The culturally and environmentally sensitive travel company is owned by Becky Woods and Rich Bloom, a married team who collectively have guided people throughout the world for over 30 years.

Becky has traveled extensively through the Himalayas since the 1980s, leading trips to every corner of Nepal. She speaks Nepali and is well-versed of the country's diverse culture and religions. When not guiding in Nepal, Tibet or Bhutan, she writes. She is the author of this guidebook, *Targhee Trails*, and *Jackson Hole Hikes*.

Rich Bloom has guided in Nepal, United States, Canada, Mexico, India, and Patagonia through Mountain Journeys and pioneer outdoor organizations such as the National Outdoor Leadership School (NOLS) and Colorado Outward Bound. He is an accomplished mountaineer, sea kayaker and whitewater boater as well as a naturalist who has worked with numerous field science schools. He is presently the director of finance for Teton Science School in Grand Teton National Park.

Becky and Rich work with a fine Sherpa staff, many of them veterans of Everest and other 8,000 meter Himalayan expeditions. Their staff prepares meals and carries out all camp duties. Porters and pack animals carry gear. You have only to carry a daypack large enough for a water bottle, a camera and an extra jacket. It is a wonderful way to travel through the highest mountains in the world.

For additional information, or to be placed on Mountain Journey's mailing list, please fill in the coupon on the following page.

YES.

I WANT MORE INFORMATION ON VISITING THE HIMALAYAS.
PUT ME ON YOUR MAILING LIST.

NAME_____

ADDRESS_____

CITY/STATE/ZIP_____

PHONE_____

Mountain Journeys

Box 623
Wilson, Wyoming 83014
mountains@wyoming.com
www.mountainjourneys.com

Order Form

To order additional copies of this book, please check your local bookstore/outdoor shop. If not available, send a check or money order to: White Willow Publishing, 1255 N. Iron Rock #6, Jackson, Wyoming 83001, in the amount of $14.95 per copy plus $1.50 for shipping. Sorry, orders can only be filled in the continental U.S. Please complete the information below:

Name_____

Address_____

City/State/Zip_____

Targhee Trails and *Jackson Hole Hikes,* both by the same author, are also available from White Willow Publishing. Please send $14.95 plus $1.50 for shipping for each copy of both titles.

White Willow Publishing
1255 N. Iron Rock Rd. #6 • Jackson, Wyoming 83001
307-733-0674 • rbloom@wyoming.com

Wholesale/Dealer inquiries invited